SEEING THROUGH
MOVIES

DATE DUE

OTHER TITLES IN THE PANTHEON GUIDE TO POPULAR
CULTURE SERIES:

Reading the News
Robert Karl Manoff and Michael Schudson, Editors

Watching Television
Todd Gitlin, Editor

Facing the Music
Simon Frith, Editor

A PANTHEON GUIDE TO
POPULAR CULTURE

SEEING THROUGH
MOVIES

Mark Crispin Miller

EDITOR

PANTHEON **B**OOKS

NEW YORK

Compilation copyright © 1990 by Mark Crispin Miller
"The Big Picture" and "End of Story" copyright © 1990 by Mark Crispin Miller
"Down the Tubes" copyright © by Todd Gitlin
"If You've Seen One, You've Seen the Mall" copyright © 1990 by Douglas Gomery
"Good Soldiers" copyright © 1990 by Pat Aufderheide
"The Last Crusade" copyright © 1990 by Peter Biskind
"Rose-Tinted Spectacles" copyright © 1990 by Stuart Klawans

Library of Congress Cataloging-in-Publication Data

Seeing through movies / Mark Crispin Miller, editor.
      p.   cm. — (A Pantheon guide to polular culture)
    Contents: Introduction / Mark Crispin Miller — Rose-tinted spectacles
/ Stuart Klawans — Down the tubes / Todd
Gitlin — Good soldiers / Pat Aufderheide — The last crusade / Peter
Biskind — If you've seen one, you've seen the mall / Douglas Gomery.
    ISBN 0-394-57491-5. — ISBN 0-679-72367-6 (pbk.)
    1. Motion pictures. 2. Popular culture. I. Miller, Mark
Crispin. II. Series.
PN1994.S47   1990
791.43—dc20   89-43231

Text design by Robert Bull Design

Manufactured in the United States of America

First Edition

*C*ontents

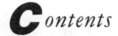

INTRODUCTION
The Big Picture   3
MARK CRISPIN MILLER

THE MEDIUM
Down the Tubes   14
TODD GITLIN

THE THEATER
If You've Seen One, You've Seen the Mall   49
DOUGLAS GOMERY

VIETNAM
Good Soldiers   81
PAT AUFDERHEIDE

BLOCKBUSTER
The Last Crusade   112
PETER BISKIND

COLORIZATION
Rose-Tinted Spectacles   150
STUART KLAWANS

CONTENTS

ADVERTISING
End of Story   186
MARK CRISPIN MILLER

NOTES   247

THE CONTRIBUTORS   265

SEEING THROUGH
MOVIES

The *B*ig *Picture*

MARK CRISPIN MILLER

"**T**HE MEN AND WOMEN who make a nation's entertainment have obligations above and beyond their primary commercial objective, which is the box office." Thus Harry M. Warner (or someone who worked for him) began an article that appeared in the *Christian Science Monitor* in April 1939. Here is its peroration:

> Our primary problem, let me repeat, is to make enjoyable box-office entertainment. No producer can slight that. But above and beyond that is an ever present duty to educate, to stimulate, and demonstrate the fundamentals of free government, free speech, religious tolerance, freedom of press, freedom of assembly, and the greatest possible happiness for the

greatest possible number. To that end our company and, I believe, our whole industry, stands pledged—now and for the future.

That was then. This is now:

"The entire marriage between us and free enterprise, quality companies and quality products, seems to be a good idea in marketing every element of the company." Thus spake, in 1989, Michael Eisner, chairman-CEO of Walt Disney Co., in the pages of *Advertising Age*—which had named him "Adman of the Year." Eisner elaborated:

> The Disney Stores promote the consumer products which promote the [theme] parks which promote the television show. The television shows promote the company. Roger Rabbit promotes Christmas at Disneyland.
> It's constant ideas.

Together these two visions of Hollywood's "duty," or agenda, tell an ambiguous story. On the one hand, it is a sad tale of success, somewhat like *Citizen Kane*—a story of high principles eventually sold out; for Harry Warner, the most pious of the moguls, wasn't faking that utopian glow. He did believe that "the motion picture presents right and wrong, as the Bible does," and that it should be used to foster Peace and Brotherhood—a vague sense of mission that pervades the Warner Bros. big productions, from *The Jazz Singer* (1927) to *Dr. Ehrlich's Magic Bullet* (1940). Whereas throughout his article the mogul refers idealistically to "mankind," "the public," "peoples of the world," "the men and women" of his industry, and so on, the Disney manager never even mentions human beings, preferring to contemplate the antiseptic "marriage" of "quality companies and quality products."

The Warner/Eisner parallel, however, also offers us another, cooler narrative—a story of smooth continuation, of predictable fulfillment: for both the high-minded mogul and the robotic CEO are instruments of the same drive for larger profits and more power. While Warner's "pledge" may well have been an honest personal credo, as a testament for his "whole industry" it was a trumpet blast of pure PR, as fine-tuned as any studio release. Even the most casual study of the old moguls' practices—as employers; as political activists; as family men; as would-be appeasers, and eventually as tools of HUAC—betrays the hollowness of that paean to American freedoms, for those colorful bosses were, above all, monopolists, just like Michael Eisner and his colorless peers.

These two ways of interpreting the Warner/Eisner contrast may seem incongruous, but together they suggest a truth, for the history of Hollywood describes at once an inexorable fulfillment and a gross decline. Louis B. Mayer and Adolph Zukor, Darryl Zanuck and the Warner brothers, Samuel Goldwyn and Harry Cohn were indeed voracious and reactionary men of capital, just as grasping, in their way, as Rupert Murdoch or the board of Time/Warner or the board of Sony. And yet that qualifier, "in their way," is crucial, for Hollywood's pioneering bosses were also antithetical to the corporate neo-moguls of today—and it was that difference that made the movies possible.

First of all, the men who built and fortified the studios did love the movies and (by and large) knew the craft of moviemaking. In David O. Selznick's epic memos, in Jack Warner's notes, in Irving Thalberg's influence, in Goldwyn's supervision, we sense a concern with cinema that was not purely economic. Even those moguls without a trace of critical discernment—L. B. Mayer or "His Crudeness" Harry Cohn—were genuinely fascinated by the movies and at times even tried (and failed) to make them better—which did not always mean just "more profitable." By contrast, the lawyers and MBAs now managing the movie business are uninterested in, and bureaucratically cut off from, the nitty-gritty of filmmaking. Obsessed with blockbusters, they prize a movie only as a multiply exploitable resource, like a vulnerable company with lots of assets. "More than ever," Aljean Harmetz reported in 1987, "the studios must think of a movie as a package of different rights, each of which brings in separate earnings."

While the moguls may have been just as avaricious as the managers now in power, their greed was modified, its impact somewhat softened, by an idealist impulse that pervaded their era in the history of capitalism. The heavy glamour of the studios' A-productions, the exquisite kitsch of their palatial theaters, the monotonous splendor of the myths sold in the fan magazines and gossip columns, at once expressed and reinforced a widespread yearning for a glimpse of heaven here on earth. Among Hollywood's Jewish overlords this upward impulse may have expressed a thwarted longing for assimilation, as film historian Neal Gabler has argued. Yet their struggle for gentility cannot account for the transcendent thrust, back then, of our entire commercial culture. The same escapist grandeur marks the images also devised, for instance, by the advertising industry, whose WASP leadership were, just like Harry Warner, given frequently to hymns of Uplift.

Their inspirational pronouncements could have been completely cynical—but even if they were (and often they were not), the fact remains that the masters of the spectacle felt obliged to make them, publicly affirming some humanistic goal "above and beyond" the search for profit; whereas for the likes of Michael Eisner, "Adman of the Year," there are no more horizons, but only the expanding universe of corporate enterprise, eternally recycling its own derivative images. Whether it's McDonald's promoting, and being promoted by, Disney's *The Little Mermaid,* or MCA/Universal's *Back to the Future* (*I* and *II*) promoted at MCA/Universal's theme park, or Time-Warner's *Batman* advertised on millions of shoes and shorts, hats and place mats, in a Time-Warner rock video, in several paperbacks from Warner Books, by a cover story in *Time* magazine, on Time-Warner's cable channel HBO, each blockbuster is made to serve as an outsize, dazzling tool for "marketing every element of the company."

In short, Hollywood's loss of vision and the new moguls' disdain for cinema reflect an enormous structural change in the movie business: the absorption of the old vertical movie monopoly, or what was left of it, into the (still-evolving) "horizontal" media monopoly that reigns today. In other words, whereas the old movie companies, controlling every phase of filmmaking from production to exhibition, made only movies, that industry (much changed) is now a major cog, or chip, within a mammoth image-generating system that includes TV production companies and syndication firms, cable distribution networks, record companies, theme parks, and numerous merchandising operations—as well as publishing companies, major magazines, and many newspapers. Such is the collective sway of Walt Disney Co. (Disney, Touchstone), MCA (Universal), Time-Warner (Warner Bros.), Sony, Inc. (Columbia, Tri-Star), Paramount Communications (Paramount), and Rupert Murdoch's News Corporation Ltd. (Twentieth Century Fox). So potent and far-flung is this new nexus of media corporations that its general product, "entertainment," is now America's number-two export item, second only to military hardware.

In several areas crucial to the movies the new monopoly, in the eighties, regained the dominance of the old studios. In 1948, an antitrust suit forced the movie companies to sell off their theater chains, through a consent decree that was pointedly overruled in 1985 by the Department of Justice, then headed by pro-trust Attorney General Edwin Meese III. At once Coca-Cola (then owner of Columbia) bought the Walter Reade chain of theaters, then MCA, Gulf+Western, and Warner Communications bought others; so the studios can now, again, dictate what gets shown, and for how long. As a side benefit such control helped the new monopoly to drive out or devour the major independent distributors—Lorimar, Cannon, New World, Atlantic, De Laurentiis, Alive, and Island, among others—that once threatened to vary the usual offerings with foreign or otherwise marginal releases. (According to *Variety,* the independents released fifty-three films in September 1987 and only twenty-six in September 1989.)

While the newly subordinated studios (again) control exhibition and distribution, they no longer plan the films themselves. This crucial process is now dominated by the giant talent agencies that handle all the major names, and that, in effect, run Holly-

wood: William Morris, International Creative Management
(ICM), and—primarily—Creative Artists Agency (CAA),
headed by Michael Ovitz. Now that the studios, writes L. J.
Davis, "behave as though they were merchant banks, financing
pictures without direct involvement in the projects themselves,"
Ovitz has assumed "many of the studios' traditional functions:
controlling casting, choosing the director and getting the script
written." With its monopoly on talent, the agency can, and does,
require that the studios take on to write, direct, and star in each
production only the agency's own clients, who are, of course,
paid what the agency demands. A clear conflict of interest, this
arrangement has boosted Hollywood's pay scale to grotesque
proportions (Arnold Schwarzenegger was, by 1989, getting $11
million per picture)—an inflationary practice that actually benefits the reigning corporations, because no smaller entities can
afford to offer any competition. And the practice also worsens
cinema in subtler ways, since the superagent packages his clients
not to make each movie that much better but only to extract the
biggest possible commission.

And so Hollywood is now monopolized even more ruthlessly
than it was by the old movie moguls. Whereas those monopolists
would often borrow each other's stars in order to enhance certain
films, the superagent doesn't need to borrow, and makes his
money even if the movie is a dud. The ill effects of this new
monopoly, and the numerous feuds within it, are kept hidden by
a wholly complementary (and, of course, highly complimentary)
cabal of PR flacks who became all-powerful in the eighties—the
"caste of *publicists,*" as one ex-journalist puts it, "who limit access
to stars and other key players in order to maximize commercial
effect." These censors preempt any "negative" news stories simply by freezing out those reporters who won't write straight puff
pieces: a tactic that has brought back, on an enormous scale, the
sort of managed journalism that, vis-à-vis Hollywood, was commonplace before the sixties. "They're in the business of black-
balling the authors they consider 'bitchy,'" notes Stephanie
Mansfield of the *Washington Post.* "They want 1950s-fan-maga-

zine coverage: positive, Pollyanaish pap." Furthering their clients' (and their own) careers, the publicists thereby serve the new
monopoly, supplying it with many column inches, or broadcast
hours, of mythic "news" about the rich and famous.

Thus has Hollywood reverted to the most oppressive practices
of yesteryear, its new, improved monopoly sustained by figures—lawyers, agents, publicists—who have emerged from Hollywood's margins to become its ruling clique. The commercial
practices that are now crucial to the movie business were also
once marginal—merchandising, for instance. "Today," *Nation's
Business* reported in 1940, "every large motion picture company
has its cubbyhole set aside for [product] exploitation within the
advertising and publicity offices." As we have seen from the
enormous licensing success of films like *Batman,* a practice once
confined to some studio "cubbyhole" has now *become* the "movie
business," while the movies themselves, at the moment of their
greatest profitability, often seem to matter least of all.

And what about those movies? How has the new monopoly
affected cinema? The six original essays commissioned for this
volume answer this important question in various ways, and with
the necessary subtlety: that is, in pained awareness of what has
happened to the movies, and yet without nostalgia. On the one
hand, this book is highly critical of today's Hollywood, whose
managers have all but ruined American film for profit's sake. But
this critique (unlike many writings about cinema) in no way
yearns for the old studio system, whose grave limitations these
essayists do not ignore. Indeed, it is precisely an awareness of
those limitations, and of the mediocrity of most older movies,
that helps us see, belatedly, the value of an earlier Hollywood's
exceptional creations—which, in turn, make all too clear the state
of American cinema today.

If there is any epoch of our film history to which these essays
point with some approval, it is not the Golden Age of MGM,
but that chaotic interregnum between the demise of the old
studio system and the onset of the new monopoly, from the late
sixties through most of the seventies. We can now perceive the

passing of that period by thinking back on the recurrent nightmare image that intensifies so many of its strongest films—an image that Hollywood has since suppressed or sentimentalized.

Back then the movies, whatever their flaws, often dramatized the dark predicament of some lone and anxious self about to be erased, drowned out, filled in, or replicated by some superior collective force: the CIA in *Three Days of the Condor* (1975), or the sinister "Jefferson Institute" in *Coma* (1978), or the cabal behind the assassinations in *The Parallax View* (1974), or the media machine that finally gulps down Bill McKay in *The Candidate* (1972), or the show biz system that chews up Barbara-Jean in *Nashville* (1975), or the unearthly virus that, in *Dawn of the Dead* (1979), turns the American people into a mass of wandering ghouls, or the alien presence that, in the remake (1978) of *Invasion of the Body Snatchers* (1956), is hollowing out the whole human race.

That chilling threat—the onslaught of some hungry corporate force—is almost wholly absent from today's movies; or rather, the movies still depict the threat, but not chillingly, for Hollywood now treats the corporate conquest of the self as something wonderful. Thus, certain dreadful images of the seventies have since recurred as cute or rousing, like the young innocent's final captivation by some hard and ravenous old powermonger—a horror at the end of *Chinatown* (1974), a cause for joy (although very lightly ironized) at the end of *Working Girl* (1988). Likewise, the sight of a woman totally *made over*, so disturbing in the last shot of *The Stepford Wives* (1975) as in the second half of *Vertigo* (1958), has—much to the greater glory of the cosmetics industry—since been made to seem marvelously "life-affirming" in films like *Moonstruck* (1987) and *Married to the Mob* (1988).

Thus have the movies, vis-à-vis corporate power, lately shifted from a tragic or subversive view to a posture both reverential and promotional. Specifically, this shift began in the late seventies, as we can now see through another sharp historical contrast. "There is one holistic system of systems!" Thus the squat CEO exhorts the awed, crazed newsman sitting there before him, in what may be the funniest scene in *Network* (1976). "One vast, animé, *inter*woven, *inter*acting, *multi*variant, *multi*national dominion of *dollars!*" the tycoon preaches suavely. *"That* is the atomic, and *sub*atomic, and ga*lac*tic structure of *things* too-*day!"* The following year saw the release of *Star Wars*—which reconceived the overwhelming corporate force, treating it not satirically but in a pious tone of pseudo-mysticism, as another old wizard preaches much the same "holistic" gospel (although in duller language) to another would-be soldier against empire: "The Force is what gives the Jedi his power. It's an energy field created by all living things. It surrounds us and penetrates us. It binds the galaxy together."

Here was one sign of an impending conquest that we can notice only now, long afterward, and whose effects on cinema these essays expose and analyze. *Network* is a key film in Todd Gitlin's "Down the Tubes." Starting with Elia Kazan's and Budd Schulberg's half-ferocious (and prophetic) *A Face in the Crowd* (1957) and ending with James Brooks's grinning *Broadcast News* (1987), Gitlin traces the movies' gradual surrender to TV and points out how bad a bargain it has been for cinema—a view that also offers us a valuable corrective to McLuhan's theory. Douglas Gomery, too, is concerned with the general narrowing of cinema, although his subject is the changed nature of film spectatorship. Focusing on corporate economics and its effect on the movie-viewing experience, "If You've Seen One, You've Seen the Mall" recounts the degradation of that experience from the days of the lavish, comfortable Roxy to this moment of the stripped-down multiplex and omnipresent VCR.

From these overviews we move on to essays that, in different ways, illuminate the backward-looking stance of Hollywood movies since the seventies. "Good Soldiers" takes a careful look at how Hollywood has refought (and revised) the Vietnam War on the screen. Pat Aufderheide sees most of those war films not as reflections of some "mature acceptance" of our recent history but as fearful efforts to replace that history with a "past" more flattering both to the Americans who fought the war and to those

who watched it—and who now watch these movies. Peter Biskind reveals a similar regressiveness in the blockbusters of
George Lucas and Steven Spielberg. "The Last Crusade" shows
how those big, simple films were devised as correctives to the
harder, more troubling Hollywood movies of the early seventies—and how, surprisingly, those directors' countercultural impulses turned out to complement, or even reinforce, the
foreign-policy agenda of the Reagan administration.

We end with two essays dealing with some crucial manifesta-
tions of the movies' new ultra-commercialism. Stuart Klawans
tackles the issue of colorization, moving well beyond the usual
lament and even subjecting it to critical scrutiny. "Rose-Tinted
Spectacles" illuminates the fierce debate over colorization by
recounting the full history of the neoclassical bias against color—
and by reminding us that the real problem is not the desecration
of the movies by their owners but the prerogative of ownership
itself. Finally, I analyze how the spirit and techniques of advertising have all but devastated cinematic narrative through widespread product plugging, a reduction of film grammar, the
incessant foregrounding of celebrity, and the repeated use of a
certain kind of happy ending—new conventions that reflect both
on the monopoly's agenda and on the public taste which that
monopoly has helped transform.

"But hasn't it *always* been like that?" No critique of today's
mass culture can (it seems) escape this question, which is usually
intended not to illuminate the issue but to shut down all debate
about it. Nevertheless, these essayists take the question seriously
and offer the only possible response: "Yes and no." As culture
critics of a certain age, we are not likely to romanticize the
Hollywood that was; and yet—as culture critics of a certain age—
we are also struck by how much "Hollywood" has changed, and
changed the world, since we were students just a few decades
ago. Although we don't look back to any golden age, we do
sustain ourselves in clear remembrance of a time when the movies held a certain promise, since denied. Over and over, what
would have seemed intolerable just a few years ago has now

become familiar, in part because the movies now are made deliberately to show us nothing, but to sell us everything. Remembering something different, and in the hope of something better still,
these critics urge their audience to look "above and beyond the
box office"—as, until recently, the movies often seemed to do,
and sometimes really did.

*D*own *the* *Tubes*

TODD GITLIN

1

"THE 'CONTENT' OF TV is the movie," wrote Marshall McLuhan. To be sure, McLuhan was promoting a general aphorism—"the 'content' of any medium is always another medium"—one of those preachments that, like many a gourmet restaurant menu, looks best at first glance. Even years before CNN, the Home Shopping Network, and Geraldo Rivera, McLuhan might have paused from his global generalization to notice Ernie Kovacs, Sid Caesar, Ed Sullivan, and wrestling—none of them exactly a movie.

McLuhan had a one-category mind. History for him was a single slipstream. There was an age of print, an age of movies, an age of television, and so on; each supplanted the other in an

apparently never-ending onrush of opportunity; there was no
room in this scheme for more than a single medium at a single
time. And therefore McLuhan didn't suggest what would seem,
at first glance, a more defensible proposition, namely that *the
dethroned medium first fights back, then accommodates.* First the outdated form practices revenge on the upstart. Then the old medium partly imitates the new, partly settles into the margins left
by the new form's triumph.

Reasons for revenge are obvious. People who derive status
and income from the practice of a cultural craft resent competition from interlopers—especially when they have to compete for
the same consumers. The longer the tradition in which the crafts-
people are working, and the more they have invested in their
craft, the more they hate the idea of adapting gracefully to the
new form—if they are capable of adapting at all.

But unencumbered by these human emotions, today's media
omnicorporations aim with considerable success to lubricate all
the transitions. They adapt with relative ease to new media and
technologies for distributing them. Gaily they decant old forms
into new technological bottles: everything for the package.
Unimpeded by any commitment to traditions or particular practices, they can pursue every technology at once, shifting production from one to another—from records to tapes to compact
disks, from theatrical movies to videocassettes—as profit beck-
ons. Each technology becomes a marketing zone for the others.

As popular culture approximates an assortment of theme
parks, American movies have become spark plugs for the wrap-
around media spectacle. The Hollywood dazzle that in the twenties, thirties, forties, and fifties regularly promoted a bit of magic
and transcendence alongside piles of myth and banality has been
blended into a vaster, blurrier, more extravagant media mix.
More and more, movies themselves have turned into coming
attractions—fodder for TV (and radio) morning shows, local and
national TV news, syndicated shows like *Entertainment Tonight,*
national magazines from *People* to *Vanity Fair, USA Today* and the
newspaper style sections, novelizations, comic books, theme-song

records, toys, T-shirts, and, of course, sequels. The sum of the
publicity takes up more cultural space than the movie itself.

On the organizational level one logical next step is already
underway—the bringing of all the components under a single
corporate roof. Thus, the Time-Warner merger and Sony's buy-
out of Columbia Pictures formalize functional cohabitations that
have been at work for decades. In this setting a profoundly anti-
establishment movie figure like Charlie Chaplin is hard to imagine (outside the degraded form of an IBM ad). Even in Europe,
let alone in the United States, serious careers making substantial
movies have become noble anachronisms.

How did American movies adapt to their diminished magnitude in the cultural firmament? In the story of the movies' absorption into the general spectacle, no subplot reveals more than the
story of the movies' accommodation to television. American
movies have coexisted with television for almost half a century
now. In the late forties the studios thought that the TV craze
would blow over and resorted to noncooperation: they refused
to make recent movies available for broadcast, and, as Tim
Brooks and Earle Marsh have noted, "many stars' contracts expressly forbade their appearance on television." When movies
finally wheeled around to address TV as a topic, they mocked it,
warned against its dangers, despised its stupidity. Such disdain,
whether in content or policy, will most likely not erupt again. By
and large the fight is over. The movies, like Europe's royalty,
have given up. On the whole they have settled for glamour and
popular culture's funky equivalent of prestige. Unable to beat
television for pure drawing power, movie people joined it, all the
while hoarding their status, sneering and imitating by turns, insisting on how special they still are.

Social status tells part, but only part, of the story. In Hollywood's pecking order, movies retain their premier (as they say)
standing. Think of the venue: movies borrow the aura of a palace
(even if the palace has been subdivided into a multiplex), while
TV is crammed into a box. TV writers, directors, and actors
aspire to work in the movies, not the other way around. In the

eyes of the movie crowd, television is second best, good for salary and security, while the movies belong to art, rich with glory.

Television, however, can afford to be generous. With little status to lose and big ratings to win, it cheerfully grants the movies their first-class standing. Television, that bottomless stomach, glories in its aspiration to devour and digest everything out there, the reality of earth and the fantasy of heaven alike; whatever else the movies may be, they are also, from TV's point of view, *something to cover*. After all, television draws a good part of its cultural power from its claim to import whatever matters—the space shot, the royal wedding, the World Series, the presidential photo opportunity, the famine, the riot, the bereaved's tears of grief, the Super Bowl, *and the movie*—into the home. The movies can make no such claim. (The big-screen newsreel, with its bombastic urgency, was a casualty of TV news: it simply couldn't compete.) As TV delights in big events, it borrows their glory, confirming them and itself in the same burst of coverage. Television not only entertains (McLuhan's premise), it gobbles and certifies; it wires the home into the world. Television triumphs by absorbing, and its absorbency apparently has no limit. There is a place for any image in its artificial sun; a place not only for the cornucopia of actual movies that spills out through cable channels and networks and independent stations alike but for Hollywood magic, the glamour and fascination of the star system itself.

The movies, having accommodated, now thrive on the attention; every March their most hallowed ceremony rambles amiably in the interstices between commercials. The Oscar ceremony aims to ingratiate by mocking itself—making the movies look good by comparison. As television revels in its capacity for self-denigration, star-hosts get off bad lines and muff others (the astute ones, like Johnny Carson adrift in a failing monologue, are sharp enough to make sport of their botches); they mock their writers and present musical numbers that are overblown past the point of self-parody; but the movies themselves, ah, the *motion pictures,* the *films,* are something else. They are taken with royal seriousness. The clips retain their hieratic aura. When each is done and the screen fades to black, the ritual applause of the assembled nominees and other luminaries confirms two things at once: that movies hold on to their magic, and that television is the means by which the populace gains access to the stars and their echoes of grandeur. Once the star-stricken, TV-packaged ceremony is over, TV news resorts to a gaga tone to regale its viewers with properly ceremonious news.

But the relative, residual prestige of movies disguises the change in their cultural position. On the whole, movies command attention one at a time—as movies, not *the movies*. Blockbusters filter into popular lore—*Rocky, Star Wars, E.T., Rambo, Ghostbusters*. Movies occasionally incite identification or controversy—*Fort Apache, The Bronx; Platoon; Colors; The Color Purple; Mississippi Burning; Do the Right Thing*. These are special events. People fumbling for common ground at parties still compare notes about movies—seeking consumer guidance and cultural community, occasionally recommending a good time. The odd movie star or style still sets hearts aflutter. But the star as type, a larger-than-life yet somehow imitable presence hovering above this role or that, personifying a way to live—Humphrey Bogart, James Stewart, John Wayne, Bette Davis, Marilyn Monroe—is virtually gone. (Today's few holdovers are negative models, figures to steer clear of—Jack Nicholson, Woody Allen.) Since the fifties the steady rituals of culture and the recognizable types in terms of whom—or against whom—people organize their identity and sense the shape of the world have been more often found on the small screen, with *Ozzie and Harriet, Father Knows Best, Leave It to Beaver, All in the Family, Charlie's Angels, Dallas, Dynasty, Happy Days, Family Ties, Hill Street Blues, Miami Vice, L.A. Law, The Cosby Show, Roseanne, thirtysomething,* and so on. With their pass at verisimilitude, it is these characters who have more often become cultural commonplaces, exemplars, and reference points. *Batman* sells $100 million worth of tickets in its first eleven days on the screen, and gives a boost to the T-shirt industry, but the audience's attachment is weak. Children make sport with the image, but the *character* of Batman becomes a touchstone for few lives. The world of the hit movie is a fantasy world which generates play but which no one expects to be real.

So the movies go on, dominated by blockbuster entertainment machines—their characters skimpy, their plots threadbare, their styles derivative, their images brutal, their significance shrinking in inverse proportion to their budgets, screaming to be heard over the endless din of television. There are many reasons for this, not least the studios' loss of guaranteed distribution and adult audiences, the consequent skewing of the movie audience toward youth, and the industry's insatiable hunger for hits. But threading throughout these other factors, television looms large in the fate of the movies. My object in the pages that follow is to ask, at two levels, how the movies have been affected and afflicted by television. First, when the movies depict television as a subject, what does this television look like? Second, how has the institution of television changed the forms and styles of the movies? In both ways television, bastard child of the movies and radio, has triumphed over its parents, leaving Hollywood to revel in revenues, publicity, passable product, and past glories.

2

At this writing, with television in more American homes than indoor plumbing, with more than half of American households possessed of two or more TV sets, with more than 60 percent possessed of a VCR and 25 percent possessed of two or more VCRs, with the average set in use roughly seven hours a day, it is hard to recall that for decades, for better or worse, movies were the centerpiece of America's popular culture.

For the movies' hold on popular attention plunged with amazing speed. In the fifties, as customers moved to the movieless suburbs and raised babies, and television rippled outward from its early hold in the urban middle classes, the movie audience plummeted. Between 1946 and 1957, movie attendance sank by half—from 90 million to 45 million per week. To put it more sharply, if we compare only the peak moviegoing years 1945–49 and the years 1960–64, average movie attendance per household sank by two-thirds—from 2.15 per week to 0.78 per week. The rate fell even faster for that part of the population over twenty-five.

Whatever might be thought about the perspicacity of capitalists when it comes to making money, Hollywood was slow to get the competitive point. The studios assumed at first that TV was a passing fancy like those early picturephones that never caught on. As it became clear that people were staying home in droves, the studios fought TV with gimmicks (3-D) and spectacles (The Robe) and slogans ("Get more out of life, go to a movie"). But they were whistling in the dark. TV, that household appliance with pictures, was indefatigable. After all, the cultural ideal was the self-sufficient home celebrating its good fortune while marooned on its private island stuffed with acquisitions. No wonder the TV set became the central good and, thanks to advertising, the main purveyor of the rest of the standard package. Like the French behind their Maginot Line, the studios got huffy and waited for the enemy to go away. That was precisely what the enemy did not do.

By the early sixties, as movie audiences continued to hemorrhage, the studios wised up. Soon, for the most part, they had transformed themselves into facilities for the assembly line production of TV "product," with movies a sideline. Major investment went into television shows to which the studios held legal title. Once they had leased them to the networks, they could lease them again, and again, into syndication—a lucrative afterlife, considering that there were hundreds of local stations, and scores of foreign TV systems, in the market for cheap product. Movie production dispersed; the studios devolved into banks for the financing and distribution of movies.

It took the makers of movies—producers, directors, and writers—a decade to recognize that they had been dethroned. Throughout the early TV years, the movies went on gamely doing what they knew how to do: musicals, comedies, Westerns, weepies, melodrama, occasional "historical" pageants, and social realism. The new wrinkle was science fiction, where the unspoken objects of alarm were the Russians and the nuclear bomb, itself the dark side of a technological cornucopia whose bright, everyday face was beyond criticism. At a time when the movies invited people to "get more out of life," there was one curious absence. The world portrayed in the movies was a world in which television was missing—although characters continued to go to the movies. Through this vast hole in the realist form of representation they laid claim to, the movies, like television itself, reeked of nostalgia. In effect, movies became commemorations of a vanishing time.

Not until 1957 did any Hollywood movies pay serious attention to television. Two movies that year broke the spell. They could not have been more different. Frank Tashlin's *Will Success Spoil Rock Hunter?*, from a play by the same name, was a teaser, an amiable sendup of the public-relations and advertising businesses, featuring mock commercials in which the image shrank to television proportions while the rest of the screen went blank—a droll reminder that the big screen was irreplaceable. Television was silly, advertising ridiculed—these were aesthetic offenses, nuisances. Their social consequences were not at issue. Still, in its mild way, *Rock Hunter* recognized that advertising and television were inseparable, and that television belonged to a way of life that had elevated banality and deception to cultural principles.

In Elia Kazan's *A Face in the Crowd* (with a screenplay by Budd Schulberg), on the other hand, TV was the very devil's appliance. The medium enshrined mendacity and mediocrity—this was not incidental, this was its purpose. Serving corporate greed and demagoguery, TV married capitalism to populism; at its heart was heartlessness. Kazan's earlier *Viva Zapata!* and *On the Waterfront* had assigned to their heroes (both played by Marlon Brando) the martyrdom to which Kazan himself felt entitled as a much-detested namer of names before the House Un-American Activities Committee. Now, as if back in the Popular Front,

Kazan, purged of communism, found a way to resurrect his populist faith—to criticize capitalism, sentimentalize the masses, and crank out a happy ending all at the same time.

Andy Griffith played Lonesome Rhodes, a small-town Arkansas drifter and home-grown populist discovered by Marcia (Patricia Neal), a former Sarah Lawrence art major who runs a local radio interview show. Lonesome strums, sings, and smolders. On the radio, when he gives a speech on the rights of women, the mail pours in. Having discovered he can sway people for righteous ends, Lonesome acquires a local notoriety. No less a national figure than John Cameron Swayze, the NBC newsman, features him. The whole town turns out when he goes off to become a TV star.

On TV, Lonesome continues to be a man of the people—in fact, a man of the left. He puts a "colored woman" on television, twits a commercial, says that the atom bomb is "important"—and gets fired. But his career is unstoppable. He goes to New York. Here he falls in with advertising men who are trying to figure out how to sell Vitajex pills. Lonesome's genius for selling turns out to be all-purpose. "Make 'em yellow," he says, and sell them sexy. As aphrodisiac, Vitajex sells.

Rhodes, the man of the people, has already become a confidence man. The line he crosses is imperceptible—that is the sinister and revelatory thing about the career of Lonesome Rhodes. The energy that catapulted him to celebrity—the fascination with power—is the very one that turns him into a confidence man. Andy Griffith was inspired casting: his open face gives an impression of intelligence, folk cunning, and innocence all at once. All he needs to be dangerous is sponsorship. And this is perhaps what is exemplary in the meteoric career of Lonesome Rhodes: he is a man without qualities. His ideas are slight. What leads him to defend women or bring a black woman onto his show? What does he mean by saying the atom bomb is "important"? It is never quite clear. His liberal ideas are gossamer, as much so as his fascist ones. Lonesome Rhodes lacks weight. He blows in the wind. His motives are unfathomable, to himself most of all. Lonesome is that quintessential American male who no sooner arrives than he is gone. He lives on, and for, the road.

Sponsorship is forthcoming, since General Haynsworth, who owns Vitajex, has decided to turn his attention to political ambitions. "My study of history," he pontificates, "has convinced me that in every strong and healthy society from the Egyptians on, the mass had to be guided with a strong hand by a responsible elite. Let us not forget that in TV we have the greatest instrument for mass persuasion in the history of the world." Thanks to the general's contacts with media moguls, Lonesome Rhodes's photo makes the covers of *Life* and *Look*. He gets on *This Is Your Life* and hosts a telethon. The general sets him up in a penthouse atop corporate headquarters.

In politics Haynsworth promotes Senator Worthington Fuller, but Fuller is an old-fashioned windbag. "We've got to face it," Haynsworth sounds off. "Politics have entered a new stage, the television stage. Instead of long-winded public debates, the people want capsule slogans: 'time for a change,' 'the mess in Washington,' 'more bang for a buck.' Punchlines and glamour." Lonesome Rhodes will be his handler—"that's just what he did for Vitajex." "This whole country's just like my flock of sheep," Lonesome boasts. He becomes Secretary for National Morale. "They're even more stupid than I am, so I got to think for 'em."

But Rhodes has grown too full of himself. The virtuous Marcia brings him down with—what else?—technology. At the end of one of his TV shows, Rhodes, thinking his mike is dead, amuses himself by denouncing the public for its idiocy. Unbeknownst to Rhodes, Marcia, in the control room, switches his mike on. The audience is shocked, and the uproar destroys his career. Rhodes flips out. At the end we see him standing on his balcony, a loner again, ranting to his applause machine. The tortoise-shelled writer played by Walter Matthau, the movie's resident sage and chorus, delivers a clunker of a speech saying, "We got wise to him. That's our strength. We get wise to 'em."

We are supposed to believe that he who lives by publicity dies by publicity. But we don't necessarily get wise to 'em before they leave their stamp on life and death, wealth and poverty, the national ethos. Seen from the present, *A Face in the Crowd* prefigures the career of another artless-looking media "personality." At just the moment when *A Face in the Crowd* was playing the theaters, Ronald Reagan was hosting *General Electric Theater* for the home crowd. Nine years later, in 1966, Reagan was drafted into the California gubernatorial race by a small group of right-wing businessmen who were looking for a prominent and reliable personality to carry the Goldwater standard into state politics. Reagan, like Lonesome Rhodes, came from the American heartland and started out left of center. Before Hollywood, Reagan, too, was a local folk celebrity and master of homespun hokum—a popular sports announcer in Des Moines. Reagan, like Rhodes, was that twentieth-century generic, the celebrity—that distinctive polyform media type, the figure who both arouses and answers to popular tropisms so primitive they cannot be easily grasped.

Nineteen fifty-seven was early. Control rooms were sloppily policed. Had security been tighter and TV technology more advanced, the moral might truly have been: in America *anyone* can grow up to be president. Thirty years later, audiences have become more "sophisticated," i.e., more cynical: a media-made president, establishing voice levels in a radio studio, could blurt out, "We start bombing Russia in five minutes," without suffering political damage. Ronald Reagan might joke about the end of civilization, but he had the good taste not to insult his constituency.

3

Two decades passed before Hollywood produced another major movie—a star vehicle—in which the workings of television were central. In the interim, Haskell Wexler's independent *Medium Cool* (1969) was a game attempt to explore the TV journalist's savvy indifference at a time when TV news was looming ever larger in national politics. For all its confused hoopla amid the

1968 Democratic convention demonstrations, *Medium Cool* made one lasting contribution: the image of the cameraman-hero "shooting" the injured motorist at the side of the freeway, just doing his job. Then *The Candidate* (1972), directed by Michael Ritchie with a script by Jeremy Larner, was the first movie to catch the dreadful merger of television, celebrity, and elections, melting ideals into patter and character into marketable personality. *The Candidate* caught something important about television: it deceives by pretending to be transparent. Claiming to show all, TV mocks democratic aspirations by closing off the discourse of politics.

But 1976's *Network* was the high point of the movies' revenge on TV. Sidney Lumet once told me that a third of the dialogue in *Network* was verbatim network material. The exact proportion doesn't matter—the film crackles with inside detail, even as verisimilitude skids into satire, which in turn lurches into soap opera, and the movie frequently loses its bearings as the genres spin. Both director Lumet and screenwriter Paddy Chayefsky had put in their years in the so-called Golden Age of TV, so their full-blooded paranoid screech carried deep industrial knowledge, even if they hyped some details. Their slash-and-burn style was suited to a world in which the likes of Fred Silverman and Aaron Spelling could rise to the heights, or depths, of television's tasteless taste-making. Unencumbered by realism, they proved realistic.

Network pivots on a contrast between the old television and the new, the old personified in news anchorman Howard Beale (Peter Finch) and news executive Max Schumacher (William Holden), the new in network entertainment executive Diana Christensen (Faye Dunaway) and higher-level corporate honchos Frank Hackett (Robert Duvall) and Arthur Jensen (Ned Beatty). Beale and Schumacher are products, or relics, of the Edward R. Murrow days of straight, gutsy, no-nonsense, world-encompassing news. As the film starts, the rumpled, bland Beale's ratings are sinking. Traditionally, the news has lost money, but the new corporate ownership now demands that the news become profitable, whereupon Beale is fired. Beale, drunk, goes on the air and announces that he's going to shoot himself on the air next week. He proclaims that "the world is a demented slaughterhouse," that existence is "bullshit," and moreover—as if this were commensurate with the rest of what is wrong with the world—that his wife yells. Ratings soar.

Meanwhile, the fast-talking, fast-walking, fast-bouncing entertainment executive Diana Christensen is prospecting for souped-up shows: "I want angry shows! I want counterculture, anti-establishment!" She sees Howard Beale as "a latter-day prophet" and obtains permission to take over the news show and reprogram it. "TV is show biz," she tells the scandalized Schumacher:

> I watched your 6:00 news today. It's straight tabloid . . . It was all sex, scandal, brutal crimes, sports, children with incurable diseases, and lost puppies. So I don't think I'll listen to any protestations of any high standards of journalism. You're right down on the street soliciting audiences with the rest of us. Look, all I'm saying is, if you're going to hustle, do it right.

Schumacher, dazzled, soon leaves his wife for the lovely Christensen, who can't stop talking about ratings even in bed, where she climbs on top of him and comes to orgasm prematurely.

Meanwhile, Howard Beale is boosting his ratings with diatribes about OPEC, inflation, recession, Beirut, crime, pollution, you name it—the words are markers of a world out of control. "I don't know what to do about it," Beale rants, "but first you've got to get mad. I want you to get up now, I want all of you to get up now and go to the window and yell, 'I'm as mad as hell and I'm not going to take this anymore!' " And all over the country, people do. The result is a 42 percent share of the viewing audience, more than all other news shows combined.

The new, improved *Howard Beale Show* debuts under entertainment division auspices (announcer cue: "How do you feel?"—audience: "I'm mad as hell!"), featuring Sybil the Soothsayer, the gossip Mata Hari "and her skeletons in the closet," and a "Vox Populi" public-opinion segment, and starring "the mad prophet of the airwaves" himself. Beale's opening-night tirade is the classic piece of anti-TV paranoia:

> Only fifteen percent of you read newspapers. The only truth you know is what you get over the tube . . . You're beginning to think that the tube is reality and that your own lives are unreal . . . You do what the tube tells you to do. You dress like the tube, you eat like the tube, you raise your children like the tube . . . So turn off your TV sets . . . Turn them off right in the middle of the sentence I'm speaking now—

whereupon he faints. The jaunty theme music comes up, the audience goes wild with applause.

Diane Christensen is riding high, and not only in bed. She has back-to-back hits in *The Howard Beale Show* followed by *The Mao Tse-tung Hour,* featuring the weekly exploits of a ragtag Ecumenical Liberation Army, which provides home movies of its robberies and kidnappings through the mediation of an Afro-coiffed Communist named Lureen Hobbs—an obvious sendup of Angela Davis. In perhaps the only representation of TV deal-making in the entire history of movies, there is an extravagant and hilarious scene in which Hobbs, the ELA, and the network lawyers wrangle over the terms of their contract (Hobbs: "Don't fuck with my distribution costs!").

Soon enough Beale reveals to his audience that the CCA conglomerate, which owns the network and which is itself the twelfth-largest corporation in the world, has been bought by a Saudi Arabian front. At his behest 6 million telegrams flood into the White House denouncing the deal. Which causes CCA chairman Arthur Jensen to call Beale into his conference room and set him straight that to "howl about America and democracy" is naïve in the extreme, for "there is no America, there is no democracy, there are only IBM and ITT and ATT and Dupont, Dow, Union Carbide and Exxon."

Beale goes back on TV with a new sermon:

> We know that democracy is a dying giant. The Communists are deader than we are . . . What is finished is the idea that this great country is dedicated to the freedom and flourishing of

every individual in it. It's the individual that's finished. It's the
single solitary human being that's finished.

Beale's ratings plummet. And therefore so do the ratings of
The Mao Tse-tung Hour. Lureen Hobbs is furious. Frank Hackett
comes up with a plan, and Christensen goes along. At the season
premiere, members of the Ecumenical Liberation Army stand up
in the audience and open fire with automatic rifles. Beale falls.
The camera rolls in for a close-up.

There is nothing subtle about *Network*'s satirical style. The
characters are mouthpieces for positions. The positions are crude
(and sometimes inaccurate: newspaper readership was then and
is now considerably higher than 15 percent). The demonizing of
the Saudis (today it would be the Japanese, and with the same
arguments—they own so much real estate, etc.) is a cheap shot,
typical of Howard Beale's ranting hodgepodge. Horror of horrors, *them Arabs* are galloping at us again; one would never find
an *American* company whoring for ratings!

Still, *Network* caught something essential about the television
business. In the mid-seventies the real world was preparing to
caricature itself. The networks had just begun to obtain overnight
Nielsen ratings for major cities; the national Nielsens, which took
sixteen days to arrive in 1961, were now being delivered weekly.
Accordingly, network greed spun into a competitive frenzy. As
Max Schumacher complains, the networks had indeed begun
expecting their news divisions to show profits—no more prestigi-
ous loss leaders for them. Local news was already what Diane
Christensen claimed network news had become—news 'n' entertainment. In real life the Symbionese Liberation Army had hi-
jacked the evening news by kidnaping Patty Hearst; and the Los
Angeles police had slaughtered the SLA live on television. Networks were not yet "in play" for corporate takeovers, but CBS
Inc. had already swallowed record stores and musical-instrument
companies to become a conglomerate, and NBC, as a branch of
RCA, was not exactly a freestanding tower of fearless journalism.

At several points *Network* measured the TV of the seventies against the "Golden Age"—meaning live drama—of the fifties. Its backward glance, of course, was somewhat brightened by the glow of nostalgia. News during much of Howard Beale's good old days was a fifteen-minute capsule lorded over (far more than today) by government spokesmen. Diana Christensen's protestation that everyone in television is a hustler was overdone—but it struck a nerve. As for entertainment, the "Golden Age," let it not be forgotten, was strictly white—and doubly censored. Starting in 1954, only a year into the "Golden Age," sponsors demanded revisions in any drama that smacked of the socially disturbing, and that same year the anti-Communist blacklist began excluding some of the most talented people. But allowing for such serious truncations, in those years an inner circle of writers and directors were able to do what they wanted (limited as TV's forms and subjects were) without having to smuggle their work through layers of bureaucracy. The Chayefsky/Lumet lament carries the pathos—and substantial truth—of any small-business complaint against the suffocating effects of the giant corporation.

Network's populist satire also prefigured major political turns of the eighties. Just as Howard Beale decried a world out of control, so was *Network* itself out of control: a pastiche of styles and ideological fragments. Beale's populism tilted leftward (anti-corporate) more than rightward (anti–welfare state) but tossed in plenty of xenophobia; his amalgam, like many a real-world populist's, was sloppy enough to be exploitable by the real-world right. A few years later, when the California tax crusader Howard Jarvis campaigned for Proposition 13, the deeply regressive property tax reform that accelerated the fiscal crisis of the state's cities, his slogan, enshrined on the bumper stickers where Californians transact their political business, was "I'M MAD AS HELL AND I'M NOT GOING TO TAKE IT ANYMORE." The distance from Beale's scattershot rants to the seething, stagy late-eighties persona of Morton Downey, Jr., is perhaps not so great.

Network, part of the post-Watergate swing against big institutions, had no easy victories to celebrate. Its critique of television was radical and paranoid. Audiences were not exempt from the logic of the situation. What spewed out was indiscriminate vitriol. The target was the entire society of the spectacle—not least the manageable mass. Thus did *Network* distinguish itself from *A Face in the Crowd*–style populism in which "the people," once they become informed, finally can't be fooled. In this respect Kazan's version of populism resembled, in fact, television's own, which presumes, through tone, voice, form of address, that television and audience are in it together—and that there's no exit.

In American television's regular tone of address, the attitudes, feelings, values of "the common people" are the bedrock standard to which all value is finally referred. Whether in the voice of Johnny Carson or Bryant Gumbel, Geraldo Rivera or Oprah Winfrey, an audience of little folks is summoned to stand against snobs, jerks, and selected big shots. In the commercial's up-tempo look and the announcer's smile, in the anchor's shy thanks and the game show host's jubilation, television flatters its audience with reminders of how fortunate they are, how deserving, to have been rewarded with television. Threading throughout television's endless appeals for viewership, its wheedling and promises, its soft sells and vague bullying ("Don't miss . . .!"), there resounds this jubilant, pseudodemocratic note of flattery. The sovereign audience is assumed to deserve all the fun it can get—but is gifted with common sense and ample choice, and therefore, once fully informed about the issues of the day, will do (and buy) the right thing.

By contrast, *Network* sets itself apart by sheer sourness. Nathanael West would have relished everything but its crude adultery scenes. In the end popular wisdom affords no redemption. When Howard Beale tells his studio audience that they don't know anything, they go wild—hit us again! When he tells them that corporate control puts individuality at risk, his ratings sink. When he is assassinated on air, there is a moment of stunned silence; then, as if on cue, the studio audience breaks into applause.

4

With *Network,* the *enragé* key was largely played out. After 1976 no other big-release Hollywood movie immersed itself so deeply in the supply side of television for more than a decade, although *The China Syndrome* (1979) deserves mention; the film's release on the eve of the Three Mile Island near-disaster obscured the fact that the plot revolved around the parallel revolts of *two* whistle-blowers: Jack Lemmon's nuclear-plant supervisor against the utility, and Jane Fonda's reporter, tired of being a happy-news "piece of talking furniture," against the TV station. Paranoia slipped into a decadent, incoherent mode in Sam Peckinpah's last film, the B-ish ostensible spy thriller *The Osterman Weekend* (1983), which lionized an investigative talk show host (played by Rutger Hauer) who brought down an evil CIA director (Burt Lancaster), but not before realizing that in a world of universal surveillance everyone is programmed. Peckinpah's bloody mess did contain one memorable line: a TV writer-tycoon (Craig T. Nelson) calls himself "a nihilistic anarchist who lives on residuals."

One worthwhile probe into TV's demand side did appear: *Being There* (1979), which extended *Network*'s view of the audience as mass society into a compatible parable. In Hal Ashby's version of the Jerzy Kozinski novel, with a screenplay by Kozinski and an inspired deadpan performance by Peter Sellers, Chance, the dissociated gardener, is a *tabula rasa,* Candide with a remote-control device. Chance's addiction to television gives him his only human contact; for the rest, he is content to pay attention to growing things. As he switches his way through the daily pastiche, from symphony to cartoon to news to game show to exercise, his unworn, almost fetally blank face is a wondrous contrast to the fragments of canned happiness stretching forever before him. Television is Chance's world; he speaks its phrases, repeats its exercises, and concludes that the world is television: he thinks he can zap away unpleasant realities (like some street toughs) with a click. When he is forced out of seclusion and ventures into the street, he assumes an intimate relation with everyone he meets—his error is to generalize television's false intimacies. Repeating what the tube tells him, he is the ideal watcher. Watching is his innocent approach to reality. "I like to watch TV" must be the most memorable of deliberate banalities.

The joke, of course, is that Chance's emptiness equips him not only as a consumer of significations but as a signifier himself. Others see in Chance (as people see in television) what they want to see: one finds him "intense," another, possessed of "quite a sense of humor." His mastery of the empty phrase destines him to become a political figure. He is as empty as Lonesome Rhodes but well meaning. In a world of blather he sounds profound. A man without history, a blank space in the archives, always aiming to please, he proves to be the ideal talk show guest and presidential adviser. (The ending is refreshingly inconclusive: the audience gets to decide whether Chance will get to be president of the United States.) His abnormal dedication to television makes him a freak, of course; but if normal people esteem him because of his television image, what does that say about *them?* As crude in its premise as *Network, Being There,* too, has the courage of its oversimplications.

5

Bright as a Dukakis button, *Broadcast News* emerged in 1987 out of Reagan's America.

Neat correspondences between zeitgeists and movies are seductive, but that does not make them false. In this case it is advisable to succumb. The shift from *Network*'s smash on the head to *Broadcast News*'s tickle under the chin speaks volumes about the course of American culture during the intervening years. *Network,* in all its venom and wildness, colored by paranoia, was an afterburn from the sixties, but more: it belonged to the cultural interregnum presided over by Jimmy Carter, a brief moment when a large general public felt indignant about the corruption and meanness of American life and the venality of its corporations. Such bitter satire, propounding to the audience that they are ignorant, complicit, even unenlightenable, still desperately seeks to enlighten.

By the time of *Broadcast News* we are well into the prolonged twilight presided over by Ronald Reagan. Corporate takeovers are greeted less by outrage than by public fascination with the entrepreneur. We have traversed the distance from harsh, even hysterical exposé, the fifties individualism of Sidney Lumet and Paddy Chayefsky overlaid by a sixties sense of apocalypse, to romantic rue, the seventies TV sensibility of James L. Brooks, whose television career as a writer was capped by *The Mary Tyler Moore Show* and whose previous directorial outing was the soap opera *Terms of Endearment.* Far more than in *Network,* Hollywood here treats old-fashioned television, the television that is fading from view, with the reverence that television usually displays toward the movies. *Broadcast News*'s nostalgia suggests that, so far as Hollywood is concerned, television—the right sort of serious, dignified television—has been repositioned upward. The movies have learned to stop worrying and love (the right kind of) television.

The plot of *Broadcast News* lines up along a single polarity—again, as in *Network,* the old, good, smart, honest television versus the new, bad, dumb, deceptive one. In *Broadcast News,* too, the bogey is the megacorporation, insatiably hungry for profits, which fires workers and dumbs the show down. (Less culpable but still implicated are the legions of pretty boys and girls in local news who stand in line for their anchor privileges.) In *Network* the transformation to tabloid TV is already far advanced; Max Schumacher and Howard Beale commune about the good old days, but those days are already good and old, two decades gone. But *Broadcast News* catches the industry in mid-convulsion; the good old days are just now passing before our eyes. This time the tone is wistful and the outcome, at least in certain respects, doubtful. The bright, frenetic, power-walking news producer Jane Craig (Holly Hunter) personifies the either/or, because, rueful about the slippage away from the serious, she also knows that

unseriousness has its seductions. Presented as impeccably professional, deploring the invasion of hard news by squishy entertainment, she will find it necessary to choose, romantically, between
the knowledgeable, trustworthy, veteran correspondent Aaron
Altman (Albert Brooks) and the up-and-coming pretty-boy anchorman Tom Grunick (William Hurt). Aaron tries, and fails, to
hold the time-honored line of seriousness against Tom and his
dumb-bunny crowd-pleasing ways. A traditional romantic di-
lemma is played from the female side: what do you do when your
scrupulous pal craves your love but the body that turns you on
is the beautiful, mindless one?

To heighten the movie's appeal, there is an allegorical neat-
ness: the public question of what gets on television, and why,
dovetails with the private question of which boy is going to get
the girl. All the better that the romance drama is appealingly
played—at least on two sides of the triangle, Hunter's and
Brooks's. Reviewers and media people were rightly impressed
that the female lead was written to be unglamorous and cast with
the unexpected Hunter. But, more, the movie was attractive
because its characters were successful, attractive people with successful, attractive troubles—people like movie reviewers. The
movie gave us professional people in the thick of their personal-
professional anxieties about romance, ambition, conflicts of purpose—for, indeed, body-over-mind dilemmas and tensions
between colleagueship and desire are built into the contemporary two-gendered workplace. Not least, the movie's nervous
tension captured the broadcast news business's everyday
rhythm—time measured against deadline; working life as a per-
petual scramble.

Not surprisingly, broadcast news people were gratified about
the realism of *Broadcast News*—felt represented by it. An NBC
producer told me that she and her colleagues left a screening in
tears. "I identify totally with [Jane Craig]," she said. "There
aren't ten frames in *Broadcast News* that aren't true." Under the
incoming regime of General Electric and in the wake of a strike,
the network had just fired or bought out the contracts of more

than a hundred news employees, many of them experienced hands; the new managements of ABC and CBS had done the equivalent. In real life budgets (for everything from foreign bureaus to perks) were being slashed, morale damaged, news ethics set loose down the slippery slope. No less a personage than Dan Rather joined a CBS picket line and signed his name to a *New York Times* op-ed piece called "From Murrow to Mediocrity." *Broadcast News* caught the network's assault on its personnel's best sense of themselves, on their prerogatives and their honor; and it did so with the gallows jokiness that pros deploy to cope with bad news. Plenty of comic lines struck home, not least a moment when two young strangers show up in the control room and, upon being accosted, explain, "We're here to play the new news theme" (when they demonstrate the silly thing, the boss intones, deadpan, "I got chills"), and an exchange in which the stuffed-shirt anchorman Bill Rorsch (Jack Nicholson in cameo) bleats to the boss, "This is a brutal layoff. And all because they couldn't win Wednesday nights," and the boss responds, "You could make it less brutal by knocking a million or so off your salary." James L. Brooks is said to have spent years hanging around CBS's Washington bureau, and he came back from the mine with a plethora of authentic nuggets: Jane resents management for cutting hotel room budgets (around this time, a CBS producer complained to me that on-the-road meal allotments had been cut by the Tisch regime); at another point Jane deplores the fact that a White House correspondent reported something another White House correspondent said and attributed it to "White House sources."

But *Broadcast News* was "believable" in a severely limited way: it gave us a media pro's own version of herself and her troubles. The movie was cramped within the industry's own view of itself. Nowhere was this clearer than in the running theme: Will "style," or "flash," in the person of Tom Grunick, prevail over "substance," in the person of Aaron Altman, as they war for Jane Craig? The narrative was stuffed with moments of truth in which this conflict reared its meaningful little head. Eventually, in case the theme had eluded anyone, Aaron punched it out for Jane in boldface—Tom, he proclaimed, represents "flash over substance. He personifies everything that you've been fighting against."

The game was rigged in favor of substantists, for Jane and Aaron not only outnumbered the stylist Tom but had most of the funny lines. (The funniest were at the expense of management and the new television dumb-down: e.g., Jane calls Aaron and tells him that all three morning shows have Arnold Schwarzenegger on, and he's live on two of them; Aaron comes back with a truly Arnoldian Schwarzenegger imitation.) "Grunick" was even outfitted with an ugly name to cancel out his good looks, whereas Altman, "old man," evoked the good old days when news was news and Jews were good at it; the name Aaron, moreover, positively rings with goodness and sincerity. (George Raft or Jack Palance could never have played an Aaron.) How, then, did *Broadcast News* tell us to recognize substance?

• During a live broadcast Jane demonstrates her professional prowess and guts by racing the clock. She can't resist a last-minute edit that will stamp the piece with a personal imprint. The edit done, her gofer hurtles, videocassette in hand, across the crowded obstacle course of a newsroom while the seconds tick away. It's a bravura piece of moviemaking, tautly edited, played for both laughs and admiration. Anyone who would go down to the wire for a triumph of artistry wins our hearts. Jane is quick, gutsy, fast-thinking, and knows how to make the organization run rings around her. But what's at stake? The piece is about a surly soldier of fortune coming home to a small town, fresh from fighting in Angola. He's not expecting "any big homecoming," he says. To nail down the point, Jane has decided to insert a shot of a Norman Rockwell painting *(The Homecoming)* from a book in her office. It is for this illustrative visual, this "gotcha" shot, that the technical staff have been driven crazy. This is the reason the gofer ends up careening through the newsroom like a broken-field runner as the clock runs out. Jane is not apparently interested in what the red-blooded boy was doing for dollars thousands of miles from home. With our own hearts in our hands, our sympathy and admiration wholly Jane's, we are not supposed to be wondering, either. We are supposed to be dazzled by Jane's ingenuity, her derring-do, and the professional click that comes with beating the clock.

• Jane and Aaron dash off to Nicaragua to report on the contras. The cameraman tells a soldier to lace up his boots. By the pro's code of good practices, this constitutes rigging. Goody Two-shoes Jane upbraids the cameraman for his stage-setting zeal. The next thing you know, Aaron and Jane are caught in a fire-fight. The result is a bang-bang piece that thrills the anchorman. There's no sign that Jane or Aaron or the anchorman wants to know (let alone wants anyone else to know) who the contras are, what they stand for, who bought their boots. What everyone wants to bring back alive is ninety seconds of *authentic* bang-bang.

• A Libyan plane has attacked "one of our bases" in Sicily. Hapless Tom is tapped to go on air live and anchor a special report, and Jane is furious. Tom doesn't know Tripoli from the Halls of Montezuma, while Aaron once spent six weeks in Tripoli and interviewed Qaddafi. On the air live, Tom is fed questions through an earphone by Jane—standard practice—and Aaron, iced out, is home drinking. But Aaron can't bear to see the network (and Jane) humiliated. Hard-headed pro and mensch that he is, he calls in with information that enables Tom to triumph. Aaron knows an F-14 is called a Tomcat; *he* knows a thing or two about the Gulf of Sidra skirmish of 1981. Tom, thus rescued, doesn't skip a beat. No embarrassing gaffes, no flubs. His muttonhead boss is delighted (nor will the military brass have any complaints). In TV terms, Tom has "gotten the story." "The story," as the script, Jane, Aaron, Tom, and the company brass construe it, is the story as the military sees it, all nuts, bolts, and tactics. The question is strictly whether the Libyan pilot was a maverick or the advance guard of a general attack. Important, of course, but not all-important. No one, not even Aaron, is interested in the history of the conflict, although Aaron does contribute the information that Qaddafi in person is "presidential."

When Tom asks an American officer, "What's it like to be in a real dogfight?," Aaron doesn't groan.

• To prove he can report a story on his own, Tom interviews a victim of date rape. For his reaction shot, he works up an on-camera tear. When Aaron deduces that Tom must have staged his tear, and tells Jane, she is shocked and enraged, and walks away from the weekend tryst they had planned.

• A tense Aaron, knowing his day has passed, challenges Tom: "Can you name all the members of the Cabinet?" Tom: "Yes, Aaron." Aaron: "All twelve?" Tom: "Yes." Aaron, master of fact: "There's only ten." He can't resist twisting the knife: "Hey, we may do capitals of the states next." Q.E.D. A real reporter knows how many seats there are around the table at a photo op. He isn't expected to know which of the ten are lining their pockets, or what the Secretary of Defense does when he's not out inspecting F-14s.

Jane and Aaron, in short, share a style *of* substance. Their news-gathering triumphs are precious thin. The Norman Rockwell painting with which Jane won our hearts, if not our minds, amounts to nothing more than a dredged-up tear transposed into an image. Trapped inside the conventional wisdom that "TV is a visual medium," she has signed up with show biz. Even Tom's ethical transgression—working up his tear in the rape interview—is not quite so unusual as the film makes out: for years, Mike Wallace reshot his *60 Minutes* questions in such a way as to pump up his inquisitorial tone and expression for the camera. True enough, it's better for a newscaster to have heard of the Gulf of Sidra and the Secretary of Housing and Urban Development than not, and indeed scandalous that the network's ratings-grubbers would promote a brainless wonder like Tom. But Tom's incapacity overvalues Aaron's credentials. Tom is such a dim bulb he makes Aaron shine.

Not that Tom is wicked. He's refreshingly unpretentious. He jokes about his manifold incapacities. A bit embarrassed at finding himself beloved because of his looks, Tom has simply battened on a social fact that is not of his devising: society, the media in particular, rates public persons by their looks, credibility by appearances. In this corrupt setting, with millions of profit dollars riding on the anchor's composure, his looks, his allover anchorness, it is his fortune (in every sense) to know, as Aaron doesn't, how to gull a gullible audience. When he counsels Aaron on the need to compose himself on camera, to limit himself to one idea per story, to say, "Trust me," to *sell* himself, he isn't an especially grasping or unpleasant character, he's nothing more than a good-looking talking head born into the right time and place.

No, the bad guys are the money-grubbing corporation bigwigs who buy up the business, don't understand it, fire some of the pros, and hamstring the others. If only cutthroat capitalists would keep out of the pros' way, the film seems to be saying, the pros would be free to tell it the way it is. It's as if, all along, the network had been doing its steady professional job—digging for facts, informing the public, keeping democracy vital—until the wicked outsiders came along to pollute the business. Healthy professionalism versus outside corruption, objectivity versus bias: this is how most of the fortyish generation of TV journalists today understand their ethical and political quandaries. *Broadcast News* is written inside that script. It *is* that script.

And in the process the movie's soft, romantic blur encourages complacency about TV news. By the time *Broadcast News* was in production, some of the Nicaragua part of the Iran-contra story—the fact that the White House was behind the contras, and that Oliver North was a key man in the apparatus—had hit the headlines (and then sunk). Television was almost entirely uninterested. Until a Nicaraguan gunner shot down the American mercenary Eugene Hasenfus on October 5, 1986, the Aaron Altmans of the networks were decidedly uninterested in even such news as had been reported about the secret mission to aid the contras. By the time the movie was finished, a great deal was known and published—albeit in fragments—about that mission. In the year when the Iran-contra story was rarely out of the news, and the American news business had plenty to answer for, Jim Brooks delivered broadcast news's love letter to itself.

But this point was absent in the commentary that swirled

around *Broadcast News*'s release in 1987. To the contrary: the film got a splendid press. It comforted those who fight for their millimeters of substance in the land of fluff. One needn't glorify the grand old days of broadcast news to recognize that the custodians of the bottom line have deprived the veterans of an intangible value: the notion that they are custodians of serious information, guardians of the public weal, tribunes of democracy. And then, too, much of the acclaim came from that most desperate of appreciations, virtually indistinguishable from condescension: this movie was at least *not embarrassing.* At a time when what passes for movie repartee are one-liners, grunts, and banalities, reviewers hastened to congratulate the principals of *Broadcast News* for sounding reasonably grown-up and literate.

6

From *A Face in the Crowd* to *Network* to *Broadcast News*—in broad strokes, this traces the movies' accommodation to their subservient position.

Part of the problem is that Hollywood movies have largely been blind to the workings of institutions. Where they excel is with villains. Thus, movies have often sneered at the assorted rogues and hacks deemed to populate newspapers, thereby elevating their own capacity to tell the truth and high-mindedly entertain in the process. Publishers have often been bloated, amoral plutocrats mouthing populist slogans about the public's right to know while they operate behind the scenes to benefit their friends. The most memorable portrait is, of course, Orson Welles's *Citizen Kane* (1941), a man whose towering inferno of an arbitrary ego is redeemed only by the sad revelation that he never outgrew childhood. There is also Angela Lansbury's scheming temptress in Frank Capra's *State of the Union* (1948), who drags her lover, played by Spencer Tracy, into Republican politics and corrupts his honorable values until he summons the nerve to overthrow her. The thoughtless, cynical reporter is another stock figure, as in Capra's *Mr. Smith Goes to Washington* (1939).

Capra, of course, resolves all difficulties with the formula of the folk redeemer who rides into the capital and cleans up the mess, whatever the amoral press may think. But if a movie is going to come to grips with television's central position in contemporary life, it has to shuck such happy-go-lucky versions of the Christ-and-the-money-changers scenario. It has to grasp the ways in which TV has saturated American life—sculpting popular images of politicians and criminals and mass movements, freedom and intimacy and the good life. Instead, of all TV's attributes, it is banality that makes for the most convenient target, as in *Tootsie* (1983), where soap opera turns out to be—you don't mean it!—silly, or *Rain Man* (1988), where game shows are fodder for an autistic Dustin Hoffman. Again, the movie automatically elevates itself by taking a swipe at show biz low life. Ubiquitous television is hard for American moviemakers to see; they have taken it too long for granted.

So it comes as no surprise that many of the best movie insights into television have come from directors who aren't American: Bertrand Tavernier in *Death Watch* (1980), a dystopia in which Romy Schneider plays a dying woman whose last days are televised; Federico Fellini's brilliant *Ginger and Fred* (1986), in which popular art has been degraded by that particularly Italian TV form, the omnibus variety show. Note, too, that television's own most trenchant self-criticism, *Max Headroom* (1987), was English in its inception and quickly degenerated in the course of its brief American serialization.

And the most penetrating recent Hollywood film about television, *A Cry in the Dark* (1988), was directed by an Australian, Fred Schepisi. The target is television's propensity to bend truth precisely because it not only invades privacy but seems transparent, impartial. Because the anguished Lindy Chamberlain (Meryl Streep) doesn't play well on the tube as she defends herself against the charge of killing her baby, she is made to appear not only negligent but murderous. She appears stiff, touchy, sarcastic; she is a religious nut to boot; she is not acting as a soap opera heroine would act. Moreover, the dingo, which she insists is responsible for dragging her baby into the bush, is a symbol of

Australian innocence. As a result, the vox populi, in a binge of nationalist fervor amplified by television, clamors for her head. Eventually the movie camera discloses to us decisive evidence which the stupid immediacy of television did not disclose to its own audience: that her baby was, in fact, as she had maintained, killed by a dingo. The point is that television's zeal to expose, reveal, and invade serves only its own self-infatuation, not the truth. This fine movie suggests that in a society so thoroughly floodlit by the white glare of television, innocence and truth are reduced to sounding their own tiny cries in the dark.

7

Small screens in the household are not automatically bad for movies. Arguably, good movies have benefited—along with the bad and the ugly—from the recent developments in video technology. Videocassette royalties and pay-cable fees, invested up front, now account for more than half of total movie revenues; and while most of these billions go for blockbusters of dubious worth, some funds do spring loose to help finance films like *The Killing Fields* that might otherwise not have been made. Public-television money, skimpy as it is, helped finance the extraordinary *Thin Blue Line.* In Great Britain films like *My Beautiful Laundrette, Sammy and Rosie Get Laid, Letter to Brezhnev, Prick Up Your Ears,* and *High Hopes,* along with theatrically released documentaries like the British *28 Up* and the Australian *Cannibal Tours,* have been financed in part by television money from the public-private hybrid Channel Four. The niches for craft and diversity ought to be more ample than in the assembly-line studio years.

And yet, overall, the movies have been overwhelmed by the sheer volume, weight, and conventions of commercial television. The effects on style have been enormous: effects of imitation and effects of compensation. In the years of their long twilight, movies have, for the most part, either *become* television or, in recognition of television's cultural dominance, settled into the niches that television lacks the technology or permission to occupy—those which exploit the size of the screen, the quality of the sound, or the absence of external censorship. Increasingly directors, stars, and audiences have been trained in television. Thus the steadily inflating supply of, and demand for, one-liners, pulse-hyping actions, up-close-and-personal close-ups, and special effects ghoulish or vicious enough to trump the last one. Samuel Goldwyn and Harry Cohn would gasp at the alacrity with which today's Hollywood hunts for blockbusters and movies deemed possessed of "high concept" (once strictly a TV cliché, meaning easy-to-grasp)—movies whose plots recombine pretested elements, and whose "essence" can be grasped in a single advertising or word-of-mouth phrase. The movie business always liked hits, going back to studio days, but today the industry has become addicted to them.

Imitation, as they say, is the sincerest form of Hollywood. The movie business admires nothing more than a winner, and what has been more winning than television? And so television has had a direct impact on movie genres: buddy-cop (*48 Hours, Lethal Weapon,* et cetera ad nauseam) and family movies *(Mr. Mom; Honey, I Shrunk the Kids)* derive from the respectively paranoid and sentimental formulas of the TV episode series. Although there were precedents on the big screen (*The Thin Man* series, among others), today's proliferation of sequels takes inspiration, if that is the right word, from TV's series as well as the financial value of bankable stars; after *Perry Mason CCVII,* why not *Rocky VIII?* Increasingly the movies have employed television actors, whose stock-in-trade consists of the once-over-lightly performance, the distinct tic, the gesture aimed in the vague direction of character. Talent aside, one reason is that the endless close-up of the small screen so magnifies any facial expression that TV actors learn to play their emotions down.

But TV's most ruinous impact has been on directorial style. Where many serious directors of the sixties and seventies served apprenticeships in early television (Lumet, Arthur Penn, John Frankenheimer, Robert Altman, Norman Jewison, Martin Ritt), many of their successors—and, crucially, the succeeding distributors and audiences as well—have developed their skills, and their standards, from post–Golden Age TV. Moreover, like everyone else, they have watched thousands of hours; TV rhythms have been engraved in their cortices. An audience attuned to hundreds or thousands of hours of cop shows and "action adventures," by the time it gets to moviegoing age, wants to see something that both is TV, with its cliff-hangers and violence, and isn't, because TV is still relatively toned down. So movies deliver something different but similar: more explicit renderings of the sadomasochistic imagination. The easy resort is to an image of some fraction of the human body—either pornography or the ingenious representation of some maimed and disfigured body part. In turn, as movie violence grows more graphic, so do even the edited-for-TV versions, as well as network series, adding to the pressure on the next round of movies to establish that they can offer something network television cannot—by raising their gore quotients. The unprecedented violence wrought in Arthur Penn's *Bonnie and Clyde* (1967) did, as Pauline Kael wrote at the time, "put the sting back in death"; it punctured numbness. But starting with Sam Peckinpah's *The Wild Bunch* (1969), and growing more grotesque all the time, movie violence has devolved into training in numbness. The likely result is a general anesthesia in the face of the actual violence of the world—an anesthesia that has become necessary equipment for steering through the thousands of limb-tearings and arterial spurts that the movies have made more common than dependent clauses.

Steve Mills, a CBS executive in charge of the network's TV movies, once told me that a particular movie was praiseworthy because it had "great jeopardy," meaning two elements: mechanically contrived suspense and the promise of bodily harm. The plot becomes a hammock slung from menace to menace. Action movies and real-life cartoons (the Rambo, *Star Wars,* and Indiana Jones serials) account for a disproportionate share of movie profits by taking bankable stars and plunking them down in "great jeopardy." Of course, television did not invent cliff-hangers; movie serials thrived on them half a century ago. But commercial television made them routine; dramatic structure was bent to keep the audience hooked through the commercial breaks. Steven Spielberg, who started out as a director of TV episodes, has built his career precisely on setting up "great jeopardy," but he is simply the most successful of the movie directors whose sensibility has been formed by, and aims to exploit, the expectations aroused by television. Like the clockwork violence of present-day children's TV cartoons, the cliff-hanger moment becomes everything and nothing: more vivid and necessary than character, sprinkled into the action to paper over vast holes in the narrative. Mangled flesh rescues a mangled plot. The severed limb recapitulates a severed continuity. Witness the extraordinary careers of Sylvester Stallone and Arnold Schwarzenegger, whose personae resemble chainsaws and whose on-screen functions are similar.

The predilections of financiers, directors, and audiences come together to ratchet the frequency and magnitude of violence upward. The movie audience remains disproportionately young and flocks to Stallone and Schwarzenegger movies; directors draw craft pride from their ability to surpass the previous round of abominations; financiers see no reason to temper the cycle and every reason not to. Studio bosses, bankers, and distributors think there is nothing more riveting than the furies of jeopardy, frights, wounds, machine-gun bursts and fireballs, car chases and crashes—and no motivation more alluring than revenge, power lust, or all-around viciousness. Their truncated sense of what constitutes a commercial movie is coarsened further by all the garish "advances" in makeup and stunts, the better to assault the imagination with picturesquely wounded or bared flesh that (at this writing) the networks will not fully permit on their airwaves—all the censored words, shark gouges, ax gashes, and machine-gun spatters that end up routinely dotted throughout even the most modest thriller.

Moreover, today's movie pace is a TV pace raised to a higher power. The point is to whisk the audience along before it can think—lest it fall through the holes in the plot. Even a movie that isn't a slasher is cut to the bone. The style derives from commercials, a major training ground for directors; from music videos, which imported the one-cut-per-second style into episode television; and from instant replay, which saves the viewer the trouble of paying attention to the rhythms of regular narrative. Not that languor is intrinsically virtuous or speed intrinsically wrong. *Hill Street Blues*'s fevered movements, when they first came along, made for a fresh look and, more important, a plot point—urban buzz, police work chaos. But the cut-and-slash, whizbang style has become a kind of violence all of its own: an addiction.

On the premise that only sensation can draw the dazed teenaged hordes out of the house, more and more movies resort to high tech. Veblen! thou should'st be living at this hour. Synthesized sound pulsates from every corner of the theater; computers design dazzling if arbitrary layouts; the physical scale of the film is meant to overwhelm (even if most people will end up seeing the movie on diminished multiplex screens); set design becomes the supreme "production value." When Stanley Kubrick deployed these crafts in *2001: A Space Odyssey* and Ridley Scott in *Blade Runner,* they did so in the service of—to use an old-fashioned phrase—artistic visions; but for the most part, advanced technology has become banal—a series of spectacular atmospheric set pieces and gestures, as in *Batman.* When Hollywood wants to compliment a production, it says, "All the money is on the screen." In aspiring blockbusters that is what one sees—the gaudiness, the concocted miracle of money.

By the same logic, the exchange of speeches more than two crude sentences long has come to be considered a longueur, a distraction from action, a turnoff for turned-on legions of teenage moviegoers. It is as if, once we acquire eyeglasses, we must puncture our eardrums—to restore balance to the sensorium. The hackwork that produces a script for George Lucas's *The Empire Strikes Back* is more marketable than the serious screenwriting that produces *Body Heat*—amazingly, the writer in both cases is Lawrence Kasdan. Writers have long been paid to dumb down, but if they start their careers thinking that *The Empire Strikes Back* is a good movie, no amount of money will train them to smarten up. For if such a tongue-tied blockbuster can make hundreds of millions of dollars, rich language often comes to be seen as incidental or, worse, an embarrassment, even a handicap—a weakening of the ramrod force of the severed image. Fatally, a fascination with the free-standing image is the premise that American directors—and, to a considerable degree, audiences—share with Jane Craig. Words are meant to fill the silences between actions, or to constitute blunt instruments of their own ("Read my lips"). Rambo's grunt passes for working-class inarticulateness, and surface gestures are left to convey the personal attributes that run-of-the-mill movies want to pass off as character. Words are not to distract from the movie's *real* business—the trademark grin or strut, the adorable android, the ambush, the wound, the chase over the San Francisco hills (spliced together from different districts, but who's counting?), the bared breast, the helicopter exploding, the car spinning out of control, the ingenious placement of gun or knife or razor or chain saw or bomb against the victim's flesh.

No recent directors have done more to devalue the word than George Lucas and Steven Spielberg. All the more poignant, then, that on receiving the Irving G. Thalberg Memorial Award for high production achievement at the 1987 Oscar ceremony, Spielberg told the assembled and a billion or so viewers, "I think it's time to renew our romance with the word." Thalberg of MGM, said Spielberg, had had great books to spin into movies, but today who reads the great books? "Movies have been the literature of my life," Spielberg said. But he had the grace to add, "I'm as culpable as anyone in having exalted the . . . image at the expense of the word." Oscar night belongs not only to misty movie memories but to TV—it would have been bad form to point out that Spielberg owes his early career to television, where he efficiently directed episodes as well as the ABC made-for-TV movie *Duel,* in which a driver is followed for hundreds of miles by a big truck, and barely a word is spoken.

The notion that movies, or people, have to choose between pictures and words is a canard, refuted by such extraordinary television as Rainer Werner Fassbinder's *Berlin Alexanderplatz* and Dennis Potter's *The Singing Detective.* Movies like *Bull Durham, Rain Man, When Harry Met Sally . . . ,* and *sex, lies, and videotape,* while far from flawless, demonstrate not only that reviewers are hungry for literacy but that good talk can make money—granted, not as much money as *Batman.* About one-third of the adult American public has gone to college, and the educated see more movies than the uneducated; still, as hopefuls keep trying to reverse the prevailing devolution, most of Hollywood has swallowed the mindless notion that sensory attributes are locked together in a zero sum: one attribute must be suppressed as the other swells.

All criticism of present trends runs a certain risk of nostalgia. One remembers fondly the dialogue of *The Philadelphia Story* or *Casablanca* and blissfully forgets a hundred clunkers. One recalls the bloated "epics" of one's youth—*Gone with the Wind, The Wizard of Oz, The Bridge on the River Kwai, Lawrence of Arabia,* whatever—through the rosy halo of selective memory. Without doubt, the studio dream factories ground out their own kind of feeble work by the gross; to deplore the mainstream of movies today is not to wish back the old days, which are in any case irretrievable. If today's entertainment machines are bleak, it is not because they are in every way worse than some golden age whose exact location shifts as it recedes. The reasons are multiple, as I have argued, but the thread—or sewage—of mainstream television runs through the whole process. The movies are bleak in precisely the ways that television encourages: pure sensation instead of narrative; gesture instead of character; the script that still bears the sutures of the committee that stitched it together. The good old days were not so good, but so what? The measure of movies' impoverishment today is not what we have lost but what we desire, what we need, what we deserve.

If
You've Seen One, You've Seen the Mall

DOUGLAS GOMERY

THE LINES WERE LONG, but there was not much else about the twenties movie palace that looked ahead to the multiplexes of today. In those Orpheums and Paramounts things were constructed on the grandest scale. The lobby alone, for instance, was often larger than six of today's whole cinemas combined. It was more than mere size, however, that made the movie palace stand out as something special. It was the fine furnishings, the massive tapestries and marble statuary, the plasterwork evocative of some "French court" or "Spanish courtyard" that, in those years, told the middle-class American viewer that going to the movies was indeed transcendent, an experience "out of this world."

Having climbed elaborate staircases, fans would enter a sumptuous auditorium that could, and always did, hold three or four thousand other eager viewers, many staring at the decorations of the sidewalls with the same awe they might have felt at a White House reception, or at a soirée held at the home of John D. Rockefeller. And the films that Hollywood released at the zenith of the silent era—DeMille productions, for example, like *Fool's Paradise* (set in Siam and Mexico) and *The Affairs of Anatol* (about the "troubles" of New York's wealthiest)—lavishly reconfirmed movie palaces as the cathedrals of a new art. Ben Hall put it best when he called the movie palace "an acre of seats in a garden of dreams." It is unsurprising that Sid Grauman called his famous picture palace "the million-dollar theatre."

None of those extravagant buildings, from the Fox in San Francisco to the Oriental in Milwaukee to Loew's State on Times Square, was exactly like any other. One can hardly say the same thing about the anonymous mall multiplexes of today. If the movie theater of the late silent era was, as well as a great place to watch movies, a luminous modern pleasure dome, itself expressive of transcendent fantasy, the cinemas today—their names based only on location—are no more than stripped-down screening rooms. Gone are the uniformed ushers, the marble busts, the spiraling staircases. Now there is nothing besides those loud images, and then the parking lot. As when visiting any other mall location, one feels that one is merely buying product. If the movies have always wavered between Art and Commerce, surely the movie palace represented Art, however kitschy and grandiloquent such art may seem today—whereas today's multiplex is among the purest tools of Commerce in the latter half of the twentieth century.

Hollywood was ten years away when Americans began to wander into the true first movie theaters, nicknamed nickelodeons in honor of their low prices. These were small, uncomfortable makeshift theaters, usually restaurants, pawnshops, or retail shops made over to look like a scaled-down version of the vaudeville theater. Outside, vast hand-painted posters announced the film fare for the day; there were no regular newspaper listings or reviews. I am not sure everyone can become as nostalgic as James Agee when he recalled, forty years after the fact, his childhood experiences of "the barefaced honky-tonk and the waltzes of Waldteufel, slammed out in a mechanical piano; the searing redolence of peanuts and demirep perfumery, tobacco and feet, and sweat; the laughter of unrespectable people . . ."

Phillip Grant, a writer not connected to the film business as was reviewer/screenwriter Agee, remembered a nickel show on Western Avenue in Chicago in somewhat different terms. A ticket booth, its colors the yellow, red, and blue of a circus sideshow, stood in front of a former furniture store. Inside, a white sheet hung at the far end of the room. Except for the light reflecting from it, the theater was pitch-black. Folding chairs provided little comfort, but then the show lasted only an hour. Directly beneath the "screen," a piano player "did his best to provide musical atmosphere" and to drown out "the loud and rhythmic clickety-clackety-click of the motion picture projector."

Grant vividly recalled the disconcerting constant chatter of the audiences, untrained in the decorum of attending the legitimate theater, opera, or ballet. Subtitles were read by the literate to their neighbors. Grant's mother's biggest complaint remains vivid and applicable fifty years later in the age of the grainy VCR image and the distorted projection at most mall movie theaters: "Ach—how the pictures jump—worse than a penny peep show in White City [the Chicago World's Fair of 1893]—it could give you a headache—how it jumps—that people should pay good money to see this—it could give a person a headache . . ."

Film has had a long history since those first flickering firemen rescued children in distress in *The Life of an American Fireman* and cowboys chased Indians across the plains of New Jersey in *The Great Train Robbery*. Film has now been proclaimed an art, even *the* art of the latter half of the twentieth century. Yet today, upon leaving one of the ubiquitous Cinema 1, 2, 3, and 4's found in malls from Northridge to Southtown, one might ask: are we any better off than those moviegoing pioneering ancestors of ours?

At the turn of the century, to circumvent existing fire laws, nickelodeons limited themselves to fewer than three hundred seats. Today the average mall cinema auditorium is half that size. Screens have replaced sheets, and stereo speakers the hit-and-miss melodies of the neighborhood piano player. But are sticky floors and ever-conversing couples so different from the conditions of the nickel show? Indeed, through the history of film the lone precedent for the cramped, boxlike multiplex of the eighties is the nickelodeon. And if we think the movies have gotten better, tell that to someone who has just paid $7 to see *Howard the Duck, Ishtar,* or *Death Wish 3* in the local Cinema 1.

However humble its viewing conditions, once the nickelodeon movement began in earnest in 1905, its rise precipitated the film industry we have today. Consider that as late as 1904 there were probably no more than twenty-five nickel theaters across the country. Three years later Chicago alone had that many. By 1910 pundits placed the number nationally at ten thousand, with one of every five adults attending each week.

"Nickel madness" rode a wave of economic prosperity. A price significantly less than was charged for even the cheapest vaudeville show drew early devotees from the poorer sections of the city. Some called them "democracy's theater," but movie house owners soon realized that the only way to expand was to abandon the working class and seek out the "discretionary income" of the then-emerging middle class.

To lure in the family trade, theater owners focused on the mother and her children. Their schedule might be such that she could treat a film show as a shopping break or an after-school activity. A theater drawing such an audience could gain a favorable image in the community and increased patronage in the evening. Through the early 1910s in city after city mothers and their children were granted special half-price afternoon admission to see films inspired by the works of Emile Zola, Victor Hugo, and William Shakespeare—a shift in programming that signaled the absorption of moviegoing into the mainstream of American life.

The theater of the "photoplay" proved so powerful that vaudeville, its cultural predecessor, was soon moribund. The narratives on the front wall—the new flickering world of dreams and images of modern life that the nickelodeon had to offer—were enough to draw an impoverished, largely immigrant audience, whatever the seating or viewing arrangements. The nickelodeon established the narrative as the dominant motion picture form. Documentaries and non-narrative experiments would forever be reserved for the rare specialized theater. Hollywood became the locus for the creation of narrative films and thus owed its very existence to the rise of the nickelodeon. But by 1915 audiences were destined to experience early feature film classics like D. W. Griffith's *Intolerance* and Cecil B. DeMille's *The Cheat* in far more luxurious surroundings.

The era of the modern movie palace began in April 1914 with the opening of Samuel "Roxy" Rothapfel's three-thousand-seat Strand Theater in New York City. It dwarfed even the finest nickelodeon of the previous decade. It offered the architectural splendor of the legitimate theater and the sight of uniformed ushers constantly scurrying about making sure everyone was comfortable in seats that rivaled the best Pullman had to sell. Between shows Roxy paraded his staff with a snap and rigor he had learned in the Marines.

The show opened with the house orchestra playing a suite of popular classical compositions (which not only set the "proper" aural tone and mood but involved no extra fees for musical rights). Then came newsreels and comic short subjects. Only half an hour into the program did the feature film begin, accompanied by a full orchestra. Newspapers compared going to the Strand to attending a reception at the White House or opening night at the Metropolitan Opera.

By 1927 Roxy had a five-thousand-seat movie palace called, immodestly, the Roxy. "Spanish" in design, it had specially constructed domes and recesses, richly colored drapery, gold- and silver-trimmed plaster detail, extensive drapes, and vast crystal chandeliers. A *New Yorker* cartoon of the day had a young girl gazing up into what all knew to be its lobby and asking, "Mama—does God live here?"

It took a family enterprise from Chicago, however, to organize the movie palace experience into a business enterprise that would prove the entertainment world's equivalent of a chain of department stores like Gimbel's or Macy's. Balaban & Katz developed the formula that brought the movie palace to every Main Street in America, and made millions doing it.

Brother Abe Balaban handled the orchestra, Barney Balaban did the film bookings, and John Balaban hired the ushers and ticket-takers, but it was Sam Katz who controlled the overall process. Katz, by all accounts a human dynamo, had put himself through school by opening nickelodeons. His goal was simple—to fashion the greatest chain of movie theaters in the world—and his success was obvious to all when Balaban & Katz merged into Paramount in 1925. The new Paramount-Publix chain drew more customers, employed more musicians, and owned more theaters than any enterprise before or since. Balaban & Katz's success commenced with the opening of Chicago's Central Park Theatre in October 1917. This mighty picture palace was such an immediate hit that Sam Katz was able to stitch together an impressive syndicate of Chicago-based businessmen to back him: Julius Rosenwald, head of Sears, Roebuck; John Hertz, Chicago's taxi king and later the creator of the first national rent-a-car operation; and William Wrigley, Jr., of chewing gum fame.

Rosenwald taught the world of retailing that location mattered. Sears, Roebuck was the first to establish a national chain of department stores, built amid the middle-class neighborhoods then springing up at the edges of America's biggest cities. No need to go downtown; shop close to your new home on the edge of town. Hertz made his fortune by making the Yellow Cab identifiable with consistent service at a low price. Hertz knew that the issue was not simply transportation but the whole package: a clean cab available night and day, a courteous and knowledgeable driver, and a fair price. Wrigley may have been the greatest salesman of his day; he sold the middle class something it really didn't need—chewing gum—through careful advertising and promotion.

From them Katz learned that through careful theater location, reliable service at a fair price, and skillful promotion, Balaban & Katz could take the movie world by storm. More than any Hollywood-based movie mogul, Sam Katz turned a fledgling leisuretime industry into the centerpiece of American popular culture. Created with new technology but always service-oriented, glorifying the past in order to popularize the first art of mechanical reproduction, the movie palaces he founded were perfect pleasure machines geared to an urban nation. In retrospect, filmgoers never had it so good.

Previously theater owners had simply followed the custom of putting theaters near older ones. Balaban & Katz constructed the locus of its power by taking the movie show to middle-class audiences who had just moved to the first true suburbs (although many were actually within city boundaries). With the help of urban mass-transit trolley and elevated lines constructed at the turn of the century, Balaban & Katz was able build its movie palaces miles from Chicago's downtown.

Take the Central Park Theatre. North Lawndale, in what was then the far west side of Chicago, had been reached by the elevated lines in 1902, and within two decades this lightly populated suburban outpost had grown into a teeming neighborhood principally populated by Jews who had fled the Maxwell Street ghetto. In the public schools the children were taught to seek upward mobility and so ate nonkosher food, attended synagogue infrequently, and spoke Yiddish only at home. As part of this process of cultural assimilation, they also fell in love with the movie show.

At the Central Park they could see Hollywood films of all types, but especially those of director Cecil B. DeMille. His *Old Wives for New, Don't Change Your Husband, Male and Female,* and *Why Change Your Wife?* taught a generation American customs. But titillating lessons in love American-style and optimal theater locations were not enough to turn the Balaban & Katz showcases into the money-making machines they came to be. The actual building, the movie palace, was carefully designed to envelop the moviegoer in a special fantasy atmosphere. It was to be a total experience from the moment one arrived, one that bore no relation to daily life—at least the daily life of the ordinary citizen—but served as an enormous link to the American dream of a better life. Of the lessons to be learned about the good life in America—one immeasurably far away, opulent, and aristocratic, but also so close that for a few hours any week one could touch it—the movie itself was only a part, and not necessarily the largest part, either. Elaborate plasterwork adorned the front of these temples of pleasure, making Balaban and Katz's movie palaces seem more substantial and impressive than nearby churches, local courthouses, or even the city's finest hotels. In time Balaban & Katz movie palaces became tourist attractions unto themselves. With a pride usually associated only with the opening of a world's fair or a new skyscraper, Chicagoans of the twenties heralded Balaban & Katz's movie palaces as wonders of the world.

The movie palace viewing experience began long before one went inside, let alone got near a movie screen. On the street one first gazed upon strong vertical lines accentuated by ascending pilasters, windows, and towers lifting high above the storefronts. The building was a rigid steel shell with an inner core on which the plaster decoration—in purples, golds, azures, and crimsons—glowed day and night under massive electric signs. These "bright-light" displays could be seen for miles by those arriving on trolleys. Here was advertising even a William Wrigley could appreciate. Behind the upright signs several stories in height, flashing their messages in a variety of colors, were the very symbols of European architectural religiosity—stained-glass windows—reminding Chicago's immigrants not only of the great churches back home but of the fact that they were about to undergo the American equivalent of a transcendental experience.

These exterior light displays made quite an impact on city dwellers so long used to gaslight. Chicago-born novelist Meyer

Levin, writing in *The Old Bunch* fifteen years later, had his characters remember going to the Chicago Theatre this way:

> As [he and his friends] turned into State Street, the Chicago
> sign blazed at them. Boy, was that a sign! It made daylight of
> the whole block. Eight stories high. Three thousand bulbs
> spelled CHICAGO!

Once inside the movie palace, the patrons wove through a
series of vestibules, foyers, lobbies, lounges, promenades, and
waiting rooms designed to impress and excite. Balaban & Katz
demanded that their architects, George and C. W. Rapp, design
lobbies to meet certain standards:

> The lobby must be a place of real interest, a place where the
> waiting throng may be transformed . . . The walls and surfaces
> of the lobby should . . . [permit] the theatregoers to get one
> vista after another, which will produce . . . a desire to gain
> admittance to other parts of the house. In other words, the
> lobby should be so designed and so equipped that the fascina-
> tion resulting from it will keep the mind of the patron off the
> fact that he is waiting . . .

In the lobby, distractions included continuous organ recitals, art
galleries, and restrooms larger than most people's homes. Unlike
the design of today's cramped multiplexes, in which excess
crowding seems the only memorable feature, the architectural
rule of thumb for the picture palace demanded that lobby spaces
comfortably hold the same number of ticket-holders as there
were seats in the auditorium.

Theater design for the movie palace absorbed elements of any
style of the past that symbolized opulence. Architects mixed design features from classical French to sixteenth-century Spanish,
from Venetian to Moorish. For their top houses Balaban & Katz
favored the "French" style, even copying the monumental stair-
case of the Paris Opera House and the grand, column-lined lobby
of the Hall of Mirrors at Versailles.

These wonder-theaters were not haphazardly thrown together
but formulated in assembly-line fashion by specialized architec-

tural firms headed by John Eberson, Thomas Lamb, and the brothers Rapp. The major theater chains never set up their own design departments but kept one of these firms constantly busy. George and C. W. Rapp, for example, had begun with Sam Katz in Chicago and then moved with him to Paramount-Publix to plan the bulk of that chain's thousand-plus movie houses. Theater owners would often contract for one set of plans and then build the "same" theater in several distant locations.

For each city the watchword was stylistic differentiation: one Oriental theater, one Egyptian theater, one atmospheric theater (with stars and clouds on the auditorium ceiling), and so forth. But as the twenties wore on, lesser chains mixed Egyptian, Oriental, Venetian, and other assorted motifs in single buildings to make sure their theaters would not be confused with the designs of Rapp & Rapp, Thomas Lamb, and John Eberson down the street.

As the exotica of the twenties brought forth fads, theaters followed suit. So in the early twenties the discovery of King Tut's tomb brought forth a wave of tabloid headlines; by the mid-twenties nearly every major city had an "Egyptian" theatre. Such competition in design differentiation faded with the coming of the Great Depression and only returned in the eighties as Cineplex Odeon brought a measure of architectural splendor back to the movie theater.

In their pleasure palaces Balaban & Katz treated their patrons like royalty, providing free child care and ushers to handle any emergency. America's robber barons had servants around the clock; in a Balaban & Katz theater so did the average moviegoer—at least for a few hours. Balaban & Katz recruited its corps of ushers from male college students, dressed them in red uniforms with white gloves and yellow epaulets, and demanded they be obediently polite even to the rudest of patrons. And the service was free, no tipping allowed.

What a contrast to moviegoing today, since the vast corps of ushers served to maintain quiet in the auditorium throughout the show. Filmgoers rarely spoke above a whisper, attentively, even reverently, listening to orchestras that often numbered more than fifty players. Movie audiences of the twenties, awed by their surroundings and supervised by scores of ushers, behaved far better than their grandchildren, who declared film an art.

To bury the vaudeville competition down the street, Balaban & Katz packaged the movie show with live entertainment. In time Balaban & Katz became the top vaudeville bookers in Chicago, even developing local talent into stars who could then play the circuit. Balaban & Katz sought to mount popular but tasteful shows that could attract the middle-class audiences who had grown up on vaudeville. In Chicago stage show stars became more famous than Hollywood stars. Consider the case of organist Jesse Crawford, whose 1923 wedding to fellow organist Helen Anderson was the talk of Chicago's tabloids. The couple began to perform together and by 1925 had their own radio show and recording contract. When Sam Katz took the pair to New York, the Chicago newspapers mourned their loss as a blow to city prestige comparable to a White Sox star being traded to the Yankees.

Sam Katz, ever the cunning entrepreneur, sought every possible angle in selling his shows to the public. None became more of an instant hit than air conditioning. The Central Park Theatre was the first air-cooled movie house in the world, providing summertime comfort no Chicagoan could long resist. Before the Central Park, despite crude experiments in blowing air across blocks of ice, most movie houses closed during the summer season. Great progress toward safe mechanical cooling had, however, been made during the first two decades of the twentieth century, principally at the insistence of Chicago's meat-packing industry. The apparatus itself was expensive and massive, including fifteen thousand feet of heavy-duty pipe, giant 240-horse-power electric motors, and thousand-pound flywheels.

Once in place, Balaban & Katz's air-cooled fantasy worlds became famous as escapes from the brutality of Chicago's summers. Balaban & Katz's publicity constantly reminded Chicagoans of the rare treat in store inside their theaters. Icicles hung from the lettering of all summer newspaper advertisements. The Public Health Commissioner of the city of Chicago, with some urging, publicly proclaimed that Balaban & Katz theaters had purer air than Pike's Peak, and that anyone with a lung disease or women in the final trimester of pregnancy ought to regularly spend time "at the movies."

The results were phenomenal. Movie trade papers noted consistently high grosses during the summer months, making moviegoing for the first time a year-round activity. Balaban & Katz had led the world to a technological marvel we now take for granted. During the twenties—indeed, into the thirties and forties—the movie theater was often the only air-conditioned building in town. The popularity of the movies themselves ought not to be overestimated in Hollywood's Golden Age, when the movie show was the only place in a pre–air-conditioned world to cool off.

Location, architecture, service, stage shows, and air conditioning helped Balaban & Katz earn millions of dollars and made the movie palace a community institution. With this five-part formula for mass entertainment, Balaban & Katz made more money than any other chain of movie houses in the world. Their theaters were filled morning to night, every day of the week, and prices sometimes reached the then-staggering sum of one dollar—for the best seat on Saturday and Sunday nights.

No one could have mistaken a movie palace for the makeshift, plain, converted storefront of two decades earlier. The coming of sound during the late twenties seemed a logical step, making the movie house America's complete technological wonder. Sam Katz had his publicists declare, "You don't need to know what's playing at a Publix house. It's bound to be the best show in town." Although no one could have imagined it at the time, the movie theater had reached its zenith, both as a site for viewing pleasure and as a community institution.

The Great Depression abruptly ended the movie palace era. With approximately one-third fewer customers, theater owners began to cut costs. First to go were the services: doormen, nurses, most of the ushers. Several chains took the halfway step of recruiting women ushers, a cost-saving, sexist strategy—or, as a manual published for theater managers in 1938 put the matter:

> In [theaters] where carpets, draperies, and furnishings are worn, and some of the luster has faded, beautiful young usherettes, attractively costumed, help keep the public's eye off the shabby spots. In small operations, usherettes can also save the management the expense of a maid.

Patrons now had to seat themselves, and as a consequence going to the movies became a much more informal experience. Gone were the pretensions of asking ticket-holders to "behave." And gone with them was much of the off-screen fantasy the movie palace embodied. From this era on, what joy and pleasure the theatrical movie-viewing experience offered were more and more restricted to the screen itself. Talking to your companions suddenly became acceptable, and no one thought it offensive to get up during the middle of the show to get some popcorn. To viewers today, the movies of the thirties often seem to have overpowering stories; but they had to in order to hold the attention of audiences in increasingly barren auditoria, only half-filled, with seemingly constant coming and going.

Once the novelty of talkies had worn off, exhibitors struggled for ways to shift the specialness of the movie experience onto the films themselves. Thus came the national craze of two-movies-for-the-price-of-one, or "duals," which we now call "double features." This was not exactly a new idea (most historians place its origins in New England in 1915), but the Great Depression led to its widespread adoption. Since a complete show lasted three hours or more, theater audiences "turned over" fewer times each day, a loss of income initially offset by increased attendance.

Surprisingly, public-opinion polls suggested that the nation thought double features a "bad idea," despite the fact that millions queued up to see them each day. Nostalgia, not for the single-feature policy but for the transcendent experience the movie palace had once offered its audiences, held sway. Opponents of double bills, however, pointed to such mundane issues as eye strain and fatigue to make their case, and in 1938 educators even persuaded the Chicago City Council to consider a law restricting the double feature.

But the greatest change in the moviegoing experience caused by the Great Depression was the selling of popcorn. During the movie palace era, movie exhibitors had steadfastly refused to sell snack foods, so long associated with carnivals, burlesque shows, and cheaper entertainments. Such considerations were swept aside with the economic calamity of the Great Depression. Money was money. Concession stands, the heart of movie theater operations ever since, blossomed during the early thirties, offering the candy, soda pop, and popcorn previously purchased from confectionery stores invariably found next to the theaters. (In the twenties one purchased snack treats before or after the show; exhibitors prohibited ticket-holders from bringing treats into the grand movie palaces.)

The pattern of introduction was gradual. First came the candy stand. That was simple to set up, since the treat was already packaged for sale when it arrived. Independent exhibitors first embraced this extra source of revenue they did not have to share with any Hollywood movie studio (as they did their box office take). Hollywood-owned theaters quickly followed. By 1936 sales of candy in movie houses had topped $10 million.

Next came popcorn. For decades vendors had sold this snack food to movie patrons from wagons positioned outside theaters. Theater owners simply moved the popcorn stand into the lobby. It was easy to manufacture, and its aroma enticed waiting customers. Best of all, popcorn was one food that Americans consumed more of during hard times. Because popcorn was so cheap, its sales went up as incomes came down and people began to substitute it for other, more costly treats.

During the late thirties exhibitors popped corn by the train-car load. The theaters associated with the largest chains, those owned by the major Hollywood movie corporations, negotiated corn purchases in bulk. Even with wages, containers, and the cost of the popping apparatus included, profit per box sometimes reached ten cents per sale.

The movie industry elevated popcorn to the status of an important farm crop in the United States. The popcorn harvest grew from five million pounds in 1934 to more than a hundred million pounds by 1940. Production of popcorn during World War II, even with extra land devoted to growing food for the troops, still exceeded four hundred million pounds per annum, more than four pounds of popcorn for every person in the United States. The movie theater industry watchword became: "Find a good location for a popcorn stand and build a theater around it."

Soft drinks sealed the bargain. During the forties, with its rich overseas markets cut off, Coca-Cola began to step up sales to theaters. By 1950 the red Coke fountain symbol was in nearly every theater lobby, at least those in which Pepsi had not beaten it to the punch. Salted popcorn made soft drinks easy to sell. To sell even more, theater owners ritualized the intermission: first one feature; then advertisements for soft drinks, popcorn, and candy; the intermission; trailers for coming attractions; and then the second feature. The early forties, with their double features, popcorn, and lack of competition from war-ravaged entertainment rivals, saw more fans stream into movie theaters than ever before or since.

All these changes meant more money in the pockets of theater owners, invariably the Hollywood movie companies themselves, but less comfort for the moviegoer. The grand movie palaces slowly and inexorably deteriorated due to lack of maintenance. Since funds for more theater construction were seldom available during the Great Depression and materials for it were lacking during the war, the nation basically made do with its existing theaters, almost all built before 1930.

But by 1950 theaters had deteriorated to such a point that the commonest viewing experience could be summed up in a single complaint: "sticky floors." That millions continued to go out to the movies offers strong testimony to the films Hollywood was putting on the screens of these aging theaters. As the movie fantasy grew more elaborate, with stars known around the world, projected in CinemaScope and VistaVision, the sites for their presentation grew shabbier and shabbier. Looking back on the thirties and forties—that Golden Age of Hollywood as a movie factory—it is now clear that the inexorable descent of the total moviegoing experience into a fantasyless factory of the mall multiplex had begun.

After the war, quieter but more fundamental social and cultural forces would make over the movie theater into what we know today. Weekly movie attendance in movie theaters in the United States crested in 1946 and then began its steady fall. By the early sixties it was half what it had been in the glory days of World War II, and thousands of formerly flourishing theaters had closed up shop.

Television alone is ritualistically blamed for this. Superficially, the logic seems self-evident. Once television programing began, movie fans attracted to this new and free entertainment form simply stayed home. Suddenly, going out to the movies came to be seen as a relatively expensive night out, often requiring a long journey downtown, a baby-sitter, and endless parking hassles. TV was so much easier, and almost as much fun.

Upon close inspection, the blame-television argument ignores the fact that in most parts of the United States television signals did not become available until long after the decline in moviegoing was under way. Only a few big cities gained TV stations in the late forties before the Federal Communications Commission halted the process with slightly more than one hundred stations on the air. In most of the United States, before the process of getting new stations going on the air commenced again in 1953, television was something one read about in the newspaper. Yet by 1953, millions had given up the moviegoing habit. Television may explain why New Yorkers abandoned the movies but not—at least initially—why the citizens of Augusta, Kansas, and Green Bay, Wisconsin, did so, too.

A more precise analysis of the decline in moviegoing might begin by noting that after World War II many Americans had new concerns on their minds. Wartime prosperity was turning into postwar stagnation, as millions of returning veterans struggled to find jobs. Moreover, those who found them took what money they had saved during the war and spent it on big-ticket items like new automobiles, unavailable since Pearl Harbor Day, not on nights out at the movies. The goal became: Move to the suburbs, leave behind city congestion and noise, and through quality schools make a better life for your children. Americans moved to new suburban subdivisions in record numbers.

By 1960, more Americans owned homes than rented for the first time in the nation's history. And Americans filled these new homes with children in record numbers. The birth rate increased as never before. Women married younger and had more children. Indeed, the most fanatical moviegoer of the past (a better educated, middle-class citizen with the time to be entertained and the money to spend on it) was now to be found in precisely the demographic cohort that most embraced the suburban ideal, the sizable mortgage, and the family of four or five children.

Suburbanization and the baby boom led to less moviegoing, and would have done so even without the coming of television (which is not to say that television was a factor of no importance in the process). Successive waves of suburbanization took moviegoers farther and farther from city theaters. Poor public transportation from those suburbs made it difficult to journey downtown, while parking was a horrendous problem in the congested city, even if one took the family car.

The baby boom meant that new parents used their free time to play with the kids. Extra income went for new toys and clothes, and in any case the family had fled the city and its attractions (including the movies) for the new world of Little League and backyard barbecues. Here is where television came in. It provided free entertainment at home for suburban children whose parents had long ago decided to abandon city life and, with it, the moviegoing habit. And it began to influence a new generation's ideas about what viewing a movie should be—informal, at all times of the day or night, splintered by advertisements, on a screen one-hundredth the size of that of a nickelodeon, one-thousandth the size of an image in a movie palace.

The American film industry was not oblivious to these trends. Its first response came with "auto-theaters," drive-ins, which had, in fact, been around in small numbers since the mid-thirties. Once the necessary building materials became available after the war, thousands of drive-in theaters opened in the suburbs. The drive-in converted a farmer's field into an open space where parked cars filled with movie fans watched double and triple features on a massive screen. By the early sixties drive-ins accounted for one out of every five movie viewers. For the first time, during one week in June 1956, more people attended drive-ins than went to traditional "hard-top" theaters, thus sealing a bargain initiated by the air-conditioned movie palaces of the twenties: peak moviegoing attendance during the summer, a trend that holds to the present day.

The movie industry, from 1952 on, sought to redefine the very technology of the medium—Cinerama, 3-D, CinemaScope, VistaVision, even Smellovision. This was the beginning of the modern era of moviegoing, in which theaters tried to become whatever TV wasn't. This included wide-screen images and Dolby stereo sound. By the end of the decade the industry had settled on the variable wide-screen format system offered by Panavision, most frequently set at 1.85×1 (versus the 1.33×1 that had been standard since the turn of the century). From the sixties on it has been taken for granted that movie theater images are wider than those offered on 1.33×1 television sets. And the sounds they offer would come from speakers bigger than most home television sets have.

But the drive-in, even with CinemaScope or Panavision, could not provide a permanent solution to serving suburban America. Or even a permanent solution to the basic comfort of the suburban TV room. Simply put, if the movie palace had been the grandest of arenas in which to enjoy watching films, the family car was not. What fantasies it held—for teens desperate to get a little privacy together, unsupervised privacy—had little to do with the movie-viewing experience. Almost its sole movie attraction was its cheapness for baby-boom families wanting the occasional night out—two dollars a car for whoever could squeeze in. As Pacific Theatres reminded its California customers: "Come as you are in the family car." Still, price, convenience, and informality could not clear the foggy windshield or improve the sounds from the tinny loudspeaker hooked to the car window, frequently falling off as someone climbed out to run to the restroom or buy more popcorn.

Drive-in ads inexplicitly reminded potential patrons of further problems. Those north of the Mason-Dixon Line, for instance, offered free in-car heaters for winter viewing. As the drive-in craze hit its peak during the fifties, some owners even built motels nearby so mom and dad could escape the kids, and so served up fantasies even less linked to films and easier to fulfill without them. (In coming decades chain motel complexes would show up, with their indoor pools, restaurants, video game parlors, and pay-per-view TV room entertainment services.) In the end there simply were too many problems for the drive-in, even one offering triple features like *Nashville Girl*, *Blazing Stewardesses*, and *Dirty Mary, Crazy Larry*. As the receipts of drive-ins began to ebb, some sort of longer-term and more permanent response to the suburbanization of America, to the TV-in-every-household life, was necessary.

Two problems the movie palace had once solved had now—again—to be addressed: location and fantasy. The movie house had to be made convenient to middle-class suburban life, and the movie-viewing experience off the screen had to be expanded. Only the first of these issues was dealt with in the coming two decades when the movie theater was put back on the map of middle-class life with movies in the mall. But first a retailing revolution of historic tenor had to take place: the coming of the suburban shopping center.

During the sixties, preplanned malls opened in record numbers around the United States. Innovative theater chains, led by General Cinema and American Multi-Cinema, worked with shopping center developers to jam in thousands of more or less prefab, undistinguished Cinema 1's and 2's into mall after mall. With acres of free parking, and easy access by superhighway, the shopping center—America's new downtown—grew to accommodate the majority of the nation's indoor screens and became the locus of Hollywood's attentions.

But this change did not occur overnight. At first, during the early sixties, one or two theaters were housed together in the parking lots of shopping centers. Gradually the multiplex, of four to twenty screens, moved inside, next to the shops for clothes or shoes such as The Limited and Thom McAn and anchor stores for everything such as Sears. Traditional one-screen cinemas in cities survived only in special situations, often near colleges. By the early seventies movie trade papers began to note an increasing number of U.S. cities that had no single-screen cinemas left within their proper borders. New York City was one exception, with a handful of art houses, from the Thalia to the New Yorker to the Regency, serving Manhattan.

What we got with the movies in the mall was as far from the golden days of the movie palace as one could imagine. A cluster of unadorned screening rooms offered only feature films and concession stands. Space was at a premium, and screens were often sandwiched in the basement. It was as if, realizing that it had lost the battle with TV and the living room, the movie theater gave up almost all pretense of the struggle at the level of architectural fantasy and the viewing experience and actually produced interiors with *less* to offer than at home. Taking their cues from the dominant trend in architecture, the new movie chains seemed to push the slogan of the international style to a new low of literalness: only function should dictate building form. The function, in the age of television, was clear: show blockbuster feature films—and nothing else. Gone was the architectural ambience of the movie palace; ushers were rarely sighted; stage shows were something that grandmother and grandfather talked about. Only air conditioning continued to add a measure of pleasure. Moviegoing in the mall was minimalist.

Viewing conditions reached an all-time low. To shoehorn as many auditoria into a corner of a shopping center, projection booths rarely lined up with the screen. That is, one booth served two or more spaces, so the image almost invariably came out with one half of the movie larger than the other (a phenomenon called keystoning). The careful film buff called ahead to find out which auditorium was being used and selected the one (if possible) in which the image was least distorted.

To further skimp on costs, theater owners inadequately padded walls between auditoria. Thus, as one tried to catch a quiet moment of *Annie Hall,* more often than not the rousing battle laser sounds of *Star Wars* poured through the wall, drowning out lines and distracting attention. Ironically, this resulted in part from just about the only area of the viewing experience, other than the films themselves, in which the film world attempted to outdo the conditions at home: sound systems. With Dolby eliminating all extraneous noises and six-foot speakers placed in every corner, as well as behind the screen, the sound in 200-seat auditoria became so good that it could have been properly accommodated only in a 3,000-seat movie palace of the twenties.

For a generation trained on home stereo and the Walkman, such sound systems made music in the movies—in fact, almost any noise—far superior to all but the best home stereo systems. To say the least, a four-inch TV speaker was simply no match. Now, finally, the images of Panavision were coupled with new, clear sound, ratcheted often to almost unbelievable levels to offer the film audiences of the eighties a new, totally enveloping technological experience. To the core teen-age audience it offered the equivalent of putting headphones on and spacing out.

Of course, the world of special effects now extended to sound tracks of unparalleled quality, and the zipping of lasers, the blasting of interminable explosions, the constant car crashes, and even the panting of couples making love poured from one all-too-small auditorium into the next. On the other hand, one almost wanted the volume turned up full, because at least that would drown out those folks talking behind you—for television had trained movie fans at home to accept constant conversation as part of the standard viewing experience. By the eighties, talking and constant commotion had become the order of moviegoing in the mall.

Other interior amenities, once taken for granted by film fans, disappeared in the age of the multiplex. Waiting in the lobby of a movie palace was a wonder-filled experience. In the multiplex, lines, through or by which shoppers streamed, often spilled out into the mall. What space there was in the lobby per se was invariably taken up by the popcorn stand, which in some cases also hawked shirts and posters, while attendants made change for the video games tucked into any corner adaptable as a "profit center."

Going to the movies had been reduced to the equivalent of standing in line at the K-Mart to buy a tire or picking out lawn furniture. Students of film history correctly note that the viewing conditions of the multiplex, save its advantage of superior sound, seemed to be a throwback to the nickelodeon era. The social experience of vast crowds in an auditorium seating thousands had been fragmented into screening rooms typically holding no more than 200.

The suburbs and television had changed the nature of film in any number of ways, none more important than this fragmentation of viewing conditions. Indeed, to draw folks away from their TV sets and living rooms, one needed a diverse set of attractions—all attempts to create *the* blockbuster. That is, so much money could be made on a single film, such as a *Star Wars* or an *E.T.*, that fashioning blockbusters became the single purpose of the contemporary film industry. But no one could predict which film would become a blockbuster and which not. So theater owners tended to construct one larger auditorium (about 500 seats) surrounded by a half-dozen of 100 seats each. Films were then tested in the smaller auditoria, and only the true blockbusters moved into the more spacious auditorium.

The multiplex put an end to folks over thirty-five regularly going out to the movies. Too many sticky floors, too many noisy teen-agers, too many *Friday the Thirteenths*. During the seventies and eighties, wily entrepreneurs sought to find viewing conditions to recapture that lost audience—or at least to capture the newer ones growing up in a world of TV around the clock. No wonder Time, Inc., transformed itself from a magazine company to a video money machine with the innovation of Home Box Office. The introduction of the home VCR in 1975 offered a simple response to the almost squalid viewing conditions of the multiplexes built during the sixties and seventies.

By the late seventies the theatrical-movie exhibition scene was at least stagnating. In a late-seventies report the consulting firm of Arthur D. Little, Inc., predicted that pay-TV and home video would imminently close nearly all the nation's movie houses. Into this economically sluggish entertainment environment stepped Garth Drabinsky, a Canadian entertainment lawyer who proposed to make going out to the movies fun again. Skillfully, through the eighties he fashioned a movie empire, Cineplex Odeon, first in Canada, then the United States, by bringing the movie theater interior as a fantasy element (on a reduced scale) back into the film experience. The splendor of the movie palace was self-referentially recalled in complexes in which eighties films also self-referentially "quoted" from the classic films of Hollywood's Golden Age.

Cineplex Odeon broke with the multiplex-in-the-mall in April 1979 by opening a $2 million Toronto complex that held eighteen auditoria. The original Cineplex (from "*cine*ma" plus "com*plex*") was a part of a new downtown mall, the Eaton Centre, which was directly linked to all parts of the city by subway, as Sam Katz's theaters had linked all parts of Chicago by elevated lines some sixty years earlier. Cineplex monitored its operations from a central computerized box office and in its ads heralded its wide selection of foreign films, revivals, and repertory favorites. Film fans were excited; Cineplex promised a smorgasbord of world cinema in downsized, postmodern theaters.

Within six months the Eaton Centre Cineplex started to make money. Its second run of *Midnight Express* set a record, remaining for sixty-eight weeks; *Life of Brian* broke that mark, lasting a year and a half. Drabinsky took his formula to Vancouver, Calgary, Montreal, and Winnipeg. By 1981 Cineplex was operating 124 screens with yearly grosses exceeding $20 million.

After scouting several sites in the United States, Drabinsky selected the movie-mad west side of Los Angeles and in July 1982 opened a $3 million, fourteen-screen Cineplex in the chic new "upright mall," the Beverly Center. To cut costs, three projectionists handled the needs of the fourteen auditoria. A massive concession stand tendered not only the usual popcorn, soft drinks, and candy but exotic coffees, imported bottled waters, and candies normally found only in Beverly Hills confectionery boutiques.

To catch the interest of cinema-saturated Los Angeles, Drabinsky added moviegoing luxuries not seen in years. The Beverly Center Cineplex, going far beyond the Canadian operations, offered a splendid art deco–inspired architectural design for lobbies and auditoria. The formula called for a Cineplex to be not simply a visual and aural experience to disappear into but a fun place to hang out, with more films than any other complex in town, a purposeful throwback to the days of Sam Katz.

The Beverly Center Cineplex proved a hit from day one, in part because Cineplex took direct aim at the fickle mentality of the American shopper. If mallgoers loved to browse and make "impulse" purchases, why shouldn't they be able to do the same thing for movies? Seven years later the company took the obvious next step and, following the lead of the retail world, began to offer credit card purchases to make "impulse" shopping for movies as easy as buying jeans at The Gap.

With so much invested, Drabinsky could not stick with a cornucopia of offbeat films and began to bid openly for potential blockbusters. When a *Batman* or *Top Gun* came along, his bookers moved screenings from one to two to three, even four auditoria to accommodate the surging crowds. Gradually fewer and fewer screens were devoted to revivals and foreign films, and so Cineplex's film selection began to offer the city the homogenized set of films viewers had come to expect from the unnamed rival Cinema 1's and 2's in the multitude of L.A. malls.

The success of the Beverly Center led Drabinsky to declare to his Hollywood neighbors that he intended to make his company the world's biggest movie chain. In 1984 Drabinsky bought out a Canadian rival, acquiring the Odeon chain's nearly three hundred screens. In August 1985 the newly minted Cineplex Odeon swallowed Plitt Theatres, a chain that dominated moviegoing in the United States from the Sun Belt to the environs of Chicago —a corporate successor to Balaban & Katz. In two bold moves Drabinsky had put Cineplex on the list of the top four theater chains in North America.

These mergers impressed Lew Wasserman, head of Universal Pictures and the most powerful movie mogul in Hollywood. Wasserman knew that the Reagan administration (under his former client, actor Ronald Reagan) had dropped the old Paramount decrees that since 1949 had banned major Hollywood companies from owning and operating theater chains. Wasserman got to know Drabinsky through negotiations to build a $10 million, eighteen-auditorium, six-thousand-seat multiplex (then the world's largest), to be located in the parking lot of Universal Studios in California. When it opened over the Fourth of July weekend in 1987, the Universal Studios Cineplex set a new eighties standard for a cinema complex, complete with stars and clouds in the ceiling of the lobby (a conscious reference to the atmospheric theaters of the twenties), concession bars that rivaled small restaurants, and two eight-hundred-seat auditoria complete with balconies. Southern Californians reveled in this new taste of filmic opulence and made the Universal Studios complex an instant success, even though the films shown there were no different from those found in nearby multiplexes.

Soon Universal and Cineplex Odeon, Wasserman and Drabinsky, were partners, the newcomer from Canada in bed with a major Hollywood studio—on Universal's part, a less than nostalgic and more than profitable nod toward the days when Hollywood ownership of movie theaters had defined the moviegoing experience. Now Universal's sleepers like *Field of Dreams* could linger at a Cineplex Odeon theater and develop an audience, while a non-studio-affiliated chain would undoubtedly have weighed the first weekend's results and jettisoned such an initially unprofitable film.

Cineplex Odeon was on a roll. Drabinsky set up his own in-house professional design unit, the first anyone in the movie business could remember since the days when Sam Katz kept the Rapp brothers busy. Carpets ordered from Europe were matched, in recurring purple motifs, to designs on ceilings and archways. Art deco schemes, complete with touches of neon, highlighted lobbies and auditoria alike. Commissioned sculpture and paintings included Alan Wood's *The Movies* for the Oakridge Mall in Vancouver and Phil Richard's *Once Upon a Time* for the Woodbine Centre in Toronto.

The business operations of Cineplex Odeon also were reminiscent of Sam Katz's management style when one mogul supervised everything, from the films to be shown to the types of soft drinks sold. Indeed, Drabinsky proudly boasted of the deals he negotiated for candy, popcorn, and soft drinks. In this sense the post–movie palace experience remained central to even the most elaborate and fantastical Cineplex establishment, for concessions stood at the heart of his movie house economies. Cineplex Odeon prided itself on markups exceeding 100 percent on popcorn, and the simplicity of the service it offered, including the near-minimum wages it paid inexperienced workers to serve its Cokes and tubs of popcorn with "Real Butter," proved a company specialty.

A handful of the newer Cineplex Odeon complexes even have formal cafés in their lobbies, where espresso, pastries, and fancy, upscale sandwiches are served. Drabinsky knew how to play the yuppie market in selected "upscale niches." Many joked that the movies only served as an enticement to come into Garth Drabinsky's fast-food operation. And the joke reflected the degree to which these complexes blended new vistas of consumption into the nostalgic repackaging of film's more opulent past. In all this Drabinsky was proving that if you combined a patina of the nostalgic movie past—no matter whether it was the art deco of the twenties or the "real butter" of the thirties—with the full present-day consumer package, from its technology of stereo sound to its credit card convenience, you could make the public not just return to the movie house but pay ever-rising prices for that opportunity. Drabinsky took an average ticket price under five dollars and in the latter half of the eighties upped it to seven and a half dollars. (The public protests over each rise fizzled fast.)

By 1987 Drabinsky had sewn up more theatrical takeovers than at any time in film history since the heady movie palace days of the twenties. He held a dominant share of the New York, Chicago, Seattle, and Washington, D.C., movie markets but feared that such a spate of takeovers and the ensuing rises in ticket prices that helped fund them could make movie fans livid. To appease them, he initiated and publicized a select number of special projects.

For filmgoers of New York City, Cineplex Odeon heralded (through ubiquitous newspaper advertisements) the restoration and expansion of the Carnegie, long one of the city's top art theaters. In Washington, D.C., Cineplex Odeon presented the political movers and shakers with a splendid six-plex near their posh homes. Its spacious lobby and marble floors and a clever sequence of spaces led to the auditoria, comfortable seats, and good-sized screens. It was fitting that in November 1988 George Bush, Dan Quayle, and their families would make their first public post-election "informal" appearance at a premiere held at the Cineplex Odeon Wisconsin Avenue Cinema.

Cineplex Odeon in its ads tried to be everywhere. Drabinsky even negotiated a deal to offer coupons on the back of Chex cereal boxes to save patrons "up to" 50 percent on movie tickets. Drabinsky even commissioned a special section of *Variety* for Cineplex Odeon's tenth anniversary, therein announcing his authorized biographers. In turn, Cineplex Odeon began to regularly screen others' ads (for Club Med and American Express, to name but two campaigns) before the features, initially in places like New York and Washington, D.C., to choruses of boos and howls of protest.

Although he lost control of his cinema empire late in 1989, when the history of the movies is written a hundred years from now, Cineplex Odeon's Garth Drabinsky will most likely be remembered for showing a stagnant theatrical film industry that there was still a profitable place in the American consumer package for a new version of the total film experience, on and off the screen. Drabinsky showed the film industry that the coming of cable TV and home video need not close down the movie house—that within the confines of late-twentieth-century capitalism and culture, going out to the movies to see blockbusters such as *Batman* and Indiana Jones films could be a "unique" cultural experience, and that there was still room for more offbeat fare such as *Blue Velvet* and *Black Rain*.

A revolution in how Americans watched movies began in the late fifties at home with the appearance of TV's "Late Show." The television set as home movie theater commenced in 1954, when eccentric billionaire Howard Hughes agreed to sell the films of his studio, RKO, to television. Millions took notice when these titles were showcased by WOR, a non-network New York television station, on its "Million Dollar Movie." *King Kong* became a celebrated classic; *Citizen Kane,* playing over and over, was "discovered" and soon hailed as a great (maybe even the greatest) American movie. A new generation of dancers was inspired by the extraordinary grace and charm of Fred Astaire and Ginger Rogers in *Top Hat* and *Swing Time.*

But the "Late Show" hardly proved perfect. Silent films were only occasionally presented—and then at the wrong projection speed—and so film fans raised on TV too often thought that movies made before 1929 consisted of the flickery movements of a Charlie Chaplin or a Buster Keaton running around "too fast." Except for a wave of British titles shown in the late forties as

Hollywood withheld its wares, foreign films have made infrequent appearances on television.

Far more significantly, feature films were normally "re-edited" to meet television's time requirements and advertising needs. Making over films for telecast did not begin with colorization; revision began as soon as films were first shown on the tube. Anonymous schedulers trimmed films to fit prescribed blocks of time, often butchering narrative, character, and cinematic beauty in the process.

So it was a historic moment in the mid-fifties when the major Hollywood movie companies released their pre-1948 titles to television. For the first time in the sixty-year history of American film, movie fans were able to view—with perfectly good homemade popcorn at hand—a broad cross-section of the best and worst of Hollywood talkies. No better example of the importance of this can be found than MGM's and CBS's experience with *The Wizard of Oz*. Unbelievable though it may seem today, that film lost money in its initial release. Through TV *The Wizard of Oz* became the most watched film in Hollywood history.

Watching movies on TV continued the movie theater trend toward informal viewing. No need to get dressed and be on one's best behavior as in the movie palace. In any attire, while eating or even trying to nap, people could watch movies in the same comfort as listening to the radio or reading a book.

So popular were these "late shows" that soon the TV networks ached to show post-1948 Hollywood features in prime time, but this required agreements from the Hollywood craft unions. In a precedent-setting action the Screen Actors Guild, led by its president, Ronald Reagan, went on strike and won guaranteed residuals for televised airings of post-1948 films. On September 23, 1961, NBC premiered "Saturday Night at the Movies" with *How to Marry a Millionaire*. Ratings were high. Of the thirty-one titles shown during this initial season, fifteen were in color. NBC especially liked the color titles because its parent company, RCA, was looking for ways to spur sales of its color television sets.

Thereafter TV screenings of recent Hollywood movies generated record ratings; Alfred Hitchcock's masterwork *The Birds* was watched in 1968 by nearly 40 percent of the nation. *The Bridge on the River Kwai* and *Cat on a Hot Tin Roof* found new life on television. On television, as at neighborhood theaters through the thirties and forties, second-runs proved as popular as anything the small set had to offer.

But the limitations of such TV screenings opened other potentially profitable view-at-home possibilities for those who wanted to see theatrical films at their full length and unsanitized by some network vice-president. As cable TV spread across the United States during the seventies, millions quickly signed up on HBO, where, for the price of three movie tickets, one could see uncut, uncensored films around the clock for a complete month. Millions who had deserted the movies in the mall became fans again, only at home.

Cable TV offered other treats. In a bold move in 1985, for instance, Ted Turner with his cable SuperStation in mind temporarily purchased MGM, not for its current productions but for its library of old films. To many film buffs Turner may only be remembered as that evil, awful colorizer, but to the folks in TV-poor North Dakota he will be remembered for bringing the film classics of the thirties and forties into their homes through his TNT network.

And yet with HBO one still had to adjust one's schedule (some fans getting up at 4:00 A.M.) to see a particular favorite film. Sony resolved that problem in 1975, when it introduced the Betamax half-inch videocassette recorder. An enthusiastic public snapped up so many machines that by 1989 fully two-thirds of U.S. households were equipped either to tape movies off the air at any hour (for viewing at some more convenient time or for safekeeping) or to rent and watch any of the thousands of films now available on tape.

By the mid-eighties there were so many movies on cassette that their titles filled multivolume reference books. By the end of the decade about four hundred new prerecorded tapes were being released each month, three-quarters of which were Hollywood feature films. Brian De Palma's *Scarface,* a bust in theaters, was rediscovered on video by an entirely new audience, just as a nation of TV-viewers had rediscovered *Citizen Kane* three decades earlier. In 1986, for the first time, the revenues from home video sales and rentals exceeded the entire take at the box office, even with more than twenty thousand screens functioning nationwide.

While we now have more, however, often it amounts to less. True, with a VCR we can have as many "screenings" as we want—but each viewing brings us a diminished film, for the movies have been panned, scanned, and otherwise distorted to fit our TV sets. Some may remember the magnificent, swooping pans and dollies in Sergio Leone's *Once Upon a Time in the West* (1969). Unless one has access to a theater equipped with the proper anamorphic lenses (and can find a projectionist who knows how to use them), there is simply no way to see, much less appreciate, a work that many deem the greatest wide-screen movie ever made—and the same is true of numerous other large-scale masterpieces, from Nicholas Ray's *Rebel Without a Cause* (1955) to Stanley Kubrick's *2001: A Space Odyssey* (1968). Sadly, more and more viewers are seeing these cinematic wonders in TV versions that suggest great paintings chopped off at the sides, blown down to minuscule proportions, and displayed through a sheet of smoked glass.

The reputed savior of the TV industry, high-definition television, seems so promising precisely because it can provide, in the home, images that have the clarity of a movie properly exhibited and in the correct aspect ratio. However, none of its proponents claims that HDTV can restore the size and scope of the theater screen—not even the diminished screens that hang in so many of today's mall cinemas.

It is not surprising that during the eighties, the age of home video, millions of Americans would still faithfully line up for the right movie, a *Batman* or a *Beverly Hills Cop,* paying as much as seven dollars to watch something that they knew would eventually be much cheaper on cassette. The great filmmakers of our day—Ridley Scott with *Blade Runner* (1982), Stanley Kubrick with *Full Metal Jacket* (1987)—take full advantage of the scope, texture, and sound that are possible only in a theater.

Nevertheless, as far as viewing conditions are concerned, the best is behind us. There is no way for us ever to return to the glory days of Balaban & Katz. The thrill of those vast images, projected in a "palace" built especially for your community and rich with lavish extras, is one that we can never rediscover. Sadly, the movie palace, a building made not just for profit but to purvey a pleasure multisensuous and seemingly transcendent, soon went the way of all the other transitory niceties of American culture: it was extinct the moment it became unprofitable. Our cinematic interiors are subject to the same inhuman forces that have changed the movies, and that also work on us, who keep on watching.

*G*ood *Soldiers*

PAT AUFDERHEIDE

RAIN OR SHINE, weekday or weekend, they file into the trough of the Vietnam Memorial in Washington, D.C. They emerge somber and shaken from this monument to inchoate sorrow, and there are always more behind them. Some, hoping to make a connection, leave behind mementos; more than 12,000 personal objects left there are now archived in perpetuity. Nothing better symbolizes how Vietnam has hovered in the American popular consciousness—unavoidable but inexplicable, a horror to be grasped only at the level of adding up the dead one by one.

It took Americans until 1982 to erect a monument to the Vietnam War. It took longer still for the makers of American movies and television programs—those avenues through which history becomes part of popular consciousness—to find a way to transform discordant political passions and unbearable images into entertainment. Only in the later 1980s, after periods of filmic silence and false starts, did the war become the subject of a subgenre, one that could be called the "noble-grunt film."

The noble-grunt films have been widely heralded as a sign of the maturing of the American audience—an audience finally ready for brutally frank images of the war the way it was really fought. But they are better seen as reconstructing the place of Vietnam in American popular history, away from a political process and toward an understanding of the war as a psychological watershed. Indeed, they speak more eloquently to the psychological plight of the average moviegoer today than to any reality of the war years. Just as the Vietnam Memorial enabled a public acknowledgment of personal mourning, films and TV shows of the later eighties evinced a sense of loss and a recognition of the need for grief.

These films had often been in the works for years, even decades. They got made, though, only when public opinion turned toward sympathy for Vietnam vets, and when Vietnam had become a topic for retrospectives and for academic research. And this shift in the social mood occurred as it was becoming apparent that America's international role had changed, when not even calling for "morning in America" could obscure the onset of imperial twilight.

We waited a long time to begin this transformation of Vietnam into a digestible element of popular consciousness. The war itself, *New Yorker* writer Jonathan Schell noted in 1969, was strongly marked by a sense of dreamlike unreality: "This may be partly because Vietnam is the first war to be shown on television, but we believe that there are more important reasons. A man dreaming is caught up in a reality that is entirely his own creation." The self-created reality to which Schell referred was grounded in assumptions so deep they often appeared simple fact until they were challenged. Novelist and vet Philip Caputo recalled, "America seemed omnipotent then; the country could still claim that it had never lost a war, and we believed that we were ordained to play cop to communist robbers and spread the political faith around the world." Historian Loren Baritz neatly summarized the beliefs with which Americans had entered the war: "Our national myth showed us that we were good, our technology made us strong, and our bureaucracy gave us standard operating procedures. It was not a winning combination."

No, it wasn't. The Vietnam War took the easy confidence out of America's self-image as a good-neighbor world cop, the Lone Ranger of international policy, a cowboy tall in the saddle against a world teeming with sneaky Indians. Even when President Reagan later evoked these images, there would be invisible quote marks around them, as if foreign policy were only a late-night movie.

The war also bitterly divided social groups and generations, and out of the social turmoil surrounding the war came a deepening of cynicism and disbelief in an effective relationship between citizenry and government. The crisis of American international authority so boldly symbolized by the taking of hostages in the American embassy in Iran, and the Iran-contra scandal, deepened a sense of rupture without signaling new directions.

The Vietnam War marked a messy end point to "the American century" in popular culture. "The sixties" has become a talismanic reference to that rupture in expectations and self-image, and the sixties reevaluation that hit late-eighties media always referred to Vietnam. You could see it in the movies—for instance, in *The Big Chill,* all about people caught up in the era without having been actors in it and nostalgic about anti-war atmospherics. The film's popular reception testified that millions who were merely present in the era remained psychologically unaccounted for long afterward.

In the late eighties that very sense of confusion became the psychological center of films and TV programs about the war. Films as different as *Platoon* (1986), *Full Metal Jacket* (1987), *Good Morning, Vietnam* (1987), *Hamburger Hill* (1987), *Gardens of Stone* (1987), *84 Charlie MoPic* (1989), *Off Limits* (1988), *Dear*

America (1988), *Casualties of War* (1989), and TV series like *Tour of Duty* and *China Beach* have carried into film what author C.D.B. Bryan described for literature as "the Generic Vietnam War Narrative." This generic narrative features combat units in tales that chart "the gradual deterioration of order, the disintegration of idealism, the breakdown of character, the alienation from those at home, and finally, the loss of all sensibility save the will to survive." There is something terribly sad and embattled about these films and TV shows, even in their lighter and warmer moments. They celebrate survival as a form of heroism, and cynicism as a form of self-preservation.

The noble-grunt films collectively recast the war as a test of physical and, much more important, psychological survival of the person who had no authority and too much responsibility. The war is seen from the viewpoint of the American soldiers in the barracks and bars, in the jungles and the paddies (rarely in the air or on water). The war is confined to the years in which the most ground troops were present. The battlefield has been internalized, and the enemy is not so much the Vietnamese as the cold, abstract forces of bureaucracy and the incompetence of superiors.

Vietnam, in these movies, becomes a Calvary of the powerless—not just for the grunts, but also for the viewers. The American moviegoer—a citizen-consumer who, like the soldier in Vietnam, is far from decision-making yet still accountable for its consequences—can find much to empathize with here. The moviegoer, too, is plagued with a nagging sense of guilt and suffused with a dull anger for carrying that burden. And, like the movie grunts, he or she has learned contempt for the bureaucrats above, whether at work or in government. Vietnam has thus become a powerful metaphor for tensions in American society since the war—especially over questions of personal responsibility for social conflict and political decisions. Watching the noble-grunt films, viewers can identify with characters who are misunderstood, confused, idealistic, well-intentioned, and betrayed from above.

The plots and styles of these films range widely, although they share a common focus and theme. In Oliver Stone's sentimental, elegiac *Platoon,* a young naïf (much like Stone himself, a Yale dropout and Vietnam enlistee) joins a platoon in which two archetypal warriors, the saintly, dope-smoking Elias and the bleak killer Barnes, vie for his soul. Barry Levinson's *Good Morning, Vietnam,* in a style that borrows something from sitcom rhythms and draws heavily on the talents of comedian Robin Williams, uses the character of hip, reckless Army DJ Adrian Cronauer to poke fun at official stuffed shirts and to wring poignancy out of the American's search for friends across culture and politics. *Gardens of Stone,* directed by Francis Ford Coppola, nostalgically evokes (and embalms) 1968 in an honor guard; a young recruit chafes at favors and begs to go to Vietnam, while his NCOs, heartsick veterans, try to stop him. Patrick Duncan's deliberately crude *84 Charlie MoPic* is told entirely from the point of view of the naïf behind the camera. He is recording, ostensibly for a training film, a day on patrol with a crackerjack squad whose routine tour in the bush becomes a confrontation with death and with moral questions in fighting "Charlie's war." *Casualties of War,* directed by Brian De Palma in his characteristic florid style, recounts the rape and murder of a Vietnamese farm girl by a battle-crazed squad, the newest of whose members brings them to court-martial. *Dear America: Letters Home from Vietnam,* made by Brian Couturie for HBO (which has backed many cable ventures about Vietnam), draws on music video. Its images are outtakes from network news footage, including many close-ups of soldiers; its script is a collage of letters written to relatives from the field; its sound track comes out of a still timely jukebox. The earnest TV series *Tour of Duty* dramatizes the conflicts of and relationships between field soldiers; the stylistically hipper *China Beach* sets its dramas in a field hospital next to an R&R station and prominently features the role of women who served as nurses and support staff. Stanley Kubrick's chilling *Full Metal Jacket* both fits within and breaks the noble-grunt convention, since it uses the elements of this subgenre to shape a critique of it. Hapless boys are turned into killing machines in boot camp, where one—a recruit—kills his sergeant in despair; fellow recruit Joker goes off to war and to battle during the 1968 Tet offensive.

The viewpoint of the noble-grunt film is not, in any one instance, inaccurate, although it is partial. Taken together, these films revise, even erase, our understanding of what was, historically, not so much a military as a political process. They replay history as an emotional drama of embattled individual survival.

Entertainment movies, of course, stand or fall on their ability to act powerfully on viewers' emotions. Recall Samuel Fuller's comment in Godard's *Pierrot le Fou:* "A film is like a battleground. It's love, hate, action, violence, death. In one word, emotion." Successful films tap something in the feelings of millions of viewers and express them in a way that all can share. What these films offer is the revisioning of history as personal tragedy of a particular kind. It's the agony of having the emotional battleground itself destroyed, leaving the fighters without a way to express their own pain.

In these films close-ups of the grunts' faces are a regular feature. *Dear America*'s editors, for instance, combed archives' worth of footage to find fresh faces. Often the grunts talk directly to the viewer, either in voiceover, as in *Platoon,* or, as in *84 Charlie MoPic* or in *Full Metal Jacket*'s interview sequences, frontally into the camera in self-reflexive sequences. These are the voices and faces of people who insist on finally being heard and seen. The sound and image come at the viewer with a faint whiff of the grunts' resentment at having been overlooked, and also with a certain bravado for daring to risk recognition and, ultimately, self-acknowledgment.

If this focus recognizes and validates the suffering of the men (and sometimes women) who fought, it is also the result of the filmmakers' search for acceptable heroes. That fact was made explicit by liberal journalist and Vietnam vet William Broyles, Jr., who codesigned the concept of *China Beach,* which featured women, many of whom served as nurses. "No matter how involved you get with the tangled purposes of the war and its moral confusion and its unhappy end," he said, "what they did was purely heroic."

And the search for acceptable heroes is also the search for an acceptable vision of Vietnam, one that allows for the empathic union of character and audience. (The movie industry, after all, is in business to sell tickets, not critical history.) So these films arrange reality to fit the Hollywood grunts' perspective.

Consider the portrayals of the Vietnamese. Those portrayals show boldly that we, as citizens and moviegoers (not to mention moviemakers), don't know why we were in Vietnam and are no longer afraid to admit it. Nor are we interested in finding out, in a political sense. Such questions lie with others—politicians, pundits, bureaucrats—who have already lost our trust.

Vietnam was not only an overseas war but a civil war, which Americans first entered as advisers. It was also a war fueled by anti-Communist rhetoric, both in Vietnam and in the United States. In these movies the civil war virtually disappears; differences between North and South, civilian and military, "our" Vietnamese and "theirs," evaporate. From this filmic point of view the Vietnamese are all inscrutably Other, a pervasively untrustworthy population (except as victims)—not because filmmakers have suddenly accepted the proposition that the conflict was a true people's war, as the North Vietnamese claimed, but because the whole struggle is presumed meaningless. As a soldier in *Casualties of War* puts it, the first three weeks you're "in country," you're likely to be killed because you don't know; the last three weeks, it's because "you don't care."

And so the civil war simply moves inside the platoon, where ideology and the survival of peoples is replaced by life-style, careerism, and the survival of individuals. The war itself appears typically as a chaotic, maddening exercise in tracking a mostly invisible enemy. In the absence of community or mission, the only real job left to the grunt is his search for individual integrity.

The Vietnamese typically become part of the backdrop of paranoia into which innocents are lowered, or act as plot triggers to the problem of individual responsibility in the absence of social cues. When the Vietnamese function as victims, their mortal suffering is often a trigger for the central issue, the moral suffering of the grunts. What precipitates *Platoon*'s crisis, for instance, is a My Lai–type massacre, but the massacre itself is portrayed as the direct result of unbearable tension and paranoia in the platoon—fueled when the troops uncover a Viet Cong guerrilla hidden in the village.

It's the war for the soul of *Platoon*'s naïve hero Chris that really occupies the two warrior-gods Elias and Barnes. Elias is a superlative fighter whose guerrilla tactics make him a potent warrior; Barnes's nihilistic style is far more dangerous to the group. Elias puts a stop to the massacre, overriding the death-happy Sergeant Barnes, but Barnes gets his revenge by killing Elias. Although Chris kills Barnes, there's no satisfaction in it; the civil war in the platoon has eaten away at the warrior mission. At the end of the movie Chris says in mournful voiceover, "We didn't fight the enemy, we fought ourselves, and the enemy was in us." As Oliver Stone put it in the introduction to the published screenplay, Elias and Barnes were meant to illustrate two views of the war: "The angry Achilles versus the conscience-stricken Hector, fighting for *a lost cause* on the dusty plains of Troy. It mirrored *the very civil war* that I'd witnessed in all the units I was in. [Emphasis added]"

In *Casualties of War,* American atrocities lead back to American casualties. The farm girl's suffering—filmed in a style that makes it, horrifyingly, a pornography of pity—is the vehicle leading us to the film's central tragedy: the collapse of a moral framework for the men who kill her. The spectacular agony of her death is intended to stir not the audience's righteous anger at the grunts—that role is already filled in the film itself by the moralistic new recruit Eriksson—but empathy for the ordinary fighting men who have been turned into beasts by their tour of duty. De Palma himself said as much: "It's not really [a] political [movie]. It's very emotional, and full of sorrow." The sorrow was for the soldiers; he called the court-martial scene a moment that revealed that "these are *all* casualties of the war." The film was for him about America's emotional legacy from Vietnam: "To me, the Vietnam experience is the sore that will never heal. So many things happened to these kids, and marred their lives forever, and there's no rational way to explain it."

Not that the Vietnamese can't be worthy enemies in these movies, but as such they are likely to be triggers of questions of conscience, responsibility, and conflict within the platoon. In *84 Charlie MoPic* the squad members have the highest respect for the Vietnamese as soldiers. "It's Charlie's war," they say. They don't even conceive of the war as a moral or political battlefront between them and the Vietnamese; political issues are inconsequential for men trying to survive a day in the bush. The Vietnamese, not only setting the terms of the war but fighting it well enough to threaten the Americans, set a standard for what a real warrior is. They are even enviable, for having real community and purpose, while the squad members must create community in the field and mostly out of oppositional sentiment directed against their own superiors. For most of the film the Vietnamese presence is registered only as ominous rustlings, small figures in the distance, or by booby traps, until one Vietnamese soldier is captured. The squad leader, a ferociously serious black man, forces the white, careerist lieutenant to kill the man with a knife, literally driving home the point that war means killing real people. Thus, conflicts within the army are acted out on the Vietnamese soldier's body. This acting out occurs again at the end of *Full Metal Jacket,* when the squad finally locates the lone hidden sniper who has decimated the patrol. The soldiers' arguments over killing the girl (who in the screenplay is an Amerasian) revive again the bitter divisions within the American fighting unit. In Kubrick's vision these divisions are not neatly drawn between grunts and officers but exemplify the contradictions within the values that fueled the American war effort.

The therapeutic mission of the noble-grunt subgenre—to rehabilitate, through confrontation with one's own pain, both grunts and viewers—comes out even more clearly on television, where subtleties take second place to sentimental drama. Vietnamese appear occasionally in the TV series *China Beach,* but they function as mere triggers of the series's central concern: how to maintain your humanity in the midst of chaos and pointlessness. One episode of *Tour of Duty* ends with an aborted discussion of the U.S. role in Vietnam: "The war is wrong," says one grunt. "That's not the point," says the other. And in context, of course, it's not—the point is the grunts' survival, not just physically but as caring human beings.

As vehicles back into the problems within the U.S. armed forces, the Vietnamese can sometimes be shown sympathetically, since they reveal the grunts' plight. For instance, in *Good Morning, Vietnam* the major Vietnamese characters function primarily to show how Cronauer, a Huck Finn–like individualist, is betrayed by higher-ups in his own army, and how Cronauer can hear what his superiors cannot. He forms a romantic attachment with a young Vietnamese woman and then an even deeper emotional bond with her younger brother. The boy cries out to him, "We're not the enemy—*you're* the enemy." When Cronauer does end up in danger, it's his own officer who is the real culprit, and the young boy—who works for the Vietcong but loves Cronauer—saves the hero. And so the boy's act reveals conflict within the army. The minor Vietnamese characters who fill Cronauer's goofy English classes show us that the Vietnamese can be just like us, except poorer and with funny accents; they learn ghetto jive and play improvised softball, only with melons, and endear themselves to Cronauer and the audience. We know they will soon become boat people. (*Full Metal Jacket* showcased the complacent imperialism of such attitudes, in the remark of a colonel to Joker: "We are here to help the Vietnamese, because inside every gook there is an American trying to get out.")

Vietnamese characters are more often the displaced object of grunt rage at the meaninglessness of their mission. These Vietnamese are sneaky, and they don't play fair. *Casualties of War,* for instance, opens with two battle episodes, one nighttime and one daytime, that showcase guerrilla tactics and provoke virulently racist comments from the grunts. The sergeant offers a relatively sympathetic explanation: "See, these people here are confused themselves, are they Cong or not Cong."

America's Vietnamese allies are also often shown in a way that reflects the American soldiers' cynicism and dismay. For instance, in Christopher Crowe's *Off Limits,* a film noir set in wartime Saigon, the corrupt South Vietnamese police are "mice" to the hard-bitten U.S. Army detectives. In *Full Metal Jacket* the grunts frankly despise their Vietnamese allies. Their hostility is worked out on, among others, Vietnamese prostitutes. And in interviews with a Canadian television crew one says, "We're shootin' the wrong gooks." Or Vietnamese can simply become invisible, as in *Gardens of Stone,* where Vietnam is seen only in one murky jungle shot. And sometimes they're erased, for a reason. In the making of *Dear America* HBO simply struck references to Vietnamese deaths, according to the director, for fear that such comparisons would be invidious.

The grunts, and the viewers, are almost invariably plunged into a Vietnam of alien beauty and ever-present danger, without clear boundaries. The war is murky in most battle scenes, such as in *Platoon,* where the thick jungle metaphorically overwhelms the grunts, rather than sheltering them, as do the warm dens of their barracks. (*Full Metal Jacket,* whose urban battle scenes take place during the atypical 1968 Tet offensive, is the exception.) If the field is impenetrable jungle, Saigon—symbol of the failure of the rear guard to back its field soldiers—is all riotous overcrowding and crass commercialism. Cronauer's Saigon is sunny daytime in *Good Morning, Vietnam,* while the *Off Limits* detectives mostly see it by neon-lit night. But either way, it's an unpredictable universe, seeded with booby traps, time bombs, and bad faith. In this sea of uncertainty the only real relationships, for good or evil, are among the American fighters.

Portrayals of the Vietnamese thus point to the way in which, for these films, the war isn't about "us versus them" so much as about "us versus Them within us." The "Them within us" is carefully confined. The focus is on someone up above, but not too high—not, for instance, anybody in particular in the State Department or the White House. In *Good Morning, Vietnam* the bad guys are the putz who runs the radio station and his superior, who can't see that the war is changing and that he might need someone with Cronauer's ability to help boost morale. Above them, though, is a good general, who does recognize Cronauer's value, and who intervenes in the end to rescue him. In *84 Charlie MoPic* the bad guys are middle-level officers. Careerist "L.T." delivers a speech in which he describes how combat duty is a stepping-stone to a military career. "L.T. thinks being a war hero will give him an edge as a junior exec," director Duncan said, "but the rest of the guys know they've been earning that for him." The detectives of *Off Limits,* pursuing the serial killer of Vietnamese prostitutes and their Amerasian babies, find out that their culprit is an American officer. Although the detectives precipitate his death, his crimes go undenounced because his peers protect him. In *Casualties of War* get-along-go-along officers, both black and white, block the outraged Private Eriksson's pleas for justice. (It's only when the Lutheran Erikkson runs into a chaplain—a moral voice that transcends the system—that court-martial becomes a possibility.) *Hamburger Hill*'s subject, the taking of a pointless strategic objective, where soldiers suffered 70 percent casualties, carries its implicit indictment of military officers into every scene. In TV series incompetent and corrupt officers and embassy officials punctuate the hard life of the grunts and the medical and R&R staff—a seemingly bold, but contained, criticism of higher-ups.

Grunts may be self-righteous in their contempt for the higher-ups, but they are still true to their roles and jobs. Fragging (the killing of officers by their men) is a rarity in these films, as it was not in the war. *Platoon* is the primary case, and there the murders of first Elias and then Barnes occur within the platoon's civil war. Only in *Full Metal Jacket,* where the deranged recruit murders his officer because he takes the drill sergeant's pronouncements literally (this is a "world of shit"), is fragging portrayed as a revolt against the stated mission. As in Kubrick's earlier anti-war films, *Paths of Glory* and *Dr. Strangelove,* in *Full Metal Jacket* arrogant officials carry the brunt of the director's misanthropy, although his bleak view of human folly includes the culture of the grunts— and the audience.

So the noble-grunt subgenre features intense immediate conflict and skirts attacks on the decision-makers higher up. That makes sense, of course, given the movie grunts' point of view (although real-life grunts often had a larger perspective). Even the documentary *Dear America,* which might be expected to have looser narrative constraints than a fiction feature, carefully limits its view. It does feature documentary footage of civilian officials, including the presidents, making pronouncements. But they are mere black-and-white punctuation, dramatic images of faraway authorities giving cryptic orders.

The invisibility of the real war-makers is thus built into the premise of these films. That distancing is the expression, in filmic narrative, of a long social process of erasure set in motion by President Nixon in 1972. As public protest grew over massive bombing raids and the mining of the Haiphong harbor, threatening to precipitate more huge demonstrations, and as the presidential election grew near, Nixon announced the existence of a "secret plan" to end the war. Early in 1973 U.S. troops were withdrawn. The TV networks seized on the "U.S. leaves Vietnam" theme. The war, however, continued, as did U.S. involvement. Within twenty-four hours of the peace announcement, over a hundred U.S. bombing raids had been conducted over Laos and Cambodia, and within Vietnam the civil war continued.

The "Vietnamization" of the war was a policy designed to get the war out of the sight of U.S. citizens without ending U.S. involvement in Southeast Asia. Aided by mainstream media, the strategy successfully dampened public protest, which declined with the end of U.S. troop involvement. But the out-of-sight policy did not put the experience of the war out of mind for Americans; it merely left its import unresolved.

Nor do the noble-grunt films attempt to resolve the questions swept under the rug by Vietnamization. Rather, they probe the pain of living with that lack of resolution. In their narrowly limited perspective the war becomes as confusing as it may have ever appeared to a nineteen-year-old recruit from Oklahoma.

In fact, these films do not just express but validate that confusion, partly through their very claim to you-are-there-in-the-swamps authenticity. It's perhaps most boldly asserted in *84 Charlie MoPic,* whose camera style and ambient-noise sound track are meant to convince you that you are watching unedited real life. However accurate the films may be—and the battle scenes from *Platoon* and *Hamburger Hill* (directed by John Irvin, who was a BBC film director in Vietnam), among others, have won high praise—their claim implicitly goes further than telling us what some combat soldiers suffered. They claim to tell us "the real truth" and, finally, how to feel about the war.

How we feel, by and large, is aggrieved. Aggrieved righteousness was not an attitude that began with the Vietnam War, of course. It had been building in American culture since the first flowering of consumer society. Perhaps its most widely heard spokesman today is veteran broadcaster Paul Harvey, who incarnates resentment at the decay of the embattled national self-image. He has constructed a career purveying wounded innocence, staunch patriotism, isolationism, and felt betrayal. His arrival on American radio coincided both with American dominance in international affairs and with changing life-styles in which American citizens defined themselves increasingly through personal consumption. His masterful mix of pride in power with resentment at felt powerlessness artfully expressed a general attitude that later surfaced both in the movies and in politics.

The resentful attitude toward authority that these grunts express can thus be seen as an oblique commentary on the gutting of a national democratic process in a consumer society. Anti-authoritarianism is a strong tradition in American popular culture, but the anti-authoritarianism that suffuses these films is of a special sort. It has nothing to say about authority badly wielded and evidences, instead, a collapse of faith in "the authorities." Distrust of politics in general is the corollary to that collapse of faith. Sullen grievance and self-preoccupation are accompanying attitudes—attitudes that were key to President Reagan's personal popularity and to the success of the cartoonish movie figure Rambo. They reflect at a personal level a sociopolitical reality. The public—increasingly seen even by national political party officials as a collection of demographic-marketing categories—may be polled, may even vote, and carries responsibility for and the onus of decisions made by elected officials. The decisions themselves, however, are executed by those far from the citizen-consumer.

And so the grunts in these films can do something normally forbidden to entertainment movies: lecture the audience. When they do—when the squad members bark out harsh and undeniable truths in *84 Charlie MoPic* or respond with frank vulgarity to the camera in *Full Metal Jacket*—they are, unlike their higher-ups, ready to pay for the consequences of their acts. If the fighting men are angry about the position they have been put in, it is anger on behalf of all those who, as foot soldiers in life, suffer without reward.

The grunt becomes the underdog in the war, even taking on some characteristics of the Vietnamese. The best fighters are guerrilla fighters, like *Platoon*'s Elias and the sergeants of *84 Charlie MoPic* and *Casualties of War.* They fight at the level of the Vietnamese; this time around, the Vietnam War is a ground war.

The air war that, with defoliation, made Vietnam today an ecological disaster area is usually far away. When choppers appear, they're almost always medical helicopters on a rescue mission, not on the attack. The bombers that came to dominate U.S. strategy are virtually absent, and even their effects—the craters, the burned-over ground—are rarely seen in the thick filmic jungles. Nor is defoliation much in evidence, although stripped ground appears in *Casualties of War* as a metaphor for the emotional wasteland of the soldiers themselves. The bombing that was so shocking a metaphoric instance of U.S. aggression in *Apocalypse Now,* whose effects pervaded *The Killing Fields* (about the Cambodian war and its aftermath), appears briefly—for instance, in a scene in *Good Morning, Vietnam* when a village is obliterated—or is only a forlorn reference by soldiers trapped on the ground, calling for air support. Once again, an air sequence in *Full Metal Jacket* is an exception, and a clue to the film's self-awareness. And so, of course, aviator heroes are hard to find in the noble-grunt films. *Top Gun* (1986), the major air war film of the same period in movie history, takes place not over Vietnam but over the Middle East. In *Bat 21* (1988), one film that does feature airmen, the flier falls to earth to become an instant grunt and victim of fire from both sides.

These underdog warriors fight most of all for basic humanity, responsibility, integrity within a mad situation. Chris in *Platoon* is a voice of individual conscience. The conflict over Chris—or Ishmael, the observer, as Stone calls him—forces him to grow up and "shed the innocence and accept the evil the Homeric gods had thrown out into the world. To be both good and evil." Patrick Duncan called *84 Charlie MoPic* a film to "make sense out of a vision of personal responsibility sustained by people who have never been trained to do anything but survive." The NCOs of *Gardens of Stone* spend the movie grappling with the contradictions between what they know to be true ("there is no front in Vietnam") and what they are ordered to believe. *Casualties of War* spins on the individual moral decisions of the squad in "a twisted, upside-down world in which the normal things you can believe in didn't seem to apply any more," according to De Palma.

In the struggle to remain human when your bosses aren't, cynicism is a protective device, as is irony; both mask well-armed idealism and willful innocence. The *Off Limits* detectives are modern incarnations of Raymond Chandler's last good man in a sick world, and if *Full Metal Jacket*'s Joker makes sick jokes and wears a peace symbol on his helmet, it's in the service of maintaining sanity. *Hamburger Hill*'s grunts, initially divided by race and class, have a constant and common refrain, unifying them while separating them from the higher-ups: "It don't mean nothin' " (also a common refrain during the war itself).

But the cost of such personal strategies is high. That is the central theme of *China Beach,* which builds its drama on each wounded soul's lonely alienation. Central character McMurphy, a nice girl from Kansas, has seen so much tragedy that she can't remember how to feel; she is in constant peril of "going robot."

Like the heroes of the noble-grunt movie, she and the other characters exist in isolation, clutching in the air for lost community. They are innocents damaged by experience, remaining innocent by conscience although they may, at times, be guilty by circumstance.

The noble grunts are often children (as were the real grunts of the war, whose average age was nineteen), and their vision of the world reflects it. They are often, in fact, abandoned children, with bad or absent fathers (Barnes in *Platoon,* the self-deluded drill sergeant in *Full Metal Jacket,* the dead father of *Gardens of Stone*'s orphan, and the untrustworthy officers of many such films). Their youth culture, whose rock music pervades these sound tracks, promises a substitute web of relationships for those of family and community. That is the bright hope of DJ Cronauer's musical taste, and it is a promise made wistful in the nonstop sound track to *Dear America. Full Metal Jacket* milks musical communitarianism for fierce irony, as the troops tromp back to base singing the Mickey Mouse Club song.

Locked into the hermetic universe of "Nam," these grunts have a nostalgia for home. "Home" in these films is the cuddly image of Chris's grandmother, to whom he writes in *Platoon,* or the scenes bathed in golden light of *Gardens of Stone,* or the Mom and Pop and Sis to whom the child-soldiers wrote in *Dear America,* or the Christian, midwestern town and family of *Casualties of War*'s Eriksson. It's rarely the riven civilian world in which the anti-war movement energized popular debate over the meaning of the war. About as close as you get is a scene in *Gardens of Stone,* where a cartoonish anti-war protester, one of Vice-President Spiro Agnew's arrogant "effete snobs," insults one of the NCOs.

Most of these films, of course, take place far from protest demonstrations back in America. But they are also insulated from the sentiment that did exist within the armed forces themselves, especially among African-American troops; there was resistance to officers, including fragging; and there were even *ad hoc* truces between U.S. and Vietnamese soldiers in the field. The ranks of Vietnam Veterans Against the War were filled with grunts who had been politicized in Vietnam. Even the documentary *Dear America* gives nary a hint of that side of the war. The freewheeling Cronauer's resistance in *Good Morning, Vietnam* is typically countercultural, a protest against being stuffy and old-fashioned and liking the wrong kind of music.

The roiling social conflict that the war provoked is refracted indirectly in these films. What these good soldiers suffer is abandonment by authority, answered by finding support and solidarity with each other. That is Elias's promise to Chris and the other dope-smoking buddies of *Platoon.* The black pilot tells the downed colonel in *Bat 21,* suddenly stricken with conscience, "I don't know you, Bat 21, but you don't sound like a killer. I'm sure you couldn't stop it from happening. The important thing is to put it behind you." The found buddies of *84 Charlie MoPic* cross racial and regional lines (although the cracker sternly lectures the lieutenant about how it'll be different back home), as do the buddies of *Hamburger Hill.* As that film's producer, Marcia Nasatir, put it, "Making this movie allowed us to recognize the courage and heroism of the young men who were there and who fought for each other." And that is the recognition that keeps *Tour of Duty* and *China Beach* going every week.

The problem of maintaining one's humanity, in these war films, is linked to asserting masculinity. These soldiers have been betrayed not only by their superiors but by macho warrior values that prohibit emotional expression. The contradictions they are crucified on come out in *Casualties of War*'s misogyny-on-parade atrocity sequence; in the woman-hating murders of *Off Limits;* in the contrasting characters of Barnes and Elias in *Platoon;* in Cronauer's impish refusal to be a grown-up, a man, in *Good Morning, Vietnam.* The tough-guys-do-cry stance, the pathos of boy-man protagonists searching for good fathers, the brave refusal to give in to despair so typical of this subgenre all bespeak an awareness of the end of good-soldier macho imagery.

Some say these films are recovering the masculine ethos by the back door, while others hope that they reflect expanded gender definitions in the culture. The "tormented libidinal economy" of

this era's Vietnam films, as one critic calls it, may speak as well
to a wider uneasiness in the national mood, for both men and
women. The heroic, sometimes tragic John Wayne–type character in war films was also an emblem of a righteous, sacrificing
America on the world stage. The audience today can empathize
with the grunts' struggle to find footing on uncertain emotional
as well as physical terrain. They, too, are confronted with a
chaotic and uncooperative world, terrorized by large consequences of individual responsibility, and terrifyingly lonely.

The noble-grunt movie thus joins past and present. Interest-
ingly, most of these movies take place between 1965 and 1968,
thus creating an image of a war that ignores the origins of America's investment in Vietnam in the Kennedy era and eliminates
the process of Vietnamization with which it ended. In the slice
of the war they choose, the noble grunt can take center stage, as
a figure who resonates with the embattled American consumer
now.

If any film confronted the implications of the omissions and
limitations of the noble-grunt perspective, it was *Full Metal Jacket*.
But, like Kubrick's work generally, it dealt with what Kubrick
perceives to be killing weaknesses in the human condition: the
need to create and pursue an enemy in the search for self-defini-
tion, the dangerous delusions of the idealistic and ideological.
With its black humor, savage irony, and pervasive skepticism
(particularly in its central character, Joker), *Full Metal Jacket* undercut the pieties of the noble-grunt film. It did not heroicize its
militant innocents nor render sentimental the confusion of the
powerless. Neither was it intended to frame or explain the particular historical process of American involvement in the Vietnam
War.

Arriving in a sudden burst at the theatrical marketplace, the
noble-grunt films seemed to emerge out of a long silence on the
war. But, in fact, the pop-cultural landscape had been gradually
changing to accommodate this new vision.

The World War II combat film—*Bataan* (1943), for instance—makes a convenient benchmark to measure shifts in pop-

cultural perception leading toward the noble-grunt film. It featured a group of diverse men, symbolic of America's pluralism, whose individual heroics are dedicated to group survival, whose sacrifices are justified, and whose battles and objectives are clearly defined.

The genre died a lingering death. After World War II the U.S. armed forces never demobilized, and the Cold War replaced the hot one. The American government's geopolitical interests became global, while daily life, in an age of affluence propped up by military spending, became more and more defined by consumer choices. The kinds of wars in which the U.S. government got involved after World War II did not lend themselves easily to the conventions of the genre.

War movies refracted the changing times in many ways. Already in Samuel Fuller's *The Steel Helmet,* made in 1951 during the Korean War, the combat unit had become offbeat, the "good guys" often none too good, and the protagonist alienated. By the time of the Vietnam War, the "dirty-dozen" subgenre (Robert Aldrich made *The Dirty Dozen* in 1967), with its corrupt and unheroic characters and objectives, had become entrenched. Even war epics were affected; compare *A Bridge Too Far* (1977), chronicling a debacle, with *The Longest Day* (1962), the last of the classic World War II films. The "Korea" of *M*A*S*H* (1970) was, in fact, a black-comedic displacement of the ongoing conflict in Vietnam.

The Vietnam War also touched other genres, such as the Western. Arthur Penn's 1970 revisionist *Little Big Man* and Ralph Nelson's 1970 *Soldier Blue* both used Indians as metaphors for the Vietnamese, attempting to turn the genre on its head by making whites the agents of atrocity. *Soldier Blue*'s recapitulation of the Sand Creek massacre of the Cheyennes was meant to be seen as an uneasy parallel to the My Lai massacre.

Such relatively oblique social and political references were signs of the way the war did not fit traditional values and cultural images. During the war itself major studios avoided the subject, with the notable exception of *The Green Berets,* made with the bankable weight of John Wayne behind it. When that jingoistic film instantly became more of a political object than an entertainment commodity, it proved to the studios not simply that old formulas would not contain the new realities but that Vietnam was not a profitable subject for entertainment.

And it was true that while American deaths were at their height, there was something indigestible about the war, its realities, atrocities, and images. The formulas of a film like *The Green Berets* had to be at war themselves with the deluge of images Americans saw on television, in photographs, and in documentaries that provided the most contentious images to emerge then or since about the war. (Recall such celebrated ones as that of a naked, napalm-burned child running down Highway 1, or that of a Vietcong being shot in the head.) Network TV and photographs made the "living-room war" a jumble of disturbing images, even if often framed by the interests of U.S. policy. Meanwhile leftists produced films harshly critical of Vietnam; on celluloid as in life, leftists sometimes inverted the reigning clichés, identifying with Third World guerrilla fighters and demonizing political forces at home.

As Nixon's Vietnamization policy and the air war proceeded, however, the war of images cooled down. Peter Davis's superb documentary *Hearts and Minds* (1974), with its searing assessment of the war as a policy debacle, fell victim to post-Vietnamization consensus and was rarely seen, despite winning an Academy Award. Fiction films that broke through that consensus did not send studios searching for more Vietnam scripts. *The Boys in Company C* (1977), *Coming Home* (1978), *Go Tell the Spartans* (1978), and *Apocalypse Now* (1979), for instance, all tripped over cinematic conventions and popular unease with the issues of the war. For instance, Sidney Furie's *The Boys in Company C* milked the one-of-everybody platoon formula for its melodrama and created a cognitive dissonance that it never acknowledged. Ted Post's grimmer *Go Tell the Spartans,* which charts officer Burt Lancaster's discovery that the war was unwinnable, fell between camps of opinion and failed miserably at the box office (a failure deepened by the coincidence of a newspaper strike in New York on its release).

Other films groped for a way to address the political conflicts inflaming the war. *Apocalypse Now* was a self-referential epic about American solipsism, drawing on Conrad's nightmarish *Heart of Darkness.* Kurtz's pronouncement in the film, "It is impossible to describe what is necessary to those who do not know what horror is," was prophetic. The film, an enduring box office success, was admired for its spectacular production design. The film's publicity was also aided by the way its filming had duplicated, in miniature, the war itself. But it did not reshape Vietnam in popular consciousness; rather, it deepened popular confusion in its very theme. In Hal Ashby's *Coming Home,* a morality play with a political message, the veteran-victim was redeemed by taking a stand against the war, while the intransigent officer walked out to sea. The partisan message rankled, and *Coming Home* fell into the entertainment limbo reserved for Hollywood message movies.

The themes and narrative of Michael Cimino's 1978 *The Deer Hunter,* an elegy to American-white-male bonding and a eulogy for its sacrifice on the altar of Vietnam, presaged the parade of noble-grunt films, with heroes who were survivors of their own disillusionment. The film opens with holy rituals of all-American working-class life—hunting and a wedding—filtered through the golden haze of autumn. Then community is brutally shattered in the tropical hell dominated by evil North Vietnamese, whose (invented) torture tactics identify them as subhuman. *The Deer Hunter* powerfully played on aggrieved sensibilities and feelings of betrayal. But its torture sequences and the visually spectacular celebration of its protagonists tripped over conflicts still raging about the politics of the war. The publicity these "statement" films garnered, and the relative success of some of them, did not spur studio producers to search out similar projects.

For years thereafter, in fact, movie producers of the Big Chill generation avoided the subject of Vietnam. They didn't lack material. The publishing industry was creating bookshelves' worth of Generic Vietnam War Film Narrative; many of these books were optioned by independents. But in an industry where novelty is prized far above innovation, and where risk—even with big stars and safe subjects—is always high, this subject was declared off limits.

What finally triggered the noble-grunt subgenre was the changing economics of the film industry. The studios had long since become financial brokers rather than producers, with the trump card of distribution to play. With cable, videocassette, and changing opportunities in overseas markets, new distribution outlets opened up. Small producers, and the distribution companies that burgeoned briefly in the mid-eighties, seized those opportunities, and some turned to Vietnam projects that had been stalled for years. Major distributors only leaped on the bandwagon once they had proof that a Vietnam film—one cut down to a more comfortable size and rid of the contentiousness of the war itself—would sell. And *Platoon,* financed by the English company Hemdale and distributed in 1986 by mini-major Orion, sold very well.

Thematically as well as economically, the ground was being laid for the new Vietnam films in the decade preceding the noble grunt's emergence on screen. George Lucas's *Star Wars* (1977), a self-conscious epic, established the imperial hero as an underdog warrior for justice. There the good (read: American) guys were a guerrilla force against "the Empire." *Star Wars* and the ensuing films in the trilogy transported the underdog-warrior theme into space. There power and innocence could be conjoined easily with individual heroics, and the burden of empire could be dumped on "them," the bad guys, whoever they were. The trilogy also asserted other elements soon to become familiar in the noble-grunt film: the missing or bad father (Luke Skywalker's dad turns out to be villain Darth Vader), bungling bureaucrats, male bonding.

At the same time that *Star Wars* was breaking box office records and giving back to us an "us" that could win on screen and in space, Americans on the ground were being buffeted with bad news. A nation that, with an energy shortage in 1973, had been given a taste of the end of affluence now faced international humiliation when Iranian students kidnapped U.S. embassy personnel in Teheran in 1979 and held them for more than a year. "America held hostage!" blared the television sets in millions of homes. It seemed as if the specter of Nixon's "pitiful, helpless giant" had taken on flesh. Environmental crises further ate away at the image of a nation both preeminent and righteous.

When Ronald Reagan assumed office, he seized upon a reason for the precipitate decline in American prestige: "the Vietnam syndrome." More, he promised a new dawn, a morning in America. And he proceeded to conduct international affairs as if he were reading a film script, altering reality to fit needs. Nazi SS soldiers at Bitburg became "victims" as much as the concentration camp dead. The tiny island of Grenada, completing a small landing strip for tourism, became an invasion threat to the U.S. and the object of an invasion. The rantings of the bizarre dictator Muammar Qaddafi became a justification for the first overt American attempt to kill the head of another country. The Nicaraguan contra forces became freedom fighters for democracy.

No matter what the outcome—even when hundreds of Marines died in a terrorist attack on a barracks in Lebanon—Reagan personally garnered support because he resolutely played the role of ordinary American, outraged and aggrieved. The decision-maker, the power-holder, projected the attitude of a put-upon victim of decision-making. It was a brilliant psychological ploy for a president who depended on popular support while exercising policies that were often unpopular and sometimes secret.

Reagan found a movie hero to match his own public persona, one to whom he proudly compared himself: Rambo. It was an interesting choice for the powerful man who played to fantasies of righteous vengeance among those who felt themselves powerless. Rambo was the perennial righteous underdog, the survivor of alienation and rejection.

Rambo—a pre-adolescent boy with Nautilized muscles, a

wounded giant in chains, who, although he breaks the chains, can never be healed—was also the figure who paved the way for public acceptance of the noble grunt. Sylvester Stallone had initially played the character in *First Blood* (1982, directed by Ted Kotcheff). John Rambo was a vet with post-Vietnam shock, who acted out the nihilistic rage of the forgotten man, among other things wasting a local police force contemptuous of war-torn vets. The first film ended downbeat, with Rambo going to prison. *Rambo,* the 1985 film directed by George Cosmatos, picked him up there, breaking rocks in a hellhole whose value for the battered and betrayed vet is that "here at least I know how I stand." And it transformed Rambo from psychotic to savior.

The plot, larded with explosive action sequences, revolves around a secret mission to find MIAs (missing in action). The choice of target is significant; the question of whether any living Americans remain in Vietnam has lingered in public consciousness as a kind of objective correlative to our lack of closure about the "Vietnamized" war. Rambo, too, is a symbol of the war's unresolved end. He's a ghost in the machine, like the MIAs. When his mentor Trautman warns him, "The old Vietnam is dead," he says, "I'm alive, it's still alive, ain't it?" And, indeed, Rambo gets to rerun history in this movie, which allows him to refight the war alone.

Refighting the war had been a staple of prisoner-of-war and MIA films such as *Uncommon Valor* (1983), *Missing in Action* (1984), and *Braddock: Missing in Action II* (1985). Playing successfully to audiences more interested in action than in Vietnam, they celebrated the (usually officer-status) prisoner of war. *Rambo* departed from the formula by making the action hero a rejected marginal, an outsider returning to battle. Focusing on the hero's sense of loss and his hurt at being misunderstood broadened the film's appeal from the male, action-oriented crowd to general audiences.

The character of Rambo crudely but effectively combined elements that expressed power and powerlessness, making him both victor and victim. And it helped complete the reversal that *Star*

Wars had begun in space—a reversal that helped tame the war to entertainment proportions. "We" became "them," the underdogs, guerrillas, embattled victims.

Crucial to Rambo's stance as innocent betrayed is his childish character. At the outset Rambo asks Trautman, in a way that combines deference and petulance, "Sir . . . do we get to win this time?"—as if this were a children's game in which he had been cheated (and as many Americans felt they had somehow been cheated by the outcome of the war). Throughout the film Rambo is the victim of repressive father figures. The bad fathers are the military and civilian bureaucrats who want to bury the POW/MIA issue. Trautman is too enmeshed in the system to protect him; he, too, falls victim to the schemes of the higher-ups. When Trautman discovers that Rambo has been betrayed again, he says of the mission, "It was a lie—just like the war."

Abandoned by corrupt or ineffectual officials, Rambo assumes the role of guerrilla fighter played the first time, and successfully, by Vietnamese. But he's a superguerrilla (part Indian, part German, he is thus part "primitive," part supercivilized). He skulks through the jungle half-naked, and his tools are a peculiar mix of high and low tech. He rips up scenes with submachine guns seized from his Vietnamese captors. He blows up enemies with a bow and arrow—but the arrows are tipped with explosives. And he always falls back on his lucky hunting knife. His victories in action are a boy's orgasmic fantasy of power, not just liquidating the enemy but annihilating the very landscape.

Vietnamese in this born-again war are both victims and villains. Rambo's liaison is a young girl, who falls in love with him; her dream is "Maybe go America—live the quiet life." She doesn't make it, dying in Rambo's arms. (Of course, she must die—Rambo is too much a child to be a lover.) The Vietnamese military men play a high-tech, big-operation game that evokes the the U.S. war effort. Armed with sophisticated equipment, in charge of elaborate camps, they also use air power against Rambo. This is a film in which helicopters do attack—Vietnamese helicopters (one of which Rambo commandeers).

Rambo plays not just hero but a holy figure on crusade, and images evoke that connection. For instance, we see him crucified on an electrical torture apparatus (echoing our first close-up sight of an MIA, also in a Christ-like agony). When the girl dies, Rambo holds her in a *pietà* position, the image joining themes of holy suffering and righteousness.

Rambo's ultimate triumph is as much over the corrupt bureaucrats as over the Vietnamese; after returning to base with the MIAs, his last act of violence is to machine-gun the corrupt bureaucrat's equipment and threaten his life. But even in victory Rambo is condemned to obscurity; the heroic innocent remains the victim. Rambo's guerrilla war has a special poignancy because he is the unacknowledged secret defender of American values. "All I want," he tells Trautman with choked anger at the end, "all *they* [pointing to the rescued MIAs] want, and every other guy who came over here and spilled his guts and gave everything he had wants, is for our country to love us as much as we love it."

Rambo is the tragic image of an America wounded by circumstance. Life has not been fair to Rambo, or to America. The film's legacy was not so much in its muscular action sequences—although they guaranteed it enduring international success—as in the image of a vet wronged but right.

Just how well *Rambo* fit the times was evoked when Lieutenant Colonel Oliver North testified in Congress during the Iran-contra scandal. His demeanor recalled the same petulant, self-righteous, hurt-little-boy attitude that Stallone expresses at the beginning of the film. Ollie North's behavior as a member of the National Security Council also had parallels with Rambo's. He, too, was a cowboy of foreign policy, having "learned" from Vietnam to do it right this time, demonstrating contempt for lines of authority in the name of patriotism.

The Rambo age of presidential image politics came to a end with the 1988 election. George Bush did not have the style, skill, or will to reverse, in his personal presentation, the image of power as Reagan had done so deftly. He did, however, invoke the specter of Vietnam in his inaugural address. "That war cleaves us still," he said. "Surely the statute of limitations has been reached . . . No great nation can long afford to be sundered by a memory."

The movies, however, had already re-remembered Vietnam, in the process transforming the social cleavages to which Bush referred into smaller, far more manageable psychological ones. They had cleared the way for the next phase of reimagining the Vietnam experience on screen: the part where the vets come home. Even as Bush called for a kinder, gentler America built on local volunteerism and a rebuilding of community spirit ("a thousand points of light"), Vietnam vets in the movies had come back and were learning to live again.

For the major studios the moment of the noble-grunt film had, by 1989, passed. Few post-*Platoon* films bore out the box office promise of *Platoon,* and, of course, the genre itself was limited in its profitability. Although Lee Iacocca linked patriotism and Chrysler's new Jeep Eagle line in an ad preceding *Platoon* on videocassette, the advertising, licensing, and marketing possibilities of the noble-grunt films were clearly never going to match those of a *Star Wars* or a *Batman.*

But the process of learning to live again in the wake of the war was still a hot Hollywood subject, with such projects as Oliver Stone's *Born on the Fourth of July* and Norman Jewison's *In Country.* The unpredictable, violent psychotic vet of films like *Taxi Driver* (1976), *Tracks* (1977), *Rolling Thunder* (1977), and *Who'll Stop the Rain?* (1978)—embodiments of the disjunction between national self-image and experience—had been virtually read out of movie scripts by the late eighties. That was in part because of lobbying by veterans' groups. But it was also because the violent irruption of Vietnam into the American self-image had been successfully transformed into a sturdier image of decent but powerless Americans doing their best to survive the decay of community around them.

In the later eighties movies about returning vets did not put the issue of the vet's political judgment at the center of the story, as *Coming Home* had done so uncomfortably. Now the issue was the plight of the vet attempting, in the midst of a shattered community at home, to recover from the shattering of community in Vietnam. In films like *Heartbreak Ridge* (1986), *Distant Thunder* (1988), *Jacknife* (1989), and *In Country* (1989) the vet is the symbol of an America scrambling for its moral and psychic footing. All these films stress the pathos of the man who suffered and was scarred, who performs the heroic act of returning to life, and who calls into question the macho John Wayne image that got packed into the baggage along with the rifles in Vietnam.

In these films veterans have buried themselves for long years in grief or dull withdrawal. They are alone with memories and values that no longer fit. Clint Eastwood's *Heartbreak Ridge* presaged some of these later themes. In it hero Tom Highway—survivor of not one but two meaningless wars (Heartbreak Ridge was the Hamburger Hill of Korea)—stubbornly clings to his outdated Marine machismo as if time had stopped. In *Distant Thunder,* directed by Rick Rosenthal, the protagonist is a "bush vet" hiding out in the Northwest rain forest with other survivors. In David Jones's *Jacknife* a vet hides out in his house, drinking away his future. *In Country,* directed by Norman Jewison, features a vet who can talk only to his war buddies, taking refuge from bad dreams and bad memories in his ramshackle family home.

These vets hide from an unfriendly, unfeeling world where the rules have changed. Tom Highway pores over women's magazines to try to figure out why his wife left him, and suffers lectures from younger officers who remind him that it's a time of low-intensity peace. The bush vet of *Distant Thunder* must listen to a redneck's smarmy anti-vet rantings. The vets of *Jacknife* live more with their flashbacks than with the trashy, complacent world of civilian consumer life. The vets of *In Country* think they're uncomfortable relics of a past no one wants to remember; proving them right, a dance honoring them draws few of the town's residents.

The therapeutic help of family and buddies helps these vets

once again to love themselves. *Distant Thunder*'s bush vet, after venturing from his hideout with the aid of a friendly woman in town, gathers the courage to live again with the help of his son, who reveres him for his high-school sports record and who wants to be proud of him for his war record. In *Jacknife* the vet finally comes to terms with the secret horror he's been living with—the death of his buddy, one of a trio, in combat. The other surviving member of the trio finally makes him relive the moment and thereby abandon the search for blame; in the bargain he, too, rejoins society, winning the heart of his buddy's sister. A vets' therapy group also helps the two remaining buddies face the rest of their lives. *In Country*'s vet finds closure, and the beginning of a new life, when his niece—whose father had died in Vietnam before she was born—and her grandmother persuade him to visit the Vietnam Memorial to see the names of their dead on the wall. His coming to terms with his past is also the beginning of a new life for his niece, who has been haunted by the mysterious past.

The earlier *Heartbreak Ridge* is not nearly so sentimental or optimistic. Of course, it came out at the emergence of the noble-grunt subgenre, when public sympathy for the vets was still in the process of becoming pop-cultural currency. As well, Clint Eastwood is a postmodern macho man, playing both to that image and against it. *Heartbreak Ridge* raises both eyebrows at its archaic hero. Tom Highway recovers his self-esteem by going to battle in Grenada, but it is a silly little exercise, and he returns home, as Eastwood later said, "a warrior without a war, without any place to go . . . Where he goes, who knows."

Born on the Fourth of July (1989), on the other hand, raised sentimentality to a battlecry of betrayal. The crippled survivor-hero (Tom Cruise as Ron Kovic) rages against his impotence, which director Oliver Stone has said symbolizes the plight of America today. It is a fate brought on by a macho Marine re-cruiter, a steely commander who denies him his remorse at killing Vietnamese civilians and his own man, and most of all by a Catholic mom who sold him on simplistic patriotism. Aided by antiwar vets, Kovic finally comes "home" when he delivers a

speech at the 1976 Democratic convention, although home will
always be, for him, pathetic impotence in a wheelchair.

Whatever happens to them, these vets are survivors of a general breakdown of community. Their heroism lies in their choosing to forgive themselves, improvise a future, weather hostility
from a few unfeeling civilians, and accept the acceptance of many
others.

We are on our way, in the movies, to forgiving ourselves not
for anything the U.S. government and forces did in Vietnam but
simply for having felt so bad for so long. It remains to be seen
whether this is a cultural landscape in which, as some hope, "we
can find new determination to brave the opening expanse," or
the platform on which new castles of nostalgic delusion will be
built—or both. Either way, it is a profoundly personal matter
rather than a political or historical one, emotionally predicated on
a sense of loss and propelled by a therapeutic tone of self-help.

The Vietnam movies of the later eighties expressed and helped
to shape a consensus that the event was not a war but a tragedy.
This tragedy was not political, and it was certainly not shared by
or with the Vietnamese. It was entirely ours—the grunts of history, the innocents, the powerless ones, the "good soldiers." The
enemy was not over there but above us, somewhere in the cold
regions of policy and commerce, those regions beyond the control of the consumer. We have been abandoned, these films told
us, and must heal ourselves. The war is over, but the damage
remains. Distrust, alienation, a loss of history, and a huddled-over
sense of self-protection are our legacy.

The
*L*ast
Crusade

PETER BISKIND

THERE'S A DRAMATIC MOMENT at the end of the "origins" sequence of *Indiana Jones and the Last Crusade* where the young Indy, having seized the coveted Cross of Coronado from the bad guys, turns it over to the sheriff for safekeeping; the sheriff, however, is in cahoots with the bad guys and gives it back to them—much to Indy's astonishment. Indy, here played by River Phoenix, a child of the sixties (his parents were hippies), learns the *echt* lesson of the sixties: don't trust adults, particularly those in authority.

George Lucas and Steven Spielberg, who between them conceived, produced, and directed *The Last Crusade,* were also children of the sixties; their movies, despite their slick, formulaic sheen, are surprisingly personal (it's no accident that Lucas's hero is named Luke) and so are permeated by countercultural values. *Star Wars,* for example, was a generation gap drama that sided with the kids. With its conflict between the weak rebels and the powerful Empire, it couldn't help evoking Vietnam and the attendant moral and political crises amid which Lucas and his generation came of age. Lucas has said that the Emperor was modeled on President Richard Nixon, which makes the Empire equivalent to the United States, Darth Vader to, say, Henry Kissinger, and the rebels to the Vietcong. Or, on an even more personal note, as Dale Pollock pointed out in *Skywalking,* his book on Lucas, the Empire is the monolithic studio system that thwarted him at every turn, while the Emperor and Vader stood in for appropriate studio executives.

With the appearance of Yoda in *The Empire Strikes Back,* the Vietnam analogy, which functioned as a subtext for the first film, became more intrusive. The gnomic Jedi master is wrinkled, old, and wise and lives in the jungle. When E.T., Gandhi, and Mr. Miyagi *(The Karate Kid)* made their movie debuts a few years later, the resemblance among them was striking, leaving little doubt who Yoda was: a closet Asian. After all, he was colored, small (underdeveloped), "ugly" (non-Western), and mysterious ("inscrutable"). If the Emperor was Nixon and Vader was Kissinger, Yoda had to be Mao or Ho Chi Minh, the Spirit of the Third World. (In a review of William Kotzwinkle's novelization of *E.T.,* social critic Ariel Dorfman described the pint-sized alien as "more like a small savage from the third world . . . than a Milky Way wizard. There is no [other] reason why . . . he should get drunk, why he never proceeds beyond pidgin English ["E.T. phone home"] such as . . . countless Indians have stuttered . . . .")

Lucas's idea of the Third World, however, was patterned on Northern California, where he lived, not Vietnam, where the war was fought; Yoda's cryptic Zen-speak recalls its dreamy, druggy, ecologically correct counterculture the same way Princess Leia's Guinevere hairdo and Pre-Raphaelite white gown suggests such quaint Northern California institutions as the Renaissance Faire, not to mention the ornate art nouveau concert posters of the sixties. It was these values Lucas was trying to pass on to the next generation of teen-agers, in the guise of Luke.

This Northern California ambience was most pronounced in the Moon of Endor sequence that concluded *Return of the Jedi.* With its dense forests of sequoias and its feisty, fuzzy-wuzzy Ewoks who defeat the Empire's technology with slingshots, crossbows, rocks, and homemade booby traps, Lucas gives us his most vivid picture of Vietcong guerrilla warfare, Marin County–style. The authorized novelization describes the Ewoks as "cadres" attacking in "human waves" and criticizes the Empire (the First World) for wrecking (aka defoliating) the greenery of Endor's moon, described as "dying from refuse disposal, trampling feet, chemical exhaust fumes." With the members of the Alliance and their teddy bear Ewoks gathered around a campfire at the end of *Return of the Jedi,* the Vietcong in the sky became Boy Scouts on the ground. The Empire is defeated by a children's crusade, an alliance of teen-agers and teddy bears—in other words, the sixties. Nature, in the sixties equated with communes in the woods, Native Americans, and untrammeled innocence, defeats culture and civilization, which were widely regarded as both corrupt and corrupting. *Return of the Jedi,* where these themes are most pronounced, represents the greening of *Star Wars.*

However, this Luddite, anti-technological strain was present in Lucas's films from the start. Apropos of his 1971 proto–*Star Wars, THX-1138,* Lucas once said, "I was fascinated by the . . . idea of rocket ships and lasers up against somebody with a stick. The little guys were winning and technology was losing—I liked that." Therefore, the trilogy pits the battered Millenium Falcon and the rebels' one-man fighters against massive Imperial Star Destroyers, Imperial Walkers, and the like, and, more important, the mysticism of the Force against the arid rationalism of the Empire, whose officers even sneer at Darth Vader's old-time "religion." When Luke is zeroing in on the vulnerable reactor core of the Death Star at the end of *Star Wars,* Obi Wan

Kenobi's ghostly voice advises him to turn off his guidance system, close his eyes, and rely on the Force, which he does. These
films prefer the heart to the head, feeling to thinking.

But it was, after all, 1976, not 1967, when *Star Wars* went into
production, and times had changed. Lucas was nothing if not a
creature of his era; if *Star Wars* was permeated by countercultural
values, it embraced regressive values as well, attitudes that
looked at once back to the old cold war of the fifties and ahead
to the new cold war of the eighties. It was during the fifties, of
course, that the Hollywood studios, along with their genres,
began to crumble under the successive blows of the consent
decree of 1948, television, the blacklist, and the increasing
power of stars and talent agencies. Nevertheless, the conventions
that governed Hollywood films survived well into the sixties.
The ideology that underlay these conventions can best be described as centrist, which is to say, the films situated themselves
within society and from that vantage point regarded the world.
They preferred culture to nature, consensus and inclusion to
polarization and exclusion, but quarreled among themselves over
the best way to achieve these goals. By far the greater number
of "corporate liberal" pictures (usually big-budget A-movies)
espoused nonauthoritarian, persuasive (often therapeutic) methods of social control, while a smaller number of "conservative"
films preferred force. At the extremes, a handful of right- and
left-wing films attacked society as the enemy, often in the name
of nature against culture, and resisted or actually fought social
control.

As the sixties progressed, however, the Vietnam War split the
consensus of the center into right against left. Fifties-style centrist
spectacles like *Cleopatra* bombed at the box office, while anti-
Establishment films like *Bonnie and Clyde,* whose politics would
have made them marginal in the fifties, broke attendance records
and redefined the mainstream. Suddenly it was okay to attack
hitherto cherished values. On the left, killers *(Bonnie and Clyde),*
bank robbers *(Dog Day Afternoon),* lunatics *(One Flew Over the
Cuckoo's Nest),* draft dodgers *(Alice's Restaurant),* and hustlers

(Midnight Cowboy) were regarded with sympathy, if not outright enthusiasm. Robbers and Indians were in; cops and cowboys were out. On the right, James Bond and Dirty Harry waged violent war not just on the scum who made the world a dangerous place for decent folk but on wimpy government bureaucrats who tied their hands with legal restraints. As cold-war liberals like Arthur Schlesinger, Jr., liked to put it, invoking William Butler Yeats, whom they oddly regarded as the poet laureate of consensus, the center had given way.

Since there existed no more than rudimentary alternative ideologies to support them, the newly respectable "extremist" films of the sixties—made by the so-called New Hollywood directors like Stanley Kubrick, Arthur Penn, Sam Peckinpah, Sidney Lumet, Robert Altman, and Woody Allen, some of whom had come up through television—most often made their points in a purely negative fashion, by picking apart mainstream genres that in any case had vanished when the consensus that supported them disintegrated. By the end of the fifties, sci-fi was no longer a viable genre, and it would be almost a decade before it momentarily reemerged in the form of *2001: A Space Odyssey.* War movies disappeared after the Korean Conflict, and when they finally surfaced in the guise of *Catch-22* and *M*A*S*H,* they were virtually unrecognizable. Westerns, traditionally the hardiest of Hollywood genres, were systematically dismantled by anti-Westerns like *Little Big Man, McCabe and Mrs. Miller, Buffalo Bill and the Indians,* and *The Missouri Breaks,* and even more conventional Westerns like *The Wild Bunch* and *Butch Cassidy and the Sundance Kid* were so pessimistic that the genre had no place to go. But this was a dangerous strategy in a narrative-based mass medium like movies, and when the counterculture itself began to wither away, and Carter won the presidency in 1976 on a platform that called for consensus and renewal, these "extremist" films gradually lost their audience, one that was fast growing younger and to whom the Vietnam War was rapidly becoming ancient history.

The next generation of directors, the "movie brats," were predominantly products of Los Angeles film schools. Lucas, Spiel-

berg, and their young colleagues set out to restore or gentrify the
genres they had learned to love in school. In the case of the *Star
Wars* trilogy, this meant combat, sword and sorcery, Western,
and, most important, sci-fi. Beyond specific genres, movie brat
directors sought to revive the idea of genre itself. But to breathe
new life into exhausted action formulas, it wasn't enough to put
out the occasional sci-fi flick or Western (they invariably
flopped); it was necessary to renovate the whole system that made
genre possible, to restore, as Lucas put it, the naïve sense of
romance, "awe," "wonder" that had accompanied the birth of
the silents. If in *2001,* at least in its first half, Kubrick had demystified space travel by picturing space ships tricked out in hum-
drum HoJo decor, a drab extension of the friendly skies of
United, Lucas not only wanted to remystify it, he wanted to
remystify film itself.

Lucas achieved this goal by harnessing the dazzling, high-tech
mega-effects pioneered by *2001* to the old action genres—really,
the kids' matinee serials of the thirties—with their simple, functional narratives. He skipped at least a generation, turning his
back on the anti-genre (and anti-war) films of the seventies, to old
World War II films, with their unambiguous attitude toward
combat. With what has often been called its "machine esthetic,"
Star Wars was both a product and a celebration of the technology
that had made the Vietnam War possible. Its spectacular depic-
tion of bloodless dogfighting in deep space sanitized and estheti-
cized combat, in a manner all too reminiscent of the air war over
North Vietnam.

The magic of the trilogy's effects lies precisely in their
verisimilitude, and their success depends largely on creating the
illusion that we are entering a futuristic world that actually exists.
Whereas for many of the anti-genre directors of the late sixties
and early seventies the screen was a mirror that reflected moving
images back on themselves, in the *Star Wars* films the screen was
a window on a world of spectacular "realism." According to
effects wizard Richard Edlund, speaking of the all-important
opening shot of the monumentally large and immaculately de-

tailed Imperial Star Destroyer drifting into the frame from above, "If somebody sat down in the theater and saw this monstrous thing come over the screen and keep coming and coming, and they were awed by that, then we had our audience just where we wanted 'em. But if they laughed, we were dead." According to Pollock, "Edlund shot the opening sequence five times until he was sure nobody would laugh." Despite Edlund's success in achieving what appears to be photographic verisimilitude, however, the effects are rarely naturalized. Because of the dynamic play of scale and speed, they never appear commonplace or overly familiar.

Star Wars looked back to the golden age of movies in other ways as well. It rolled back the sixties by employing actors with square-jawed, Waspy good looks like Mark Hamill and Harrison Ford who had been relegated to the unemployment lines in the Nixon era by "ethnics" like Dustin Hoffman, Al Pacino, and Elliott Gould. In employing a new generation of relatively unfamiliar nonstars like Hamill, Ford, and Carrie Fisher, Lucas succeeded in creating the perception that the films were newly minted, that he had started over, reinvented the movies.

At the same time, the *Star Wars* films embraced the simple values of heroism and old-fashioned individualism and revived a kind of Manichean, back-to-basics moral fundamentalism suggestive of the Reagan era yet to come. "I wanted to make a kid's film that would strengthen contemporary mythology and introduce a kind of basic morality," said Lucas. "Everybody's forgetting to tell the kids, 'Hey, this is right and this is wrong.'" It's no accident that Lucas referred to the Empire's foot soldiers as "storm troopers," invoking a time when it seemed easier to tell good from bad. *Raiders of the Lost Ark* and *Indiana Jones and the Last Crusade* carried this further, portraying the bad guys as literal Nazis. The immediate past of the Vietnam War was presumably too complicated to deal with directly.

The Indiana Jones films were always to the right of the *Star Wars* trilogy. They shamelessly revived and relegitimated the figure of the dashing colonialist adventurer who plunders and pillages antiquities from Third World countries for First World collectors. The end of the title sequence of *Raiders,* with a white man (Indy) being flown out of the jungle a hairsbreadth ahead of a bunch of spear-chucking natives, not only brings to mind the myriad of naïvely racist jungle movies of the thirties but also evokes the "fall" of Saigon; this light-hearted, veiled allusion to what, after all, was the most painful and humiliating episode in recent American history was the screen equivalent of Reagan's soon-to-be-notorious flippancy about life-and-death world issues.

One of the basics Lucas tried to restore was the primacy of narrative, or at least an eighties semblance of the classic narratives of the thirties and forties. In 1968 Kubrick messed with narrative in *2001,* and in the seventies other directors like Penn, Altman, and Dennis Hopper followed suit. Penn experimented with a variety of anti-narrative devices, while Altman employed elliptical, dreamlike, and associative strategies. Moreover, as Richard Maltby argues in his book *Harmless Entertainment,* by the seventies the aesthetics of television, with its open-ended, soap opera/ series–influenced anti-narrative orientation, which tended to privilege performances over storytelling, finally penetrated the movies, entirely transforming, say, a film like *Nashville* into a series of discrete tableaux whose order could be reshuffled at will without any apparent damage to the narrative. At the same time, and to the same end, the enormous clout of stars ("bankability"), which had helped to destroy the studio system in the fifties, delivered the coup de grace to what was left of narrative in the seventies. Movies became little more than occasions for star turns: Woody Allen's monologs broke free of the story to address the audience directly in *Annie Hall* and *Manhattan,* and Marlon Brando's scene-stealing, baroque, and extremely mannered performances similarly became ends in themselves, like his wonderful, weird bounty-hunter-in-drag number in *The Missouri Breaks,* which left then-lesser light Jack Nicholson the mundane job of pushing the plot forward. As Maltby puts it, "in the New Hollywood, a star's enactment of him- or herself . . . became sufficient justification for a movie, and performance . . . assumed the cohesive function previously fulfilled by narrative." Movies in the seventies were not so much acted as performed; they were presentational, not narrative.

Presentational cinema like Altman's found favor with critics but not audiences. (Hollywood suffered from a box office slump throughout the early seventies.) And even the critics lost patience with films like *The Missouri Breaks.* At a point where the anti-genre movies had lost both their popular and critical following, Lucas came along and imposed two-dimensional performances on his actors, trying to subordinate both acting and effects to story, lending the films a stripped-down, streamlined feel. Mark Hamill was not about to disrupt *Star Wars* by lisping, wearing a dress, and upstaging the robots. After a decade of cinematic mannerism, audiences appeared to be relieved that the dog once again seemed to be wagging the tail.

Not only did Lucas attempt to reestablish the primacy of narrative; the kind of narrative he used was linear, direct, and traditional, which is to say, it gives the impression that it is transparent—the stories appear to tell themselves. They are straightforwardly chronological, without complicated flashbacks that weaken the narrative thrust or make the plotting hard to follow. Devices with which seventies directors had drawn attention to their narrative strategies were forsworn or suppressed. The artifice that, say, Francis Ford Coppola later used in *One from the Heart* is repudiated; artifice, like the kind displayed in the Jabba the Hutt sequence in *Return of the Jedi,* is decadent, associated with the bad guys.

In borrowing, combining, and recombining elements from both right and left, then, the *Star Wars* trilogy breathed new life into the ideological consensus of the center on which their conventions depended, and succeeded in doing in the realm of culture what the Carter Restoration had, with only partial success, attempted in the realm of politics. It was crafted (intentionality aside) to appeal to members of the disaffected Vietnam generation and draw them back into the fold. It created a new consensus that included both proto-preppies (Luke et al.) and, as junior partners, an assortment of outsiders and loyal "minorities": Chewbacca, R2D2, and C-3PO, and, in *Return of the Jedi,* an astonishing array of weird-looking aliens, as well as Lando, an actual (nonmetaphoric) black man who becomes a general in the rebel army, in the same way that the actor who played him, Billy Dee Williams, became one of the few black entertainment figures to play a role in the Reagan campaign during the 1980 presidential elections.

BOYS IN SPACE

At the end of *Close Encounters of the Third Kind,* Spielberg's second blockbuster, the blessed and much anticipated event finally occurs: the alien ship gently touches down in a panoply of colored lights, accompanied by a crescendo of orchestral music, as a bunch of dumbstruck Earthlings watch in silent amazement. Since this film, itself a much anticipated marvel of techno-movie magic, is on one level as much about its own construction and reception as about its ostensible subject—visitors from other worlds—it's not hard to equate the space ship with *Close Encounters*–the-movie, and the enthralled mortals with the blissed-out audiences who greeted the movie with similar awe.

For Lucas and Spielberg, those spectators in *Close Encounters* were the model audience. Although the agenda of *Star Wars* was nothing if not ambitious—to refurbish consensus for the seventies and after—the trilogy had other, bigger fish to fry, and its influence was vastly more profound. It attempted nothing less than to reconstitute the audience as children. Lucas said he wanted to make a film for "the kids in all of us." As Alan Ladd, Jr., put it, when he was head of Twentieth Century-Fox (which produced *Star Wars*), Lucas "showed people it was alright to become totally involved in a movie again; to yell and scream and applaud and really roll with it."

To infantilize the audience of the sixties and empower the audience of the seventies, to reconstitute the spectator as child,

Lucas and Spielberg had to obliterate years of sophisticated, adult moviegoing habits. *Star Wars* came on the heels of nearly a decade of wise-ass, cynical, self-conscious moviemaking. And it wasn't only Hollywood that thumbed its nose at mom and apple pie; after Vietnam, Watergate, and attendant traumas, parody and irony were running rampant throughout popular culture, whether in reflexive, hip TV shows like *Saturday Night Live* and *Mary Hartman, Mary Hartman* (even the title was self-referential) or "adult" comics, both overground (*Spiderman* and Co.) and underground (*Mr. Natural* et al.), or punk music (the Ramones). But it was the New Hollywood, fueled by the influence of innovative European directors like Jean-Luc Godard and driven by a gang of Young (and not-so-young) Turks working under the aegis of the so-called "baby moguls" eager to tap countercultural dollars (and score a few points for the "revolution" at the same time), that was most deliriously self-reflexive.

The directors whom Lucas and Spielberg were rebelling against characteristically distanced their movies from their audiences. Penn was fond of using spectator surrogates within his fictions, observers like the anthropologist in *Little Big Man* whose study frames the story, inevitably reminding audiences that they, too, are watching a "story." But there are few spectator figures in the *Star Wars* trilogy; in fact, watching (and its ethical correlative, disengagement) is attacked as immoral. When Han Solo refuses to assist the rebels in the crucial battle that concludes *Star Wars,* when he becomes a spectator rather than a participant, he's being selfish and is punished for it. Darth Vader, the Emperor, and the Empire's generals spend so much time watching the action on video screens that they're defeated by the rebels, the doers who act rather than look.

Likewise, in the Indiana Jones films there are precious few spectators, and those who do look quickly become participants, like the Cairo natives in *Raiders* who initially provide the passive backdrop for the chases in the bazaar but eventually intervene, saving Indy from the Nazis by surrounding and shielding him. Similarly, in the nightclub scene that opens *Temple of Doom* the distinction between spectators and performers breaks down in pandemonium, and Indy and Willie escape, one performer and one spectator indissolubly linked, their roles reversed, as performer Willie becomes spectator in Indy's world and spectator Indy becomes performer. And, as a spectator, Willie loses the inviolability her performance confers upon her, becoming increasingly at risk.

It's telling that in the climactic scene of *Raiders* the movie camera plays a cameo role, the first and only time it does so in the six movies, explicitly drawing a connection between making movies, possessing whatever it is Indy's looking for (in this case the Ark), unlimited destructive power, and guilty seeing, which must be punished. When the Ark does its thing, the camera is incinerated, the Nazi spectators have their eyes burned out, while Indy and Marion survive only by averting their gazes. Moreover, the unusual presence of the camera is a surprising bit of self-consciousness that can't help but allude to the cinema of self-consciousness that Lucas and Spielberg rejected.

Controlling, manipulative director figures in the *Star Wars*/Indiana Jones films are invariably bad. In *Star Wars* Vader is the director, choreographing complicated movements in space from his screen in the control room of the Imperial Star Destroyer. In *Raiders* the director is Belloq, the Cecil B. De Mille who orchestrates the unveiling of the Ark and is destroyed, while Indy, a potential competing director, survives by dint of being immobilized, prevented from directing. In *The Last Crusade* the millionaire Donovan is the producer, who coerces a reluctant Indy into "directing," that is, conducting the search for Henry Jones and the Holy Grail. Dr. Else Schneider, not at all a reluctant but an aspiring, wannabee director, is the villain. Lucas and Spielberg were, of course, the real directors, and therefore the message of their movies disguises and contradicts the realities of how they were made and consumed. The demonization of metaphorical director figures within the movies creates the illusion that the movies are directed by no one. The movies are transparent.

This pattern of denial, or deniability, as it was called on the political level, operated in other ways as well. As we have seen, the *Star Wars* trilogy contained a pro-nature message, while at the same time it was both a testimony to and a triumph of technology. In *Raiders* the act of watching is rendered dangerous as the spectators within the movie who have the misfortune of seeing the Ark in action are killed, while (so that) the real spectators (the audience) can indulge in the pleasure of watching. Whereas *The Last Crusade* begins by offering up an origins sequence to reveal the roots of Indiana Jones–the-character, in reality Indiana Jones–the-movies concealed their origins. Lucas and Spielberg succeeded in contradicting the message by the medium, and, in so doing, they did in fact manage to remystify movies.

This is not to say that Lucas's and Spielberg's movies entirely rejected self-consciousness. The one vice that movie brat directors never could quite resist was making allusions to their favorite TV shows or classics from film school. Lucas bowed in the direction of *The Searchers* and glanced at *Dr. Strangelove* (Luke's mechanical arm). The kind of self-consciousness displayed by Lucas and Spielberg was most often self-congratulatory and narcissistic. As in *Close Encounters,* or the beginnings of *Raiders* and *Temple of Doom,* where the mountainous Paramount logo dissolves into reel mountains, it celebrated itself, whereas the self-consciousness of the seventies was self-critical and Brechtian. It deconstructed and demystified itself.

Lucas's new aesthetic of awe did succeed in infantilizing the audience, not only by overwhelming it with sound and spectacle, not only by attacking spectatorship within the films, but also, on the narrative level, by punishing cynicism, eliminating or suppressing elements that contributed to irony and critical self-consciousness. Lucas had always been quite clear on this score. He explicitly said he wished to exclude the traces of camp that had crept into those genre exercises that did persist into the sixties and seventies, most notably the James Bond films. "Lucas insisted that his cast never play a scene for camp humor, even if his script seemed to call for it," wrote Pollock. Said Lucas, "It wasn't camp, it was not making fun of itself. I wanted it to be real."

The most important part of this program involved attacking and discrediting adults while valorizing children and childlike qualities, particularly "innocence." By the post-Altamont mid-seventies, as the flower-power revolution of the sixties had started to fade, a jaundiced view of childhood had become *de rigueur* among many of the older genre-bashing directors. Sam Peckinpah led the way in the late sixties with *The Wild Bunch,* a film that turned the traditional John Ford Westerns upside down. In Ford's *The Searchers* (1956), primitive, seemingly amoral Indians massacre a family of settlers, who are identified with the values of civilization, and kidnap a girl (Natalie Wood). John Wayne, hell-bent on revenge, sets out to destroy the Indians. Years later, when he finally catches up with them, he tries to kill the girl, in the belief that she has been terminally corrupted by her Indian upbringing: nurture over nature. The film, however, partially repudiates the Wayne character, and sides with those who want to reintegrate the girl into the settler community, in the conviction that she is salvageable: nature over nurture. By the time *The Wild Bunch* was released, thirteen years later, the Indians had become an outlaw gang of senior citizens, now victims rather than killers, and (white) civilization had become totally corrupt, no more so than in its children, little lords of the flies, who open the film by tormenting scorpions. But these same children were Lucas's primary audience, and when he alludes to *The Searchers* early on in *Star Wars* (the massacre of the family farm on Tatooine), he's telling us that it's Ford's vision he's endorsing, not Peckinpah's.

If revisionist directors like Peckinpah, Penn, and Altman treated the legends Ford cherished as lies, Lucas wanted to reestablish their authority. And he brought children, often peripheral observers in the films of the seventies, to center stage. For Lucas, Spielberg, and the other movie brats, barely more than kids themselves, children were essentially good, adults generally bad. Adults behaved poorly in the sixties; they sent children off to die in war. In the late seventies the children would have their revenge. Indeed, adults in the Lucas and Spielberg films are invariably either punished, like the ones in *E.T.* who, as Dorfman points out, are the real aliens, or redeemed through infantilization, like the hero of *Close Encounters,* who sheds his family (along with his adult responsibilities) to end up, in essence, playing in the sandbox, building towers out of mud and mashed potatoes.

In the *Star Wars* trilogy most of the adults are consigned to the Empire, certifiable heavies for whom death by blaster is too kind a fate. Like Darth Vader, Lucas's Ur-adult, grown-ups in these films are shrouded in darkness, in mystery; they're opaque and filled with secrets. (The fact that Lucas used James Earl Jones's voice for Vader and had Billy Dee Williams play the duplicitous Lando in *The Empire Strikes Back* makes a good deal of thematic, if not racial, sense.) Luke even accuses kindly old Obi Wan Kenobi of lying to him on the subject of his father's true identity, and Obi Wan resorts to some lame adult double-talk in self-justification. The Empire typically exercises elaborate strategems to trap the rebels, whereas the rebels are open and straightforward. When they do resort to trickery (spies misinform them that the Death Star II is not yet operational), they fail. When Luke makes use of disguises, as he does in the Jabba the Hutt sequence, he's always discovered. Adults are complicated and self-divided; for them, appearance often belies reality. Whereas Luke is open and transparent (we can see from his face that he's pure of soul), Vader is hooded, masked, and closed. When Luke finally removes Vader's helmet, his head looks like a white slug that's been living under a rock, a pale embroyo, a proto-fetus. His good side, which Luke claims he senses, the kernel inside the shell, the reality behind the appearance, is an infant.

It's no accident that Vader's "real" self, his innocent self, is imagined as an unformed adult. In these films not all adults are bad; some, like Lando (and Natalie Wood in *The Searchers*), can be redeemed by nurturing their natures, that is to say, their childlike characteristics. The best example of this process is Luke himself, the films' teen-age identification figure. It is striking that, although the *Star Wars* trilogy foregrounds the story of Luke's maturation and education in the mysterious ways of the Force (in other words, his development into an adult), the real significance of the films is the opposite: the way this process is thwarted, aborted, and denied. Or, to put it another way, to grow up in these films is to return to childhood.

The abyss that divides children from adults is—in Lucas's eyes—sex. Therefore, sex, like adulthood, is bad news. As Pollock points out, in Lucas's earlier *American Graffiti* "adolescence was the Force—hard to understand, even harder to control. 'This is a dangerous stage for you, Luke,' Ben [Kenobi] warns another teenager. 'You are now susceptible to the temptations of the dark side [of the Force].' " To resist the dark side of the Force, Luke has to spiritualize himself by sublimating (in war) and later suppressing his erotic and aggressive impulses (which tend to be equated). The measure of Luke's maturity, his light-sword, is, as Dan Rubey suggests, an all-too-obvious symbol of power and sexual potency: "You carry it in your pocket until you need it, then press a button and it's three feet long and glows in the dark." At the end of *Star Wars,* Luke is confidently piloting his fighter, streaking through a correspondingly vaginal canal or trench so that he can launch his "missile" into the "womb" of the female Death Star.

But during *The Empire Strikes Back,* Darth Vader lops off Luke's arm, none too subtly "castrating" him; by the time Luke gets to *Return of the Jedi,* he gives up his light-sword and leaves the dogfighting to others while he attends more directly to his Oedipal needs—his struggle with his father. He's well on his way to becoming a monk (he's wearing sackcloth in his climactic confrontation with his dad and the Emperor), a passive Moonie, a First World Yoda. Although resolving this generational conflict is supposed to be the route to adulthood, it doesn't work out that way for Luke. He has merely learned to live with and internalize castration; when he renounces his light-sword, he voluntarily accepts what was earlier imposed by force from without. In the upside-down developmental framework of the trilogy, to submit to the dark side of the Force is to become an adult; Luke must resist, choosing endless childhood over childhood's end.

It follows from this imperative that, rather than becoming man enough to win Princess Leia from his rival Solo, Luke discovers that Leia is his sister. In the psychosexual universe of *Star Wars* she must turn out to be his sister, because Luke must be protected from even a hint of adult sexuality. In order to give this prohibition dramatic weight, sex must be, and is, portrayed as dangerous.

The Jabba the Hutt sequence that leads off *Return of the Jedi* represents a striking intrusion of the sixties adult *Heavy Metal* magazine brand of sci-fi; and Leia, suddenly sexualized in her revealing Barbarella outfit, must be rescued not only from Jabba but from her own sexuality. (During the production Lucas strove to desexualize Carrie Fisher by binding her breasts with gaffer's tape. "No breasts bounce in space. There's no jiggling in the Empire," said Fisher.) The Jabba episode culminates in an explicit *vagina dentata* fantasy, as Luke and his pals have to walk a phallic gangplank into the pullulating maw—festooned with long, curved teeth—of the giant Sarlacc in its "nesting place." A more nightmarishly explicit image of threatening female sexuality would be hard to imagine.

When Luke renounces his light-sword, he not only relinquishes his sexuality, he gives up power as well. In the fifties power was a no-no; cold-war ideologues associated it with Stalinism. Power had no place in a democracy; people did what they were supposed to do not because they had to but because they wanted to. In the sixties, when the culture shifted to the left, the spectacle of the world's strongest nation waging (near) total war against a small peasant society confirmed the bad rep force already had; it was no longer Stalinists who abused power but democratically elected American leaders, adults who burned Vietnamese with napalm abroad and crushed flowers with guns at home. In order to grow up into childhood, Luke must relinquish power. At the same time, however, despite this unsavory legacy, in the post-Vietnam period force had to be relegitimated. After all, when *Star Wars* was released, the Ayatollah was just about to precipitate a crisis that would go far toward the miraculous transformation of America from a bully to a victim, erasing what testy hawks, impatient for the return of the cold-war martial spirit, dismissively referred to as "the Vietnam Syndrome." (There is even a hostage crisis in *Return of the Jedi* where Jabba holds Leia and Luke's robot pals.) So there is never any doubt that force is necessary to defeat the Empire; it is only that adults (Lando et al.) and extra- or subhuman aliens (the bug-eyed "monster" who commands the rebel fleet) must do the dirty work for Luke while he attends to more consequential matters. Moreover, Luke's solution is to forswear force in favor of the Force, i.e., relinquish personal power in favor of an impersonal power for which he bears no direct responsibility.

The last adult candidate for infantilization, and therefore redemption, is Han Solo. He is older than Luke (he calls Luke "Kid"), more sophisticated, cynical, self-interested. He's a right-wing Clint Eastwood–type individualist who rejects collective values, the claims of community—or, contrarily, a left-wing (the two were often interchangeable) Jack Nicholson do-your-own-thing free spirit (*One Flew Over the Cuckoo's Nest* won an Oscar for Best Picture the year before *Star Wars* was released). He's also the kind of person who could be expected to sneer at *Star Wars*. In other words, he's the adult viewer surrogate inside the picture. (Again, on a personal level, he is Luke/Lucas's "older brother" and mentor, Francis Ford Coppola, by whom Lucas apparently felt betrayed when Coppola took *Apocalypse Now,* which Lucas had helped to develop and hoped to direct. Like Han Solo, Coppola often called Lucas "Kid.") As such, Solo is too powerful, his pursuit of Leia too threatening. He has to be immobilized by carbon freezing in *The Empire Strikes Back* before he can become a full-fledged member of the Alliance, which is to say, his development, growth, process of maturation have to be dramatically and demonstrably arrested.

During the course of the three films the relative positions of Solo and Luke are reversed. In the beginning Solo is the dramatic focus of the story; he's the more powerful of the two, as indicated by the fact that he saves Luke's life. By the end Solo has almost disappeared from the plot, which now focuses almost exclusively on Luke. Moreover, Luke saves Solo's life; the boy becomes more powerful than the man. Even though Solo is eventually rescued from carbonization, he's learned his lesson. He has been turned into a wimp and is even obliged to apologize to Leia for a fit of jealousy.

BOYS WILL BE BOYS

In the Indiana Jones films Indy is more like the older Han Solo than he is a Luke. (There is no Luke figure in these films, but to compensate, *Temple of Doom* adds a kid, Short Round, to beef up preteen identification.) Like Solo (and Luke), he has to be prevented from growing up—instead of evolving into an adult, he has to devolve into a child. Early in *Raiders* Indy accuses Marion (Karen Allen) of having come between him and her father, his mentor, inverting the usual Oedipal triangle in which the father comes between the son or daughter and the opposite sex. From Indy's point of view, in other words, the ideal relationship is one that a girl can only disrupt—presexual male bonding between father and son. Nevertheless, Marion is the perfect partner for Indy. She is a tough-as-nails, male-identified woman; that is, a presexual tomboy. In her first scene she wears pants, runs a bar, and beats a hulking Nepalese peasant in a drinking contest.

But as the plot careens along, Marion is divested of her "masculinity" by the lechery of the villainous French archaeologist Belloq. Whereas Indy treats Marion like an irritating kid sister, Belloq treats her like a woman. In fact, so great is Indy's aversion to an adult romantic relationship with Marion that he virtually gives her to Belloq by refusing to rescue her when he has the opportunity. Belloq, who knows a good thing when he sees one, dresses her in a revealing gown and tries to get her drunk. But her burgeoning sexuality must immediately collide with the prohibition against adulthood that goes with the territory of these films; so no sooner does she flash a calf than she must be terrorized with a frightening fantasy of predatory masculine sexuality, the male analogue of the *vagina dentata* scene in *Return of the Jedi*. Marion, still dressed in Belloq's white satin dress (now an index of her vulnerability rather than of her sexual power), dangles over a mass of writhing snakes, her panties blinking whitely in the dim light as her legs scissor back and forth. Spielberg presents Marion and the audience with a powerful equation of sex (again, read adulthood) and mortality in the striking images of snakes slithering first through the open toe of her shoe and then the eye sockets of a skull. The process of sexual awakening, in other words, has become a slippery slope leading to violation and death. Even when Indy and Marion merely play at parenting, it ends badly. Once in Cairo, they "adopt" a monkey and lightly allude to it as their baby. As it turns out, their monkey is a bad baby, a spy for the Nazis. Indy and Marion can't have children, of course, because they are children.

Belloq is the adult in *Raiders*. He's worldly, corrupt, and cynical—in short, a mercenary. The search for the Ark is nothing if not a Faustian quest for knowledge and power, and it is essentially Belloq's quest. Indy is innocent of power, as he is innocent of sexuality. It's the chase itself that engages him; the outcome is unimportant. He's a process kind of guy, and he's always safest while he's looking. He can even excavate for the Ark right under the noses of the Germans, who don't, or can't, see him—until he finds what he's looking for and loses his innocence, at which point he's inevitably plunged into jeopardy: Belloq is there to seize whatever it is he's found. Belloq is always able to do this, of course, because while Indy is innocent, Belloq is not. He's allied to the Nazis and has no qualms about exercising power.

Indy himself is an adventurer, a guy who can punch out the heavies and read glyphs, too, the intellectual as man (rather, boy) of action, Richard Perle (or Pipes) as Andy Hardy. Belloq keeps insisting that he and Indy are alike, and he's partly right. In their climactic confrontation, where Indy demands Marion, the two men, ostensibly mortal enemies, call each other by their first names and speak a language of intimacy that only the two of them can understand. Belloq is the adult Indy and therefore makes the wrong choice (the Ark over Marion, power over love) and has to die because, once again, power is dangerous. (On the other hand, as in the *Star Wars* trilogy, power is hardly renounced; the good guys merely want it for themselves.)

In *Temple of Doom* Willie (Kate Capshaw) starts out in a dress, a femme woman plucked out of a nightclub and plunged into the jungle, thereby punished for her explicit adult sexuality. She's also culture, thrust unceremoniously into nature. She can't ride an elephant, can't stand the disgustingly "primitive" food, and so on. Indy treats her like a nuisance (à la Marion), but she teases him for not acknowledging that she is a woman and that he's attracted to her. It's the old battle of the sexes, or the sexless, in this case, and Willie has an uphill struggle. Sexual encounters between the two are characteristically interrupted and delayed, and, moreover, suffused with an aura of danger. One of their few sexually tense scenes, where Indy and Willie each waits for the other to make the first move, is interrupted by an attack on Indy, which then segues into another *vagina dentata* sequence in the underground Spike Chamber. In the film's final scene Short Round rains on Indy's and Willy's parade by spraying them both with water (from a phallic elephant's trunk, yet) as they embrace, making the audience view the traditional romantic clinch from the point of view of a bored, playfully hostile, and suggestively jealous child. Worse, when Indy falls under the Thuggee spell, he nearly lets Willie die, and it's hard to resist the notion that this is his true desire, his unconscious wish. He'd rather see her dead than make love to her.

The dominant metaphor of *Temple of Doom* is the enslavement of children. In *The Disappearance of Childhood* sociologist Neil Postman argues that the idea of children as a distinct species, a breed apart, different in kind from adults, is a product of industrialization and the rise of schooling, of which laws prohibiting child labor were a by-product. The enslavement of children, which in *Temple of Doom* consists of forcing them to work at the kind of adult hard labor prohibited by these laws, is, in effect, an attack on the idea of childhood. Thus, when Indy frees them, he metaphorically rescues not just children but childhood. From another perspective, the child-slaves are the audience, made miserable by the serious adult films of the seventies, awaiting a director who will restore the innocence, joy, and laughter of old-fashioned, uncomplicated moviegoing.

The Last Crusade is said to be the final installment of the series, so it is fitting that in it Indy has at last grown up. Indy has been supplied with an instant childhood (in the "origins" sequence that leads off the movie) as well as a father with whom he ostensibly comes to terms, the implication being that he is now an adult. But, as in the Star Wars films, growing up in the worlds of Lucas and Spielberg is problematical at best.

The origins sequence is liberally studded with not-so-veiled allusions to the dangers of growing up. It opens like a Western in Monument Valley, Spielberg's version of Lucas's homage to John Ford. But it quickly becomes clear that what we think are the cavalry are Boy Scouts. After a shot of a phallic rock formation that looks like Devil's Tower in Close Encounters (another example of the series's self-referential narcissism), the film suddenly cuts to a "primal scene" of sorts, redolent of forbidden voyeurism of taboo activities. It's reminiscent, even in its camera angles, of the scene in the underground cave in Temple of Doom, where Indy, hidden behind some rocks, looks down on the illicit activities of the Thuggees. Here little Indy, also in a cave, watches an older version of himself—wearing what will become, when he "grows up," his characteristic leather jacket and fedora—discover the precious Cross of Coronado. Later, in an action sequence where Indy lies flat on his back on top of a circus car full of rhinos, one of the animals pokes its horn through the roof; it comes right up between his legs. Having dropped in on a lion in another car, he fights phallus with phallus, grabbing what will become his signature bullwhip off a wall to defend himself. With this riot of battling phallic images, you don't have to be Freud or Lacan (or Joseph Campbell) to tell what's going on. In one scene he's got the Cross of Coronado stuffed into his belt. When a bad guy grabs for it, a snake (brother to the one that had

crawled from his pants a moment earlier) slithers out of his
sleeve. The suggestive proximity of Cross, snake, and private part
makes explicit what the two previous films had only implied: the
power of the coveted object of the quest, be it Ark, Ankara Stone,
Cross of Coronado, or Holy Grail, is the power of the phallus,
or, better yet, dad's phallus.

Enter dad, the new element in *The Last Crusade* formula. Although Indy's dad, Henry Jones, is more appealing by far than
Darth Vader, he has been, like Vader, a bad dad, significantly
"missing" throughout much of the picture, in the same way that
Vader is "missing": Luke doesn't even know for sure he is his dad
until the third installment of the trilogy. Here Indy and his dad
haven't spoken in twenty years.

In *The Last Crusade* both father and son compete, after a fashion, for the same woman: Dr. Else Schneider. The state of grace
(innocence) that protected Indy in the first two films is compromised. After two installments of *coitus interruptus,* Indy actually
has sex with the female lead, played by Allison Doody. As we
might suspect, both he and she have to be taught a lesson. Unlike
Marion in *Raiders* and Willie in *Temple of Doom,* Else has a strong
sexual presence and the moral ambiguity to go with it. In a script
move of striking economy, she embodies the marriage of the
Belloq and the Marion characters of *Raiders* (what would have
happened if Belloq had succeeded in seducing Marion?), and in
her the themes of power and sexuality converge. Like Belloq, she
is obsessed by the quest for power; also like him, she has no
scruples and will do anything to get her hands on the Grail,
including allying herself with the Nazis. And, like Marion, she
is, of course, a woman. But, unlike Marion (and Willie), as an
archaeologist and adventurer herself, she is Indy's equal, more
grounds for her eventual demise. Suggestively, she comes to
life—animated and decisive—only when she reveals her true
Nazi colors. In the same way that going over to the dark side was
to become an adult in the *Star Wars* films, so here (for Else,
anyway) becoming a Nazi is to become an adult—or vice versa.
After she slips from Indy's grasp and falls to her death, the same

scene (in, for Spielberg, an unusual exercise in didacticism) is repeated, this time with dad in Indy's role and Indy in Else's role. Else's death has taught Indy a lesson; unlike her, he chucks the Grail and grabs dad's hand with both his own, enabling dad to lift him to safety. In other words, he turns his back on the quest for power—but not, characteristically, before he's had a taste of it (the holy water has mended dad's wounds).

When Else, unmasked as the proto-Nazi, unreconstructed ends-justifies-the-means-er that she is, falls to her death, the pre-lapsarian, presexual male bonding between Jones *père* and *fils* is restored. She is sacrificed to the sacred bond between father and son so that the two can live happily ever after. Giving up Else, Indy gives up the sexual competition with dad (much as Luke gives up competing with Solo for Leia) and renounces the quest for dad's phallus.

Has Indy finally grown up or not? He has saved his father's life, has gotten his dad to call him by his real name, "Indiana," instead of "Junior," as dad was prone to do. But the lesson dad teaches him—prefer process to product, leave the Grails to the Elses of the world, the Nazis—is not unlike the lesson Luke learns in the *Star Wars* trilogy when he renounces his light-sword: give up adult aspirations and return to childhood. It's as if once Indy made his point, made dad acknowledge his adulthood, call him by his real name, he is content to revert to the comfortable role of son. Like Luke, he has internalized castration. After all, Indy's last words in the movie are "Yes, sir!"

BACK TO THE FUTURE

The *Star Wars* and Indiana Jones trilogies, not to mention *E.T.* and *Close Encounters,* raked in an unprecedented amount of money. Most of these movies rank among the all-time top ten grossers. With their toy spinoffs ($2.6 billion to date for the *Star Wars* trilogy alone), their endless afterlife on video, and their enormous influence on the subsequent video game craze, they succeeded way beyond their producers' wildest dreams. They not only enshrined their aesthetic of awe, they changed the way Hollywood did business and, therefore, how it made movies. The blockbuster syndrome probably started with *The Godfather* in 1972 and got an added boost from *Jaws* in 1975 but really took off with *Star Wars.* Once it became clear that certain kinds of films could reap immeasurably greater returns on investment than had ever been seen before, studios naturally wanted to turn the trick again, and again, and again: enter the Roman-numeral movie, product of the obsession with surefire hits. Blockbusters were expensive to make, and the more they cost, the safer and blander they became, while the smaller, riskier, innovative projects fell by the wayside.

Nevertheless, despite the megaprofits of the Lucas and Spielberg movies, and despite the wide currency of their world view, in some sense the two wunderkinder fell victim to history and to the contradictions within their own fictions. When Reagan's Strategic Defense Initiative (SDI) was introduced in the early eighties, its critics immediately dubbed it "Star Wars," meaning that it was no more than a silly screen fantasy. Ronald Reagan, blessed with a considerably keener appreciation of popular culture than his Democratic opponents, immediately understood that, given the infantilization of the electorate, this was a plus rather than a minus, and embraced the name. ("The Force is with us," he quipped.) Meanwhile, Lucas, whose consciously held politics, politics with a capital P, were still rooted in the sixties, quixotically sued to prevent the name of his movie from being used for the weapons system of choice of the newly revived cold war. He lost, of course, because the fit was perfect. There is an irony here of mammoth proportions: the culture of military/media/industrial complex that made SDI possible was the culture Lucas (along with Spielberg) had done much to create, and now it had turned around and bitten, so to speak, the hand that fed it. Moreover, Lucas had forgotten the lesson that inspired *Star Wars* and that little Indy learns so dramatically at the beginning of *The Last Crusade:* don't trust anyone over thirty.

Why was Lucas so surprised? Twelve years elapsed between

Star Wars and the release of *The Last Crusade* in 1989, an eternity
in the foreshortened hyperspace of American cultural history,
and by the time Indy rode off into the sunset, ostensibly for the
last time, a lot had changed. The propaganda of youth that had
fueled the sixties fizzled in the eighties. The high hopes of the
sixties had been left in the dust of the Me Decade, and youth had
become identified in the media with mindless self-indulgence.
Pot had turned into coke, and then crack. The idea of childhood
had changed radically from the Age of Aquarius to the Age of
Reagan. One vehicle for this change, however unwitting, were
Lucas's and Spielberg's films. By attacking irony, critical thinking,
self-consciousness, by pitting heart against head, they did their
share in helping to reduce an entire culture to childishness, and
in so doing helped prepare the ground for the growth of the
right. The kids prevailed, but the ideals they stood for had been
drained of content.

The seeds of the rightward drift were planted years earlier
with Yoda and Obi Wan Kenobi. They were the primary teachers
or socializers of young Luke, because the generation gap of the
sixties had stripped parents of the authority they needed to properly raise their kids. *Star Wars* alluded to the loss of adult authority by eliminating the older generation altogether. Luke's father
is apparently dead, his mother never mentioned, and his aunt and
uncle killed off. There simply is no Mr. and Mrs. Luke, Sr., to
teach young Luke how to brush his teeth and drive his land
speeder—there is only kindly old Obi Wan, Luke's spiritual, if
not actual, grandfather. (In the same way, the movie brats of the
eighties looked to the movies of the thirties and forties for inspiration, not to those of the sixties and seventies.) The trilogy
creates an alliance of son and grandfather against the generation
of fathers. Even at the beginning this alliance was deeply conservative. Despite the fact that Luke & Co. are referred to as "rebels,"
in essence they play a healing, restorative role, returning the
galaxy to an earlier time, before the clique of Emperor/Nixon,
Vader/Kissinger adults worked mischief in the galaxy by overthrowing the Republic. This earlier time was the pre-Nixon,

pre-Watergate, pre-sixties golden age that Carter had pledged to restore, the period that Lucas had memorialized so well in *American Graffiti* in 1973.

As the ideological abyss between children and adults disappeared, there was no reason why young and old should any longer stand on opposite sides of the galaxy. If *The Last Crusade* begins with the don't-trust-adults lesson of the sixties, it ends with a lesson of the seventies and eighties: generational reconciliation. There is no father figure at all in the first two Indiana Jones films; the father is simply irrelevant. In the origins sequence of *The Last Crusade* little Indy rushes into his father's office, clutching the Cross of Coronado to his breast. Instead of springing to his rescue, myopic Henry Jones, oblivious to the drama that has consumed his son, makes him count to ten in Greek. Dad is out of touch and, like his whole generation, has abdicated his responsibilities. Indy has to force his father to be a father.

The Last Crusade is about the rehabilitation of the over-thirty adults the sixties had written off. In it the renegade adults of the Nixon era became the avuncular, benevolent authority figures of the Reagan-Bush era. Reagan, in turn, wrapping himself in the mantle of FDR, tried to fulfill the promise of the Carter Restoration by visibly incarnating in himself the old verities from which the nation had wandered. The circle had closed; it was, indeed, back to the future.

As the politics of the movies changed, so did their deployment of basic, ideologically constructed categories. Although the *Star Wars* films endorse nature over culture, there is a distinct undertow pulling them in the opposite direction. Way back in the beginning, say, in *Star Wars* and *The Empire Strikes Back,* adults were portrayed as unemotional machines like the Imperial Guards, and Luke & Co., more than anything else, feared becoming robots like them. With his mechanical arm, Luke risked exactly this transformation into an automaton—the hard-edged Empire techies led by his wheezing, machinelike, respirator-assisted bad dad. However, in *Return of the Jedi,* released well into Reagan's first term and amid his campaign against sex in movies and softness in politics, the threat suddenly came from the opposite direction: formless organic matter, dissolution; burning and melting, rather than freezing; Jabba rather than Vader. (The turning point in this battle between mechanical culture and organic nature came when Luke's fighter sank into the ooze of Yoda's swamp midway into *The Empire Strikes Back.*)

This change paralleled a shift in attitude toward primitive and modern evident in the two trilogies. In the *Star Wars* films Third World figures like Yoda were gurus; in the Indiana Jones films the cultural backsliding of the Reagan years allowed them to revert to the traditional role of loyal sidekick (Short Round), pathetic victims (the Indian villagers), or villains (the Thuggees). In the *Star Wars* films it is advanced civilizations like the Empire that have access to dangerous, unlimited power. In the Indiana Jones films it is ancient cultures, primitive Judaism and Christianity and the Thuggees, that have access to such power. If the *Star Wars* films come down on the side of nature, the Indiana Jones films come down on the side of culture: high tech is better than low tech. The old tombs are invariably booby-trapped with ingenious primitive devices (recalling the guerrilla warfare techniques of the Ewok-Vietcong). The films also present a generous sampler of nature's little horrors—poisonous snakes, spiders, scorpions, and so on, and Indy-the-innocent-colonial-plunderer invariably leaves the tombs in ruins as he escapes by a hair.

The idea of the primitive in the Indiana Jones films, associated as it is with dangerous, out-of-control power, also stands in for the unconscious, the id, and in the same way that sexuality has to be repressed, so does the unconscious, which, by extension, happens to be the Third World. Like the unconscious, the primitive has its own language; to the extent that Indy deciphers this language, reads maps, solves puzzles, and susses out cryptic symbols, he functions as an adult. Literacy is a product of culture, not nature. Schooling initiates children into the mysteries of adulthood, primarily by teaching them how to read. But in reading the language of primitivism, not only is Indy acting like an adult, he's acting like a particular kind of adult: a psychoanalyst plumbing the depths of the (nonwhite) unconscious. (He's Franz Fanon for the eighties.) In *Star Wars* adult secrets and mysteries are linked with villainy, while youthful transparency is equated with goodness; likewise, in the Indiana Jones films the search for the unconscious is, however seductive, ultimately dangerous. The unconscious itself has to be repudiated. It is better off left untouched and untapped, and the Third World forgotten.

We have seen that Indy is safest when searching for the Grails of the world and most at risk when he finds them. The pattern of innocent quest versus guilty possession parallels the pattern of innocent flirtation versus guilty consummation on the sexual level, which, in turn, parallels the pattern of innocent childhood versus corrupt adulthood on the developmental level. This structure provides an ironic commentary on the movie brats' own achievements. It casts a retrospective glow of nostalgia over the years of struggle and a cold, self-critical light on the success that followed. Success has its rewards, but it exacts a price, tempts fate, and courts the kind of apocalyptic retribution pictured at the end of *Raiders*.

On an emotional level the Lucas and Spielberg films are most deeply engaged over Oedipal issues, so it's no surprise that both trilogies boil down to explicit struggles between fathers and sons. For as much as Lucas and Spielberg tried to indulge their Peter Pan complex and deny adulthood, with its attendant anxieties of power and sexuality, they deeply longed for it as well and struggled hard to achieve it. And when they did achieve it, when their extravagant commercial success thrust them to the pinnacle of power in a studio system they half despised (Lucas installed himself in a bucolic fastness in Marin County, far from Hollywood, while Spielberg contented himself with informal power brokering behind the scenes), they turned around and denied it all over again in movie after movie because they were deeply uncomfortable with such success.

REVENGE OF THE DADDIES

From the beginning Lucas's and Spielberg's movies were preoccupied with the search for the father, "a strong, revitalized father

figure to fill a perceived void in the American nuclear family,"
as critic Dave Kehr put it. In *Jaws* the weak father emerges as the
one man capable of dispatching the shark, while in *Poltergeist* "a
weak-willed, childlike father finally steps forward to assume the
disciplinary authority he needs to protect his family from evil."

For Spielberg the traditional father was the fount of values, the
storyteller, the "director." "Families [used to be] very, very
close," Spielberg said. "They used to gather around the reader,
or the *seer,* of the household, and in the Twenties and Thirties,
usually it was the father. And then television replaced the father."

Thus, Lucas's and Spielberg's movies were disturbed by a
profound contradiction. Much as they wished to infantilize their
characters and their audience, they also wanted to re-create the
strong father; in fact, infantilization demanded the strong father.
At the end of *The Last Crusade* Indy finally succeeded in re-
creating his father, and it is precisely this that allows him to escape
the uncomfortable role of adult. Despite all the effort Indy has
expended on finding the Grail, ultimately he doesn't need to
possess it, because he's found something more important: the
father he never had. A newly powerful Henry Jones allows Indy
to revert to infancy. He can indulge his talent for process (over
product), relinquish his role as a director, and afford to ignore
adult preoccupations with power and responsibility. So powerful
is this imperative that the moment of truth is dramatically equated
with saving Indy's life.

It's no accident that Indy's dad is played by Sean Connery,
whose James Bond movies Lucas and Spielberg grew up on. As
far back as 1977 Lucas observed that "Steve said he'd always
wanted to do a James Bond film . . . I said I had a great idea for
a James Bond film. 'It's not James Bond. It's set in the 30's and
it's about an archeologist . . . So Indiana Jones really evolved out
of Steve's interest in James Bond." Like others of their generation, Lucas's and Spielberg's cultural tastes were much to the
right of their political convictions. They were, as Godard put it,
"children of Marx and Coca-Cola." (Or, to be more precise,
children of Charles "the greening of America" Reich and Coca-

Cola.) Spielberg once said, "I love *Rambo*. But I think it is potentially a very dangerous movie." While their cultural program—
the infantilization of movies and moviegoers—was conscious and
explicit, the political implications of their program were not,
even (or especially) to themselves.

Ronald Reagan was the strong father Lucas and Spielberg
didn't know they were looking for, the ideal president for the
Age of *Star Wars*. Reagan presented himself as the protector of
children (particularly fetuses), and it was under his administration that child abuse became a major (non)issue, while his wife
made it her business to protect kids from drugs. Like Obi Wan
and Yoda, he was a blend of adult and child. (If Yoda began life
in 1980 as Ho Chi Minh, he ended life in 1983 resembling
Reagan more, thanks to Lucas's conflation of wisdom and Yoda's
Zen-like simplicity and childishness.) As such, he transcended the
ambivalence toward the father, the twin feelings of fear and love,
the need to rebel and the need to submit. He was the true
ancestor of the movie brats, a man/child who had grown up in
and on movies, for whom movies were as real as reality, a man
who looked at crime through the eyes of Dirty Harry ("Make my
day"), at Third World wars through the eyes of Rambo. Like
Henry Jones, Reagan enabled the nation to revert to infancy,
turn its back on the complicated reality of grown-ups in favor of
the back-to-basics, black-and-white, heart-over-head, fighting-
over-talking fantasy lives of children, a perspective that, ironically, had deep roots in the counterculture.

Reagan once said, "It is the motion picture that shows us not
only how we look and sound, but—more important—how we
feel." In his excellent book *Ronald Reagan, the Movie,* Michael
Rogin suggests that the lack of box office success of the anti-
Communist films of the fifties meant that Ronald Reagan was
wrong. Anti-Communism was more a top-down than a bottom-up
phenomenon; anti-Communist movies had not succeeded in colo-
nizing our minds or showing us how to feel. He adds, as an aside,
"Should movies fail in showing us how we felt, an emissary from
Hollywood not altogether successful in them would have to enter

politics and go to Washington." Reagan's journey from culture to politics represented a movement from buying tickets to marking ballots, suggestion to statement, covert to overt, unconscious to conscious. In this sense, politics was culture demystified.

Inevitably, however, culture found its way back into politics, as political parties turned to Hollywood for money, charisma, even candidates. In the same way that Lucas and Spielberg (re)-mystified movies, the movies mystified politics. As Rogin points out, Reagan's national-security policy, including SDI/Star Wars, was as much a fantasy as Lucas's movies: "It replaced the world it claimed to represent." (From Lucas's point of view, SDI amounted to Reagan's own, unauthorized sequel to the *Star Wars* trilogy. His crime was copyright infringement.) Like a movie, it didn't matter that it had no relationship to reality, because it was anchored in Reagan's personal authority. It was the man, more than the policies, people trusted. In the same way that in the mystified universe of Lucas and Spielberg their films denied themselves, so in the mystified universe of Ronald Reagan the man belied the message. And, as Reagan understood, the electorate had become an audience.

Had Reagan not existed, Lucas and Spielberg would have had to invent him. As it was, he resembled a character in their movies. Like Luke and Indiana Jones, Reagan was a man without an unconscious. As Nancy Reagan once said, "There is a certain cynicism in politics. You look in back of a statement for what the man really means. But it takes people a while to realize with Ronnie you don't have to look in back of anything." In other words, so far as Reagan was concerned, what you saw was what you got. Like Lucas's and Spielberg's heroes, he enjoyed a child-like transparency and two-dimensionality.

Reagan's career in movies petered out in the fifties, and he became the host of *General Electric Theater* on television. Reagan's relation to his policies, the man to the "movie," resembled the relationship of host to show; he "presented" his movie, directly addressing his audience in speeches and (rare) press conferences, and it was the presentation, not the movie, to which voters responded. "Ronald Reagan" was constructed as much by the logic of television as by movies, and his relation to his policies had more in common with the naïve television of the fifties than with the ironic movies of the seventies. As a presenter in a presentational mode, he was immune to the consequences of his actions.

As Maltby points out, television's open-ended, anti-narrative presentational structure diverts attention from the consequences of choice or actions to the choices or actions themselves. "Characters and audiences are required to make choices, but as they are immune from narrative, they are unaffected by the results of those choices." Thus, Reagan was able to dissociate himself from the results of his policies. In his neither-truth-nor-consequences administration he became the "Teflon president."

Nevertheless, as we have seen, Lucas and Spielberg tried to escape the presentational aesthetic. Whereas the anti-genre films of the seventies were open-ended and unresolved, the *Star Wars* and Indiana Jones trilogies struggled to reassert the prerogatives of narrative and to achieve closure. But a funny thing happened on the way back to the future: countervailing tendencies within the films defeated their best efforts. Lacking the ideological and narrative structuring that characterized the age of consensus to fall back on, the films are permeated by ideological confusion, a legacy of the seventies, and a testimony to the degree to which both narrative and closure had been irremediably compromised. Although *Star Wars* has a conventional moral framework—the education of a young man—with regard to traditional areas of contestation, like nature and culture, it is, as we have seen, completely muddled. The premise of the Indiana Jones films is that Indy is a mercenary; older consensual films like, say, *Casablanca,* would have brought him into the fold, given him something to believe in. Indy does learn something, sort of, but his education proceeds in fits and starts, and for reels at a time it is forgotten altogether.

In *Raiders* Belloq's relationship to the Nazis faintly echoes the ideological struggle between scientists and soldiers that characterized fifties sci-fi: Belloq, in his obsession with the Ark (he exclaims, "It's beautiful!" before his eyes are burned out), is not unlike the mad scientists, e.g., the naïve Dr. Carrington in *The Thing,* who sacrifice all to learn about the alien, and he's contrasted with the more level-headed Nazi officers. In the fifties, and even the sixties, there were important issues at stake: what principles would govern the coalition of the center—persuasion or force, reason or tradition? In *Raiders* the debate is carried on in a dilatory, inconclusive, spasmodic fashion. Although Belloq clashes with the Nazi officer several times in the course of the movie, sometimes he gets his way, sometimes he doesn't, and the issue is never resolved. This confusion and inconclusiveness are at least partly attributable to the weakening of the consequential, cause-and-effect structure of narrative by the wayward logic (or illogic) of the films.

Moreover, the story line of *Star Wars* often grinds to a halt entirely in order to display some astounding special effect that invariably overshadows audience concern with the fate of the humans, particularly because the actors' level of performance has been so severely scaled down. The observation often made about the film was true: not only was Mark Hamill not about to upstage the robots, but R2D2 and C-3PO continually upstaged him. Similarly, the story line of the Indiana Jones films is often interrupted by elaborate chase scenes that seem to last forever and do nothing to forward the plot. As audiences grew familiar with the special effects of the *Star Wars* films and the thrills of the Indiana Jones films, both directors were forced to pack more and more of the same into their pictures. Spielberg complained about this in 1982: "The thing that I'm just scared to death of is that someday I'm gonna wake up and bore somebody with a film. That's kept me making movies that have tried to outspectacle each other."

Spielberg's and Lucas's solution was to reemphasize conventional story values. Spielberg said, "You need good story-telling to offset the amount of . . . spectacle the audiences demand before they'll leave their television sets. And I think people will leave their television sets for a good story before anything else. Before fire and skyscrapers and floods, plane crashes, laser fire and spaceships, they want good stories." Indeed, the third installments of both these series are much more traditional than the first and depend much more on conventional character conflict and psychological realism than on thrills and special effects.

But psychological realism was never Lucas's and Spielberg's forte. Spielberg elaborated the much maligned "high concept" as a way out of this impasse. He was once quoted as saying that if the premise of a movie couldn't be boiled down to twenty words or so—the high concept—it wouldn't work. High-concept filmmaking, in which the idea drives the plot, was an antidote to the anti-narrative undertow in his movies.

Conceived serially, Lucas's and Spielberg's films also don't have the closure they might have had had they stood on their own, and the *Star Wars* films, in addition, are peculiarly presented as the fourth, fifth, and sixth of a series of nine. Spielberg acknowledged this problem and defended himself by arguing that he didn't have to provide "complete" endings. "I don't think in any of my films the end answers all the questions," he said. "Why? Why spoonfeed? Why set out a buffet?"

Spielberg also recognized that part of the problem was television, and in combating the anti-narrative influence of the tube, he had to fight his own deepest instincts. Noting that he doesn't read much, Spielberg remarked, "I am really part of the Eisenhower generation of television." He came up through television, directing there before he made features. But he once described *Poltergeist* as his "revenge" against television. And if, as Spielberg observed, television replaced the father as storyteller and source of values, Indy's reconciliation with his father has to be seen as another metaphoric rejection of television in favor of an older tradition of storytelling, that is, of the movies. Hence, the ending where all the characters ride off into the sunset, à la the old Westerns.

Nevertheless, try as they would, Lucas and Spielberg were not able to whip their movies into conventional shape. Whereas other sequalizers had to come up with situations that allowed the stars they had created in the original to strut their stuff at the expense of plot (*Lethal Weapon II* is a good example), their problem was not so much presentationalism, seventies-style, as spectacularism, eighties-style. The result, however, was the same. Narrative became hostage not to stars' wars, but to special effects. And just as Lucas's and Spielberg's insistence on infantilization had an unanticipated result—the rise of a new patriarchy inimical to many of the values these directors thought they believed in— so their attempt to restore traditional narration had an unintended effect—the creation of spectacle that annihilated story. The attempt to escape television by creating outsized spectacle backfired, and led back to television's presentational aesthetic.

Instead of rolling back the seventies, they, along with Reagan (following a somewhat different path), brought that decade to its logical conclusion. The movies of the seventies, however scornful of genre and consensus, were inevitably tied to that tradition, if only in opposition. Lucas and Spielberg cut loose entirely; they didn't restore narrative so much as empty it out. And, as usual, this contradiction had its roots in their own paradoxical attitudes toward filmmaking, growing up, success, and so on. For all their fear of seeing and insistence on punishing spectators, they were in love with seeing. Fear of sex and forbidden voyeurism implied its opposite: the rule of the unconscious expressed as spectacle, the erasure of self before the spectacle. Spielberg once said, "I want a movie to overwhelm me. I want an environmental experience, one that I cannot get from television." The striking resemblance of the last scene in *Star Wars* to the mass rallies of Leni Riefenstahl's fascist classic, *Triumph of the Will,* has often been noted; it's no accident that Lucas and Spielberg imagined adulthood as fascism, equated grown-ups with Nazis. In fact, the forbidden and explicitly demonized figure of the Nazi unexpectedly resolves all the contradictions that bedeviled these six films: the repressed unconscious finds expression as infantilizing spectacle created by the strong father, who at the same time is the director. Spielberg's most heartfelt scene is not the end of *Raiders* but its opposite, the end of *Close Encounters,* in which unlimited power is good and spectacle is enthralling. Which brings us back to

Reagan and the odd cultural confluence between him and the two directors.

Lucas and Spielberg helped make the world safe for Reagan, only to find that reconciliation with the over-thirty generation turned out to be a pact with the devil. It was as if Indy had thrown in his lot with Belloq, run off with Else, and stayed in Berlin to parlay his Hitler autograph into a job with Albert Speer. In short, it was as if Luke had gone over to the dark side. Darth Vader had won.

In most ways the Age of *Star Wars* and Indiana Jones is over. New production and distribution formations—the internationalization of Hollywood—appear almost daily, while continuing technological innovation threatens to make the special-effects work of Lucas's Industrial Light and Magic in the eighties look as dated as silent film. Neither Lucas nor Spielberg is promising another installment of their respective series; both have made noises about moving on, growing up, and so on. At the same time, and not coincidentally, the demographics of American viewers are changing. The baby boomers are growing older; the lock of the teen-age audience has been broken. High concept, while not entirely dead, has given way to so-called "adult" movies whose plots do not lend themselves to one-sentence summaries. The blockbuster and the sequel are still with us—witness the record-breaking summer of '89—but the shape and look of these movies are changing. Blockbusters will still attempt to re-create the old consensual audience relinquished by television as it became Balkanized by the proliferation of delivery systems and specialized software, even as this audience becomes increasingly fragmented by age, geography, and class.

Nevertheless, however movies evolve in the nineties, they will have to take as their starting point the massive changes engineered by Lucas and Spielberg in the eighties, just as Lucas and Spielberg defined themselves against the movies of the sixties and seventies. Anti-genre filmmaking may reemerge, but it can never take the form it did in the seventies. It will be, like *Batman,* and

Robocop before it, a kind of graft of the seventies onto the eighties, some amalgam of presentationalism and spectacularism, suffused by the apocalyptic glow of urban dread characteristic of the nineties: indeed, the world according to Darth Vader. Neither gentler nor kinder, these movies will likely be considerably more honest, and therefore more brutal, than anything in Lucas and Spielberg. If the 1930s found amusement during the Depression in fantasies of class reconciliation, the 1990s may find amusement in similarly egalitarian fantasies of mutual class annihilation.

*R*ose-Tinted Spectacles

STUART KLAWANS

THERE WAS ONCE a cross-burning where I grew up. Perhaps I should call it a twigs-and-twine-burning; the construction sputtered for a minute and then expired, even as its teen-aged fabricators ran from the scene. Still, as a gesture, it was inflammatory enough. Our neighborhood of South Chicago duplexes had welcomed its first black residents.

A few window-smashings ensued, followed by quick sales of the surrounding homes and the departure, often in the middle of the night, of families who had lived in the neighborhood for years. They didn't want anyone to know they'd sold to black people. Within three years the last white family had gone—and nobody, even two decades later, can say why it all happened.

On one level I could blame the change on material conditions. The American economy pits the marginally employed, who are mostly black, against the next highest class, who tend to be white ethnics. The latter group—what I might term the worried class— then turns racist through misinterpretation; it feels economic pressure but sees only skin color. In that sense my neighbors' racism was only a hallucination, one that made them easy prey for the hype of block-busting realtors. And, having believed the hype, my neighbors then turned their hallucination into reality. Thinking that black people make property values go down, the residents rushed to sell their homes and took a very low price.

If I hesitate to accept this explanation wholeheartedly, it's because I know too well that racism leads its own life. Economic conditions indeed aggravate modern-day bigotry, and they were no doubt at the source of racism centuries ago. Still, money begins to fade as a motive once the hallucinations begin—those visions of robbery, rape, and murder that some white people see when confronted by any black at all.

Whatever the reasons for the change in my neighborhood, then—economic, experiential, or phantasmagorical—none of them alone seems sufficient. And none has anything to do with the immediate targets of the violence: the four people who had moved into that little duplex.

So it is, if I may compare great things with small, in the case of film colorization (or, as it is sometimes known, color conversion). Why is it, when I hear people call the process an abomination, that I remember my former neighbors talking about keeping the colored out? The analogy would seem at first to be exactly wrong. The anti-colorization forces are high-minded and liberal; the process they fight against is an unconscionable fast-money scheme, like racist block-busting. Yet hype and hallucination have played their parts in the crusade against color conversion, too, and with results as little productive of the common good as a cross-burning.

Like the four people in the duplex, color conversion is more an innocent bystander than a provocateur. Insignificant in itself, the process is worth talking about mostly for the way it has raised questions about tradition, the formation of artistic canons, the nature of that curious thing we call "intellectual property," and, above all, the way economic and emotional motives get muddled in our society. These issues are weighty; the practice that has called them into question is slight. Why, then, was color conversion the occasion for the debate?

A TRIP TO THE MOON

From the beginnings of cinema in the 1890s, people added color to black-and-white films, usually by tinting and toning. These technically primitive efforts were controlled by the film's director; by contrast, the process we call colorization is carried out with computers and is controlled by people who had nothing to do with the original film. But those are not the main differences between, say, the tinted version of Georges Méliès's *A Trip to the Moon* and the colorized version of *Topper.* The most important distinction is that with *A Trip to the Moon,* technicians added colored dyes to the print of the film. With *Topper,* no film was ever altered—not the negative, not the fine-grain master, not even the most worn-out and worthless 16mm print. Colorizers begin their work by transferring a film's images to videotape. The technicians then add color to the tape with the aid of a computer. Only a *videotape* is colorized.

Through one of history's odd short circuits, the first notable success with this method also involved a trip to the moon. In 1970 the National Aeronautics and Space Administration wanted to show Congress some footage from the Apollo mission, the better to lobby for their budget request. NASA feared, however, that the legislators would be insufficiently impressed with mere black-and-white films from the moon. So they hired C. Wilson Markle, founder of a company called Image Transform, to add excitement to the Apollo mission footage, using his newly invented process of colorization.

Or, in this case, Colorization. The name is the trademark of a later incarnation of Image Transform, which Markle set up in Toronto in 1983. The following year, Colorization Inc. became part of International H.R.S. Industries Inc., a corporation formed by Norman and Earl Glick. Using funds made in the sixties in the oil, gas, and mining businesses, the Glick brothers acquired the old Hal Roach Studios and Markle's new company. Their idea, apparently, was to treat old footage, particularly that of television series, as a natural resource—to process it like crude oil and market it to distributors. "You couldn't make *Wyatt Earp* today for $1 million an episode," Earl Glick explained. "But for $50,000 a segment, you can turn it into color and have a brand new series—with no residuals to pay."

The original emphasis, then, was on television; but film could be exploited in the same way. In March 1985 the Glicks announced the acquisition of a library of 200 black-and-white films, to be distributed as colorized videocassettes. In April the Glicks declared that *Topper* would be their first colorized release, followed by the Laurel and Hardy comedy *Way Out West,* the Jane Russell exploitation Western *The Outlaw,* and Frank Capra's *It's a Wonderful Life.*

The presence on the list of Capra's film would set off the first battle, transforming Colorization from a trademark to a generic noun. But the real war would be fought over the actions of an entirely different company using a similar but distinct process called color conversion. By the time International H.R.S. Industries had announced their plans for *It's a Wonderful Life,* Color Systems Technology of Marina del Rey, California, had become very active competition and by far the greater intruder into film history.

Like Colorization Inc., CST began with an effort to alter historical documents. Its founder, Ralph Weinger, started to experiment with color conversion in the mid-seventies. He first used the process to add color to archival footage of the 1963 March on Washington for the Filmways production *King;* he also altered newsreels for an NBC-TV foray into historical fiction, *Ike.* In 1983, the same year that Markle established Colorization Inc.,

Weinger formed CST with two film-marketing executives, Buddy Young and Charles Powell. Young and Powell's Hollywood connections gave them an immediate edge over their Toronto-based rival. By early 1984 CST had worked out a deal to convert twenty films from the MGM/UA library. The only problem was that CST, unlike the Glicks' company, was undercapitalized. It wasn't until January 1985 that CST could announce *Yankee Doodle Dandy* as its first project, to be followed by *Camille* and the 1941 *Dr. Jekyll and Mr. Hyde*. As proof of its ties to the Hollywood community, CST also announced that Gene Allen, an Oscar-winning art director and the president of the Academy of Motion Picture Arts and Sciences, would serve as consultant to "ensure color quality and artistic integrity."

Despite that gesture, the CST executives were clearly as preoccupied with television as were their competitors at Hal Roach Studios. In July 1985, the same month in which it released the colorized *Topper* to video stores, Hal Roach Studios concluded pay-TV licensing deals with Home Box Office and Showtime/ The Movie Channel for a package of ten films. CST, by contrast, concentrated its marketing efforts on broadcast television. In July 1985 it announced *Miracle on 34th Street* as the first color-converted film for TV syndication. By November 176 broadcast markets, covering 90 percent of the United States, had contracted for the film; upon its broadcast at Christmas 1985 the program attracted 20 million viewers—twice its usual audience—and earned $600,000, as much as in all previous years of syndication.

THE GOLD RUSH

The broadcast of *Miracle on 34th Street* seemed to prove the assumption of the Hal Roach Studios and CST executives: TV viewers preferred to watch their programs in color. According to the studies Hal Roach Studios had conducted, 85 percent of viewers would watch a "classic" film in color but change the channel if it were in black-and-white. The colorized version of *Topper* appeared to clinch the argument: it earned $2 million by

the end of 1986, mostly from TV syndication, on an initial investment of $180,000. A broadcast of the color-converted *Yankee
Doodle Dandy* was also pressed into service to prove the point.
WDRB-TV in Louisville ran the color version in alternation with
the black-and-white in January 1987 and invited viewers to call
in with their preferences. The station reported that 67 percent
favored the color videotape, compared with 33 percent for black-
and-white.

But was any of this really proof of the underlying marketing
assumptions? As Roger Fristoe, film critic for the Louisville *Cou-
rier Journal,* pointed out, the WDRB test was seriously skewed.
The black-and-white version of *Yankee Doodle Dandy* shown that
night was actually the color-converted tape with the color turned
off, resulting in a dull, muddy-looking image. Moreover, a great
many of the people who called to vote were children; their opin-
ions, though far from negligible to marketers, could not be taken
as representative. As for the greater profits earned in syndication
by the colorized versions of films, one might well regard them
in the same light as the drop in property values in racially changing neighborhoods—they were the result of self-fulfilling
prophecies. Buyers from the various stations assumed that viewers preferred to watch television in color; therefore, they avoided
buying black-and-white programs. But they gladly paid for the
tarted-up *Miracle on 34th Street* and *Topper;* and, sure enough,
with more stations showing the films, more people watched them.

Episodes like this tempt me to define *business cycle* as a circular
argument. I should point out that the marketing executives did
have some justification for their decisions. Frank Rowley, the
veteran revival house manager who now runs New York's Biograph Cinema, says that younger viewers in particular avoid
black-and-white pictures; he has often seen people in their teens
and twenties walk out of them. But such evidence, however
telling, is anecdotal and inconclusive. Rowley also says that when
he recently showed *Gone with the Wind,* a number of people (who
were no doubt proud of their commitment to cinema history)
asked if the film had been colorized.

No one can say definitively what the public wants; nobody can even determine how much the public knows about its own desires. We can be sure, though, that the executives at Hal Roach Studios and CST and the television outlets, having bet millions on their intuition of the public's taste, would try to keep any contradictory evidence from arising. Having arranged cable-TV showings for his colorized films, Earl Glick did what he could to keep the black-and-white versions off the market. No head-to-head competition would be allowed.

Like all businesspeople, the executives at Hal Roach Studios also threw around statistics to prove their acumen. The colorized *Way Out West,* they noted, sold more videocassettes in six months than the original had over the previous ten years. Nobody mentioned that ten years before, relatively few people had owned videocassette players. Similarly, when an executive of Turner Entertainment Company later noted that the ratings had been "excellent" for its showing of *The Maltese Falcon* converted to color—5.5 percent of the audience watching television, compared with 3.6 percent for the Turner prime-time movie the previous month—he didn't bother to name the losing film. Maybe it had been *Heaven's Gate.* Nor did the executive take into account the effect of sheer novelty—people might have tuned in to the color-converted *Maltese Falcon* out of a curiosity that, once satisifed, would not have led them to watch such a production a second time.

It is certainly possible, though more difficult to prove than the executives claim, that people prefer to watch television in color. The issue, though, is not the public's taste. It's the way some executives, those with enough power to dominate their markets, decide in advance what people want, then justify their decision by noting that people have indeed bought the only available products. With entertainment, moreover, as with drugs, the product eventually creates a demand for itself. The public may be expected to want colorization once the marketers have habituated them to it.

As the debate about colorization heated up, the small, elite group of marketers would maintain steadfastly that they were really populists. Playing right into their hands, the anti-colorization group would respond with arguments about artistic merit and the rights of the individual. The hype of the marketers was about to be met by the hallucinations and misapprehensions of the embattled *petite bourgeoisie,* trying for reasons they only half-understood to keep the colored out.

FURY

Although it is now hard to recall, initial critical reaction to the altered films was favorable. Roy Hemming, a knowledgeable cinephile, gave his approval to the colorized *Topper* in *Video Review,* and Thomas M. Pryor praised the color-converted *Miracle on 34th Street* in the pages of *Variety.* From the first announcements of the process in early 1984 through the middle of 1986, most of the controversy about colorization involved a single film: *It's a Wonderful Life.* No flimsier *casus belli* had been seen since Jenkins's ear.

It's a Wonderful Life has unquestionably gained a high reputation with the public. But, since it has done so in a version edited for television, one might doubt whether colorization would be much of an insult. Indeed, to some viewers, *It's a Wonderful Life* could hardly be made any worse—it's already sentimental, manipulative, dishonest, and miscast, so what harm could a little color do? Even among the film's admirers, though, it was unclear at first whether color was a bad thing. Frank Capra himself originally consented to the colorization; in fact, according to one version of the story, he initiated the alteration. When he later withdrew his support, the reasons were possibly financial rather than artistic: Hal Roach Studios, having discovered that the film was in the public domain, realized they didn't need Capra and cut him out of the deal. Capra subsequently became a leading opponent of colorization, writing to the Copyright Office of the Library of Congress to claim that the practice distorted his artistic vision:

> I chose to shoot it in black-and-white film. The lighting, the makeup for the actors and actresses, the camera and laboratory

work, all were geared for black-and-white film, not color. I beseech you with all my heart and mind not to tamper with a classic in any form of the arts. Leave them alone. They are classics because they are superior. Do not help the quick-money makers who have delusions about taking possession of classics by smearing them with paint.

But the Copyright Office refused to intervene, for reasons I will discuss later.

Capra gained a degree of moral support from the critical community and the public; some protests erupted when the colorized *It's a Wonderful Life* finally reached the video stores. Still, there was no organized, energetic opposition to colorization so long as the chief victim was a vulgar favorite, which was best known in chopped-up form and which its own creator had wanted to alter. The real uproar did not begin until March 25, 1986—the day Ted Turner bought MGM Entertainment.

Reports already had been coming out about Turner's interest in color conversion. On March 6, 1986, MGM and CST announced a three-year, $18 million agreement to color-convert 100 feature films; the agreement would be effective as soon as MGM merged with the Turner Broadcasting System. Three weeks later Turner completed the acquisition, paying MGM $1.2 billion for its library of 3,650 films, which included the RKO and Warner Bros. libraries as well. The principal outlet for these films, obviously, was to be Turner's cable superstation, WTBS; but he soon showed an interest in selling them to fellow broadcasters. On May 19 Turner announced his plans to market 24 color-converted films to television stations on a barter basis, under the umbrella of Color Classic Network. The films in question included the much-heralded *Yankee Doodle Dandy, White Heat, Captain Blood, High Sierra, The Maltese Falcon, Father of the Bride,* and *Dark Victory*—on the whole, a more distinguished group of films than any that had been proposed before.

At this point the crusade against color conversion began in earnest. Not only were the films in question more significant, and more numerous, than any before, but they were being marketed by a man who was, as Vincent Canby remarked in the *New York Times*, the closest thing anyone had seen in years to Howard Hughes. Until this stage, control over the major private film libraries had resided with relatively low-key money managers, most of whom operated out of Los Angeles and New York. Now an absurdly wealthy swashbuckler from Atlanta had come in, answering all challengers with the soon-to-be-notorious statement "The last time I checked, I owned those films. I can do whatever I want with them . . ."

Curiously enough, the initial protest came from across the ocean. On June 12, 1986, the Directors Guild of Great Britain issued a statement, signed by 18 filmmakers, protesting colorization and asking for their government to protect a limited number of "classics" from the practice. The leader of this effort was the honorary president of the Guild, Fred Zinnemann, the expatriate American director of *High Noon* and *From Here to Eternity*. As it happened, Zinnemann both announced the major themes of the protest and foreshadowed something of its conclusion. He declared, in subsequent statements, that he would not object to seeing 99 percent of films colorized, but that 100 American and 75 British films should remain unaltered. The proportion of U.S. to U.K. films seems a bit odd, given that the statement was coming from a representative of British directors. But the more important point is that this was the first proposal for a government-approved list of film "classics." Zinnemann justified the proposed list by charging that colorizers "are tampering with the work of a man who is an artist . . . [T]he problem is that you cannot talk morals with money people."

Thus a British-based director announced, long-distance, the terms for the coming debate. They were to be art against commerce, morals against money, in the service of something called "classics." Zinnemann did not go so far as to define a "classic," but he evidently believed the number of such items could be specified *a priori*, in convenient blocks of 75 and 100.

By August, American filmmakers had mobilized. Woody Allen, who was to become a principal spokesperson against colorization, called it "an ugly practice, totally venal, anti-artistic and against the integrity of every filmmaker. Without the director's consent it seems to me a criminal mutilation of his work." George Stevens, Jr., adopting the same line, complained, "Here you've got some computer technician who's going to tell us what color some scenery was in 'Rebecca,' as if Hitchcock had not expressly chosen to make the film in black and white, which he did . . . It becomes a distinctly different experience, and those of us who are around have some sense of protecting the work of people who made films but are no longer here to protect them."

But, while putting forth the argument for artistic integrity, Stevens touched on a second point, which was both crucial to the coming debate and rarely mentioned in it. "Classic films are going to be principally accessible over television and in video cassette," he noted. "People can't go to the archive and see the original print. They'll see the film the way it's marketed, so therefore the films will be essentially inaccessible in black and white." Shortly thereafter Nicholas Meyer expressed the point even more strongly: "History lives on tape, not in seldom-visited museums." In other words, according to these directors, there is no history of film *on film*—there is only television. So much for the artistic integrity of the medium.

A psychoanalyst might say that this was the chief act of repression in the crusade against film colorization—the repression of film history. To understand why this was so, it might be useful now to describe what happens when a film is seen on television, even in the best of circumstances. Let us imagine a viewing of an old film on public television or videocassette, without cuts or interruptions, in a faithfully restored version, and, of course, in black-and-white. How is the television version different from the movie?

First, on television you lose part of the film's image. Since the aspect ratio of the film—the proportion of its height to its width—may be different from the aspect ratio of the television screen, technicians generally prepare the film for video by a process called *scanning.* They search each frame of the film for the safe area—the part of the image that contains most of the information—and match it with the safe area of the television screen. In short, they reframe the picture. This is a common practice even with films that have an aspect ratio identical to television's, since the safe area in video is somewhat tighter than it is in film. If you were watching a video of, say, *The Battleship Potemkin,* you would find the compositions subtly altered. Shots in which you should see multiple levels of the ship, with sailors scurrying everywhere, would be reduced to a simple core. Just a trace of a ladder would remain, as a dark margin at the top or the side of the screen, to remind you of what Eisenstein had so carefully composed.

A related practice, *panning,* is used when even scanning won't fit the principal elements of a shot into the allotted space. Wide-screen pictures often feature dialogues between actors who have been positioned at opposite sides of the frame. Television, though, does not allow you to see both at the same time; so, in the process of transferring the film to videotape, a technician pans back and forth from one actor to the other, introducing camera movements where before there had been a static shot.

More damage comes from the difference in resolution between film and television. Film can show much finer detail. Objects are clearer and better rounded; the shadows and the boundaries between objects are recorded with many more gradations of light and dark than on television. So, in the video of *Potemkin,* things would seem a little fuzzier than they should, edges would be a bit too sharp, the shadows would not have enough depth.

Someday, we are told, high-definition television will solve that problem. We might even see television screens that match the aspect ratios of films. But there is one more crucial difference between film and television: the quality of the light. A television screen glows from within; a film screen flickers with reflected light. Compare *Potemkin* in a theater with *Potemkin* on television, and you will see that an essential quality of the image already has been altered—the sheen and the shimmer are gone. In their place is a phosphorescence, which in a sense might just as well be colored as black-and-white.

To put it simply, adding color to a videotape does not so much introduce a change as merely aggravate an existing alteration. Even an ideal public-television broadcast of *Potemkin*—without cuts, without commercials, and without color—would be no more than a reminder of the film. And ideal broadcasts are rare. So, going back to the protests of the filmmakers, one notes that they already had a long history of grievances against television. "We made the first mistake in agreeing to the chopping up of films to fit the two-hour television format," Stanley Kramer said. "If directors had their way," Woody Allen said, "we would not let our films be tampered with in any way—broken up for commercials or shortened or colorized." But, of course, films had been cut and interrupted and panned and scanned for years. Why choose to fight now, over colorization?

In fact, directors had been upset for years about the way their films were broadcast. I am told that Joseph Mankiewicz used to keep a notebook in which he recorded every alteration of his films on television; and he was not alone. For years the Directors Guild of America had compiled its members' complaints about panning, scanning, and editing. But there were no public campaigns against these practices, and the DGA seems to have made no concerted private effort against them until 1981. According to Elliot Silverstein, who was chairman of the DGA's negotiating team, the directors campaigned actively that year for a creative-rights clause in their new contract with the producers' organization, the Motion Picture Association of America (MPAA). The campaign arose because of the editing of films for syndicated television; Milos Forman, leading the drive, had just seen his version of *Hair* broadcast with seven of the songs cut. Although the DGA failed to achieve a creative-rights clause in the 1981 contract, the directors agreed that their battle had just begun. "There was a direct bridge between those negotiations and the campaign against colorization," Silverstein explains. "We were looking for a platform."

Or, as Stanley Kramer put it, the directors thought of colorization as "the straw that broke the camel's back." This "sinful" practice became the target for protests "because it's so horrible and preposterous and more acutely noticeable by audiences . . ." True enough; but I want to suggest some further explanations.

First, the presence or absence of color in an art object, as I will explain below, has had a lot to do with our notions of "classicism." Colorization was no more "acutely noticeable by audiences" than the slapdash editing that television had practiced for years, but it did figure more directly in the filmmakers' inherited notions of what was "artistic." Second, the domination of television over film had become complete with the advent of cable and the videocassette recorder. More and more, films were being put into theatrical release just long enough to make them marketable on cable and in the video stores; and even during their week-long theatrical runs, they were shown on multiplex screens that were scarcely bigger than a television. This was good business for almost everybody, the members of the Directors Guild included; but it also was a source of some anxiety for the people who claimed to champion the "classics." They, too, were profiting from the consignment of film to the place of "classics"—the museum. Hence the denial that there was a history of film outside of television; hence the pretense that colorizing a videotape was the same as altering a film; hence the attempt to "save films" by prescribing just how they could be mutilated on video; hence the attack on Ted Turner, who so neatly concentrated in his own person the triumph of TV over Hollywood.

I do not mean to suggest by any of this that colorization is aesthetically neutral. I, too, find it obtrusive and absurd. But I notice that the people who complained about the falsification of history—another of the standard charges against color conversion—had been silent while Ralph Weinger altered the record of the March on Washington, while C. Wilson Markle invented colors for the surface of the moon. I notice that the directors, though rightly upset about the way their films were broadcast, had not failed to cash their checks. Since the coming of television, the principal organizations for filmmakers had concentrated not on artistic preservation of their work but on getting as great a share as possible of the profits. That was entirely appropriate—it's what a craft guild is supposed to do. Problems arose only when the filmmakers had to shift the battle from money, which everybody in America understands, to morals.

With colorization, the guilds and unions for the first time took a public stand on artistic grounds. I applaud their effort; but I also note that the fight turned out to be as chaotic as a real battle. As the record of the controversy shows, emotions and economics became hopelessly muddled; opportunities were fluffed and issues buried. Ultimately the filmmakers lost, and so did the public.

THE GANG'S ALL HERE

In September 1986 a committee of the Directors Guild of America urged that the organization put itself on the record against the "cultural butchery" of colorization. In October the Guild's board of directors voted unanimously "to use its full resources to stop the colorizing of black-and-white films" and to file a brief with the Copyright Office of the Library of Congress asking that copyrights not be given to colorized films. At virtually the same time, the Writers Guild of America West and two locals of the International Alliance of Theatrical Stage Employees (Camera Local 659 and Costume Designers Local 892) joined the crusade. Also in October the American Film Institute held a "spirited, emotional press conference" at its Los Angeles campus, thus joining the DGA in leading the crusade. The American Society of Cinematographers, the Western Regional Board of the Screen Actors Guild, and the National Council of the Arts also took up the cause. Asked why the third group—an advisory body for the National Endowment for the Arts, and therefore a governmental agency—should take a stand, NEA chairman Frank Hodsoll replied that "our charter is concerned about encouraging national progress in the arts. I don't think that the colorizing of films is progress in the arts."

By November the uproar had grown so great that an attorney for CST threatened to bring suit against the Directors Guild for restraint of trade. A public-relations firm, Rogers & Cowan, resigned the CST account rather than be associated with color conversion. The highest emotional pitch, though, had yet to be reached. Let the veteran Hollywood reporter Aljean Harmetz describe that moment, as staged at a news conference by the Directors Guild:

> "HOLLYWOOD, Nov. 13—Seated in a wheelchair and cradling his oxygen tank in his arms, John Huston today denounced the 'colorization' of his classic film, 'The Maltese Falcon,' by the Turner Broadcasting System . . . 'It would almost seem as though a conspiracy exists to degrade our national character . . . It's as though our children have been sold into white slavery, and now the Turner organization has dyed their hair.' "

As Vincent Canby noted in the *New York Times,* the anti-tinting crusade had taken on a "tone of righteousness . . . which is harmless in itself but also promotes a sense of clubby elitism that prevents us from seeing the matter clearly." In a pair of columns written in November 1986, Canby tried to correct that defect by putting forward the critical community's most cogent argument against color conversion, in language that was witty but reasoned. If colorization was to be taken at face value, as an aesthetic issue, this was no doubt the best case to be made against it:

In *Topper,* Canby wrote, the ghost of Marion Kerby "seems doomed to stalk the earth in a slinky, beaded evening dress and matching evening shoes, dragging behind her what looks to be a nearly floor-length ermine wrap." These are the sort of glamorous, thoroughly impractical clothes which are not only hideously expensive but which can be worn exactly once. In the black-and-white film, "Marion's dress and shoes appear to be silvery white." In the colorized videotape, though, "Marion wears an evening dress and shoes tinted a shade that might best be described as grayish lingerie-pink. The ermine of the wrap looks to have been downgraded to grayish rabbit fur. What was once the acme of Hollywood sophistication has become something to give

Diana Vreeland nightmares . . . The awful truth revealed by the new 'Topper': Marion Kerby hangs out in thrift shops.''

Similarly, in the color-converted *Yankee Doodle Dandy* the flag is "not red, white and blue but orange, beige and the sort of sickly blue by which boy babies are distinguished from girl babies in hospitals." Not only are the hues crude—comparable to those of Republic Pictures' old two-color process—but the image as a whole is obscured. "One feels as if one is watching a movie through a large, not awfully clean fish tank. Only the guppies are missing."

Canby admitted that the technicians might someday find a way to clean the tank and produce acceptable hues. But that would not clear away the essential objection: "Black and white films aren't automatically better or worse than color films. They are *different.* They provoke different responses." As for the argument, advanced by the colorizers, that films are essentially commercial items and therefore the rightful property of the producers (or any subsequent owners), Canby agreed that most films aren't art: "They're get-rich-quick schemes, vanity productions, tranquilizers, attempts to cash in on fads, industrial products. This is something that people like Mr. Turner know, and that those of us on the other side of the fence tend to ignore, if not to forget." Still, tastes change. "If not today, [films] might be art tomorrow." It is therefore necessary to fight against colorization, since the practice is likely to accelerate the disappearance of older films from the market. Color-converted tapes will drive out black-and-white, just as videocassettes have driven out 16mm prints, so that everything will end in television. "Great, good, bad and indifferent movies—they'll have become the 20th-century's Gutenberg Bibles."

OUT OF THE PAST

Since the argument has once again ended in the vaults of "seldom-visited museums," perhaps this is the moment to ask two long-deferred questions. Where does film history really reside? And is that history endangered?

The answer to the first question is the same now as it has always been: the history of film lives in very few places. Through the 1940s, the principal resource for cinema history, among filmmakers and audiences alike, was their memories. Film societies were rare, revival houses all but unknown. In a sense the history of film began in this country only in 1935, when the Museum of Modern Art founded its film library—the first archive of motion pictures in the United States to organize regular exhibitions and circulate films of the past. Even then, despite the Modern's influence, the situation throughout the period of "classic" American cinema was dismal: once a picture had played through its initial run, it generally would disappear. And that disappearance was likely to be permanent. For not only did Hollywood and the public at large consign all but the latest films to oblivion, but the pictures so discarded were literally doomed to destruction.

Until 1950 almost all motion pictures were made on a highly unstable nitrate-based film stock. When exposed to air, the nitrate combines with oxygen to form nitric acid, which dissolves the surrounding areas of film and thus accelerates the decay. In effect, the film eats itself. First it turns gummy; then it crumbles into a flammable powder. This deterioration is inevitable. Of all the films made before 1950, fully half have vanished.

So, to answer the second question: the history of film really *is* endangered. Organizations around the world are busy saving what they can: cataloguing a multitude of older films, which often are in disarray; storing those films in conditions that will retard the inevitable destruction; and transferring as many nitrate-based films as they can to modern safety stock. But this work, carried out under the auspices of the Fédération Internationale des Archives du Film, is happening very late in the day and under considerable difficulties.

As Ronald R. Haver, curator of film at the Los Angeles County Museum of Art, said at the height of the Turner controversy, "No professional film archivist has come out against colorization . . . Colorization isn't about film. It's video. Our cultural heritage is very safe in the archivists' vaults." Or, rather, our heritage *would* be safe, if the archivists had enough money and time to preserve their holdings.

I would argue that the crusade against colorization, which ostensibly was conducted to rescue film history, wound up by damaging it. The crusaders encouraged a misallocation of resources; public funds that might have gone toward preservation were spent instead on an ineffectual, token effort to combat colorization. Meanwhile the devilish colorizers, Turner included, turned out to be supporters of film history in spite of themselves. Colorization actually "is a boon to preservation," as Haver said, "because it requires [the colorizers] to make a pristine black-and-white print and negative if the original was on nitrate film." But, in the atmosphere of hype and hallucination that surrounded colorization, Haver's point was all but ignored.

"Colorization is a mindless obscenity that obliterates and destroys films"; it is a "shameless mutilation of films"; it "is destroying our film history foot by foot." That was the tone of the debate as late as February 1989, when you would have thought the worst of the name-calling would be over. Or, if people had not regained a sense of civility, at least you would have expected them to know that colorizers don't even touch films, let alone "obliterate," "mutilate," and "destroy" them. When I encounter such a combination of emotionalism and willful ignorance, I suspect what's being lost is not the history of film but an awareness of history itself.

What's lost is a memory of that time when people saw their films in theaters, rather than on television screens. I myself began to learn about film during the 1960s, at the tail end of the period Phillip Lopate calls "the heroic age of moviegoing." I remember the Clark Theatre in Chicago—open twenty-three hours a day, and educational during every one of them—and the Elgin in New York, and the film societies that met in classrooms and church basements and anywhere else you had a 16mm projector and a group of people who wanted to argue about Samuel Fuller. I remember the friends who were acquiring their own film libraries, despite the impediment of law; I remember the friend of a friend in California who was caught stealing prints from Roger Corman's studio and promptly received a job offer from Corman. Back then it wasn't enough to see films. You had to touch them, too; which is one of the reasons I still cannot feel any respect for videocassette recorders. You don't thread a VCR.

But, like everyone else who partook of the now-vanished mystery cult, I feel some gratitude toward television. Let Andrew Sarris—a much more distinguished cinephile than I—tell the story: "In those days a film enthusiast took what he could get when and where he could get it. And for a time television was pouring out the product helter-skelter. When you have stumbled up to attics and down to cellars and hunched over film institute moviolas around the world, you could become almost maudlin over catching a hitherto unseen Garbo or Sullavan in the relative comfort of your living room."

Three points need to be made here. First, television is a *substitute* for film. Second, the substitute is necessary only because the films themselves are, and always have been, scattered and scarce and endangered. Third, the "helter-skelter" of television programing can be of value in itself, since it matches an essential element of film history: its quality of being an aesthetic free-for-all.

Why did we argue back in the sixties about Sam Fuller? Couldn't we see that his pictures were crudely written, badly acted, emotionally brutish, intellectually void? Of course—but they were inventive and surprising and wildly vital at the same time. Some of us elevated *Shock Corridor* above all the self-conscious art of Ingmar Bergman, while others thought Sam Fuller's films were as bad as they looked. But, in the moviehouse darkness, who could enforce standards of taste? Twenty years after its release, the most despised B-movie thriller could suddenly take on the aura of a Sophoclean tragedy; the most admired big-budget drama could turn into kitsch. From this the less inquisitive among us drew the conclusion that all aesthetic judgments are relative, that nothing more could be said than "Tastes change." The more critical were jolted into thinking historically. The

fluidity of people's judgments about films; the sudden reversals
in taste; the near-impossibility of asserting that a given picture
was better than another in and of itself—all this led us to believe
that the jumble of film history had to be seen *as history.* Or, to
quote Andrew Sarris again on the subject of colorization:

> Old movies *are* the past, and it will take more than colorization
> to bring them up to date. A whole array of attitudes and values,
> good and bad, has to be decoded for old movies to be ap-
> preciated or even tolerated for their comparable modesty and
> discretion. Film history is history as much as it is film, and if
> young people are not interested in history, they will drift away
> from old movies, even those drenched in glaring color.

This way of looking at art—not just at film but at literature and
music and painting as well—does not rule out the possibility of
making aesthetic judgments. But it *does* lead away from the soft-
headed glorification of a handful of works, the ones I have insisted on putting in quotation marks as "classics." That strange,
ahistorical category has dominated the debate over colorization
from the beginning—from Capra's declaration that his pictures
"are classics because they are superior," to the request by the
Directors Guild of Great Britain for governmental protection of
a limited number of "classics," to John Huston's statement that
colorization was "as great an impertinence as for someone to
wash flesh tones on a da Vinci drawing." (The more common
comparison was with painting a mustache on the *Mona Lisa.*) It's
remarkable, though, that nobody tried to define "classic" as the
word is applied to films—perhaps because the result would have
been double-talk: the "classic" Hollywood era began with the
coming of sound, taking into account that some silent movies may
be considered "classics" if enough people have heard about
them, whereas the talkies until 1932 were rarely "classic" at all;
and this golden age lasted through World War II, although the
musicals remained "classic" through the fifties; and these films
(which were always shot in black-and-white, except when they
were not) had to be feature-length A-pictures from the big stu-

dios, even though some B-pictures and shorts have subsequently been recognized as "classic," for reasons only the French understand.

To be intelligible, then, the debate about colorization must open onto the much larger subject of classicism—including the odd circumstance that we think of the "classics" as colorless.

THE LAND THAT TIME FORGOT

The word *classic* first appeared in antiquity as a socioeconomic term; it denoted a first-class, tax-paying citizen of Rome. As first applied metaphorically to works of art, it implied something at once reputable and familiar—the aesthetic equivalent of, say, a precinct captain. Gradually, the term became associated with the authors that were taught in schools; and that was the true beginning of what we call the classics.

In the schools of the Middle Ages the *auctores* were an odd lot: pagans and Christians, great poets and windy versifiers, antique writers and writers of the recent past. There was no distinction between Virgil and "Homerus"—the latter being the name given to an unknown Latin interpreter of a chunk of the *Iliad*. The classics, then, were simply a reading list, drawn up without respect to subject matter, literary merit, historical period, or even the identity of the *auctores*. To revise Frank Capra's characteristically thoughtful construction: these works were "classics" not because they were superior but because they were taught.

The concept of the "classics" that directly concerns us developed at a later date and applies to the visual arts; but, like the literary concept of the "classics," it is thoroughly ahistorical. Moreover, the visual "classics" came into being through a process very much like colorization: the transfer of an image from one medium to another, accompanied by greater and lesser degrees of alteration.

For over three centuries the "classics" were a small group of antique sculptures to be found in Florence, Naples, and Paris, but first and above all in Rome. The core of these "classics" was the

collection put in the Belvedere sculpture court at the Vatican by
Pope Julius II. There was no particular plan to Julius's collecting;
he mostly knew he wanted old sculptures and left it in part to
chance to decide which those sculptures would be. In 1503, when
Julius had the Belvedere villa incorporated into the Vatican, his
architect Bramante built more niches in the court than there were
sculptures to fill them. He and Julius evidently felt that something
would turn up. Sure enough, in 1506 the *Laocoön* came to light,
was immediately recognized to be the very work praised above
all others by Pliny, and was brought to the Vatican to take its
place with sculptures of all periods, originals and copies alike. To
quote Francis Haskell and Nicholas Penny, whose account I am
following, "installation in the statue court was of itself sufficient
to act as a consecration of quality. As with some other collections
since, the location, and the reputation of the proprietor, provided
more of a guarantee than might be warranted by a detailed and
impartial observation of what was actually exhibited."

The real history of the Belvedere collection begins later,
though, in 1540, when François Ier of France, feeling that he, too,
needed some antique art, dispatched his court artist Francesco
Primaticcio to Italy, to take molds of the most famous statues in
Rome. The result was a set of bronze copies, installed in the
palace of Fontainebleau. These reproductions "provided the first
example of that international recognition—later to be acknowledged everywhere in the Western world—of a canon of artistic
values which was embodied not just in some vague concept of
antiquity, but in certain specific works of antiquity."

How did the concept of that canon spread? It did so through
prints (which were more or less fanciful), through sketchbooks
(which were equally unfaithful), through plaster casts. There
were even ceramic copies, with polychromed glazes; the English
made copies in lead, as garden statuary. These versions of the
sculptures were not so much reproductions as distortions. The
works themselves in the Vatican were distorted through "restora-
tions"; and on top of that, nobody, for two centuries, bothered
to ask about the history of these statues. It wasn't until 1722 that

the English writers Jonathan Richardson, Senior and Junior, noted that the works of the greatest antique sculptors had not survived and that we were actually seeing copies. That conclusion was generally ignored, though, until the publication of Johann Joachim Winckelmann's *History of Ancient Art* in 1763–64. Only then did people begin to distinguish one period from another and to separate the original from the copy.

By that point, though, the ahistorical concept of the canon was firmly embedded in people's minds, along with the image of classical art as smooth, polished, and *white*. Now, in ancient Greece—which was the source of our models—the most important sculptures were not marble at all but bronze. What's more, even the marbles were colored. In the words of one scholar, "Hair, eyes, lips, and dress were certainly painted on Classical marbles, and we are only less sure about whether or how often flesh parts might also have been tinted . . ." If we think of classical sculpture as white, then, it is because "We too readily project into Classical antiquity expectations about marble sculpture which have been formed by the practices of Renaissance and Neo-Classical artists, who saw Greek sculpture in polished Roman versions, stripped by time of any paint or accoutrements which might sully the pristine, breathing white."

We have known since the excavations of Pompeii and Herculaneum that antique taste, rather than being chaste and restrained, was closer to the decorative spirit of the average Greek coffee shop. But even today you will not find any museum curators willing to paint the marbles in their collections or to improve the antique bronzes by adding copper to the nipples and silver to the teeth. The notion of the polished, pure-white antique statue is too much a part of our cultural heritage—just like the related, and equally false, notion of the unique masterwork as the timeless standard by which all other art must be measured.

When the anti-colorization group spoke up for film "classics," then, they were indeed partaking of a long tradition—a tradition of misapprehension and superstition. The film "classics" were a mixed lot, belonging to some ill-defined past. They were of a limited number; Fred Zinnemann's slots for 75 or 100 pictures, to be named later, corresponded neatly with Bramante's niches in the Belvedere court, for sculptures to be discovered later. And, of course, the "classics" could not have color. *Heaven Can Wait, Nothing Sacred,* and *Becky Sharp* are all pictures from Hollywood's greatest era; all of them are arguably superior to *It's a Wonderful Life.* But those three films are in Technicolor. As Andrew Sarris asked, why was there no talk of mutilation and desecration when they were shown on television in black-and-white or rotten color, as they were for many years? The answer, I would suggest, is that to the classic-minded, those films were *supposed* to look bad. That was the proof of their antiquity and virtue.

Now, it is a matter as negligible as a producer's heart whether the people who were fighting against colorization had a deep understanding of classicism. It *does* matter, though, that they got so wrought up about their hallucinations that the fantasy, having taken on a life of its own, came to dominate the debate. It did so, I would suggest, because of a fundamental trait of our society: Americans have no commonly accepted terms in which to ground their arguments about artistic endeavors and moral rights. Our society has never acknowledged the civic importance of either category; and so public discussions that touch on those issues will almost inevitably take off into the clouds.

In that sense Ted Turner held a clear advantage over the anti-colorization forces. Perhaps he sounded crass when he talked about his plans; but he was nevertheless expressing the central belief of American society: I own it, therefore I can do what I want with it. What could the anti-colorization people substitute for America's greatest good, the right of private property?

MR. SMITH GOES TO WASHINGTON

From November 1986 through spring 1987 the colorization war was fought mostly in the press. Then came two major developments in Washington. On May 13, Representative Richard A. Gephardt (D-Mo.) introduced H.R. 2400, known as the Film

Integrity Act of 1987. The act was intended to establish moral rights for film artists—that is, to guarantee a limited form of copyright protection to a film's creators, in addition to its present owners. Principal among moral rights is the ability to prevent material alteration of an artwork. The second development, on June 19, was the decision by the Copyright Office of the Library of Congress to extend its protection to colorized films, as "derivative works."

These two events were as alike as a butterfly and a bulldozer. The Gephardt bill was a well-meaning but quixotic effort, motivated a bit too obviously by its sponsor's ambitions. Gephardt, who was pursuing the Democratic nomination for president, used his sponsorship of the bill to borrow a little Hollywood glamour. (In the same way, one of his rivals for the nomination, Senator Al Gore of Tennessee, got some notoriety and sex appeal from the widely publicized efforts of his wife, Tipper, to censor rock 'n' roll albums.) The decision of the Copyright Office, on the other hand, was substantial. In fact, it gave the colorizers everything they had wanted.

From the beginning, colorization and copyright had gone together. As C. Wilson Markle said in 1984, "It's only feasible to convert to color if you own the world rights, since the cost would be prohibitive for small markets." Hence the effort by Hal Roach Studios to colorize films in the public domain, such as *It's a Wonderful Life.* The Roach executives were hoping the Copyright Office would recognize the addition of color as "new creativity," thereby making the videotape an "original work of authorship." Turner, of course, was playing a similar game. He might have hesitated to pay $1.2 billion for a film library if the pictures had soon lapsed into the public domain. By converting them to color, though, he could get a fresh copyright, which would be valuable for years to come in the broadcast and cassette markets. In both cases, then, the companies were trying to conjure private property out of the public domain.

In September 1986 the Copyright Office asked for public comment on the question of registering copyrights for colorized films. The Directors Guild filed a brief against such copyrights; the MPAA (representing film producers) joined with Turner and CST in arguing for the copyrights. When the Copyright Office ruled in favor of the producers and colorizers in June 1987, it did not, however, end the conflict. That ruling failed to address the issue of moral rights, which had been raised not only by the Gephardt bill but by other legislation as well.

The issue of moral rights had come up repeatedly since 1986 in the context of congressional debates over U.S. membership in the Berne Convention for the Protection of Literary and Artistic Works. Membership in the 1886 Berne Convention would help prevent piracy of American works, so Congress was moving toward a revision of the domestic copyright law, to bring it into accord with Berne. In the words of Leon Friedman, a law professor at Hofstra University who is counsel to the American branch of P.E.N., this would finally bring the United States into the twentieth century with regard to copyright law. The big publishers and broadcasters were happy enough to see this happen, since it meant their properties would be better protected internationally. But, predictably, they lobbied against American adoption of a key provision in the Berne Convention: the recognition of the moral rights of the creators of those properties.

This was the situation in March 1988, when the House Subcommittee on Courts, Civil Liberties and the Administration of Justice set up hearings on the issue of moral rights. In particular the hearings focused on the Gephardt bill and on similar legislation, introduced by Representative Edward J. Markey (D-Mass.) and Senator Edward M. Kennedy (D-Mass.), creating moral rights for painters, sculptors, and graphic artists. When Steven Spielberg and George Lucas testified in favor of moral rights, the five senators on the panel replied that they would support only a limited expansion of the copyright standards.

The issue of moral rights was thus badly stalled; Representative Robert Kastenmeier (D-Wisc.), chairman of the Judiciary subcommittee that deals with copyright, tried to put the issue to rest by commissioning the Copyright Office to study the question of moral rights in film colorization. Bear in mind that nine months had passed since the Copyright Office had recognized colorization as new creativity; little could have been expected from a further study. But, then, the issue still made good press, and the DGA was still agitating for some recognition of moral rights.

Such was the situation in May 1988, when Representative Robert J. Mrazek (D-N.Y.) began circulating a draft of legislation intended to limit the rights of film owners to alter their property. The following month Mrazek persuaded Representative Sidney R. Yates (D-Ill.) to introduce the legislation as an amendment to an appropriations bill for the Department of the Interior. Legislation regarding copyright—and this was clearly such legislation—is properly the concern of the Committee on the Judiciary; nevertheless, the Mrazek-Yates amendment was introduced through the Subcommittee on Interior of the Committee on Appropriations. This was not just improper—it was sneaky, too. The strategy, which had been worked out in collaboration with the Directors Guild, was intended to catch the opponents of moral-rights legislation off guard.

The strategy worked—perhaps too well. In late June 1988, while Gephardt's moral-rights bill was moving toward a vote in the Judiciary committee, various parties interested in the Mrazek-Yates amendment met privately in the office of the House Majority Leader, Representative Thomas S. Foley (D-Wash.). Foley told the DGA and MPAA representatives to reach an agreement so that some form of legislation could proceed. As Jack Valenti, president of the MPAA, later admitted, his organization then accepted the Mrazek-Yates bill in principle, for fear that the MPAA did not have enough votes in the House to stop the Gephardt legislation.

Wrangling over the details continued for several weeks; but with the DGA-MPAA agreement, the effort to create moral-rights legislation had effectively been abandoned. On June 30, Kastenmeier excused the procedural irregularity of the Mrazek-Yates amendment, thus opening the way to its passage. He declared that Mrazek-Yates had "settled for the foreseeable future" the "matter of moral rights in the motion picture context"— which, of course, it had not. As Mrazek himself admitted, the amendment left the central issue unresolved, while the report that Kastenmeier had commissioned from the Copyright Office was still to come. But, since the House was unlikely to deal with those problems during the 100th Congress, Mrazek cooperated with Kastenmeier, saying that he wanted to move ahead with his own legislation. Congress, he said, should "show Jimmy Stewart and the American people that they care about American movies."

So, with that clear-headed justification, the Gephardt bill was abandoned in favor of the Mrazek-Yates amendment, also known as the National Film Preservation Act of 1988. On September 27, 1988, President Reagan signed the Mrazek-Yates amendment into law; on October 31, 1988, he signed the implementing legislation for the United States to become party to the Berne Convention. The latter bill explicitly stated that the legislation neither expanded nor reduced the moral rights of authors— which is to say, that moral rights still would not be recognized in the United States.

The colorization war had ended. Its final echo was heard on March 15, 1989, when the Copyright Office finally issued its study of colorization. Unexpectedly, the Office called for Congress to enact a uniform federal system of moral rights for creators; moreover, the study recommended that the principal director and screenwriter of a film be accorded moral rights in the work. Any material alteration of a film, including colorization, would then require the consent of the authors. But these recommendations, however novel, did not really go very far. The Copyright Office advised that the principle of moral rights be applied only to new works; existing films, which means all the ones that are likely to be colorized, would still be at the mercy of their owners. In addition, the enactment of a federal system of moral rights is currently regarded as politically impossible— the big publishers, broadcasters, record companies, newspapers, and film producers are simply too powerful a lobby. Though legislation to extend some form of moral rights for visual artists will be introduced again in the 101st Congress, it would have been more likely to pass when the colorization debate was at its height, during the 100th session.

Instead, the principle of "I own it, therefore I can do what I want with it" remained inviolable. All the DGA gained for its hard work was a National Film Preservation Board, which is to select up to seventy-five theatrical motion pictures for inclusion in a National Film Registry. The pictures selected, if colorized, will then have to be labeled as materially altered. They could still be broadcast with commercial interruptions, though, without having to bear any warnings to the consumer.

As of this writing, the first twenty-five films have been announced. Eight of them were made in color—nine, if you count the tinted sequences in the earliest picture on the list, *Intolerance* (1916). Such is the victory achieved by the anti-colorization crusade. The United States will get an official list of seventy-five "classics," many of them fully immune to colorization. They will be "preserved," to use the language of the legislation, by sticking labels on videotapes. The cost of this will be $750,000, spread over a three-year period. And what does the federal government spend annually on *real* film preservation, to keep the pictures in the archives from crumbling? It spends just over $355,000. Over the previous seventeen years the government had spent only $6 million to preserve our film heritage; now it is going to spend three-quarters of a million over just three years, essentially to make a list of America's seventy-five most popular old movies. I write those words and once more recall my former neighbors, who rushed to sell their homes at a loss rather than live next door to black people. The colored, after all, drive down property values.

I AM A FUGITIVE FROM A CHAIN GANG

This has been a characteristically American story.

In other nations, values besides the right of ownership sometimes enter into public discourse. The works of French filmmakers, for example, have been protected by law since 1957; that protection was extended as a courtesy to John Huston in 1988, when a court ruled that the color-converted *Asphalt Jungle* could not be shown on French television. In America, though, it is an anomaly to speak in official terms of artistic values and the moral rights of authors. We are free as individuals to admire such values, but as a nation we respect only property.

In terms of our film heritage, this has meant that the profits made on films remain private, going to the various rights-holders; the burden of preserving those films, though, has been shifted none too efficiently onto the public. Mary Lea Bandy, director of the Department of Film of the Museum of Modern Art, notes that only Walt Disney and MGM, out of the major studios, have been careful to preserve their libraries. The others either neglected their collections, thinking it too costly to preserve the films, or passed them on piecemeal to the four archives of nitrate feature films (MoMA, the Library of Congress, George Eastman House, and the UCLA Film and Television Archive). "By and large," Bandy says, "the companies gave the films to the archives for copyright protection and to save the storage costs. The films were stored, catalogued, and preserved with public funds. Meanwhile, the rights-holders had access to those materials for redistribution, theatrical presentation, and home video. It's been the archives' dream that the rights-holders would provide additional financial support for the keeping of the collections." But that, if I may say so, is not the American way. We believe in private profit but public liability.

Of course, if you run a small business or a family farm, it's still possible to go broke in America. For larger enterprises, though, the concept of risk is becoming outmoded. As I write, the Bush administration is preparing to spend $300 billion over a thirty-year period to cover the bad debts of the savings-and-loan industry. The owners of the 500 savings and loans in question would have been welcome to keep whatever profits they might have made. Their investments went bad, though, and so the public will cover the loss.

In the past the federal government would assist failing businesses but not simply absorb their debts. During the Depression, the Reconstruction Finance Corporation helped to recapitalize firms that were facing bankruptcy; the firms had an obligation, though, to repay the RFC. The government has also helped businesses by changing the tax laws, as it did with American Motors Corporation in 1967; and it has provided loan guarantees. The biggest of those bailouts, of course, came in 1979, when Congress approved $1.5 billion in loan guarantees for Chrysler Corporation. In that instance Chrysler repaid its notes within four years. The corporation also paid the government over $300 million to buy back rights to its stock, arranged for its workers to acquire 16 percent of its common shares, and put the head of the United Auto Workers on the board of directors. In other words, the public got something back for its investment in the company.

In the Reagan-Bush era, though, the trappings of modesty have fallen away, and naked capitalism stands before us. The savings-and-loan bailout will be financed through thirty-year bonds, with most of the interest to be paid by the Treasury— which is to say, the taxpayers. This will mean a cost to the public of approximately $225 billion; and the public will receive virtually no control or profit in return. As a currently unfashionable writer once put it,

> the laws of appropriation or of private property . . . become by their own inner and inexorable dialectic changed into their very opposite . . . [P]roperty turns out to be the right, on the part of the capitalist, to appropriate the unpaid labour of others or its product and to be the impossibility, on the part of the labourer, of appropriating his own product.

Just so, the American public has been made to pay for the preservation of films (though not consistently or in very large sums) yet has no control over the pictures, other than the right to draw up a list of seventy-five favorites. In countries such as France and England (even Margaret Thatcher's England) the nation's film heritage is both a public responsibility and a public resource. In the United States the public has no rights to the films in the archives and (not surprisingly) only a confused understanding of the costs of their preservation. That, rather than the addition of color to some videotapes, is the scandal of our film industry.

Having abandoned the concept of commonwealth, we are reduced to hoping that private interests will somehow coincide with the public good—a proposition so absurd that I would feel embarrassed, at this late date, to point out its falsity, were it not the dominant ideology of the United States. We have twice elected Ronald Reagan to the presidency in the belief that unrestrained greed would benefit society at large; yet, from 1979 through 1987, while the personal income of the wealthiest Americans rose by over 15 percent, that of the poorest dropped by almost 10 percent. In fact, during the Reagan era nearly half of the American people saw their incomes decline. Still, we continue to worship the faceless god called Market—a jealous god, who forbids us to lust after morals.

Perhaps, then, there are two lessons to be learned. The first, as seen in the history of the Mrazek-Yates amendment, is that our efforts to create social policy will fizzle, so long as we never challenge the idea that private property is absolute. The second lesson—which is rather more painful to draw—is that the pursuit of private gain sometimes *does* lead to public benefits. It is no pleasure to throw oneself on the mercies of Ted Turner. But, there being no other choice, we should acknowledge that this undignified, unreliable, undemocratic method sometimes pays off.

Even the outspoken opponents of color conversion have had to admit that Turner is doing some good. For example, he is transferring about 200 nitrate films from the RKO library to safety stock. Turner's detractors seem to think this a piddling effort. But, to put it into perspective, consider that it costs about $10,000 to preserve a feature film. Turner is thus planning to spend an estimated $2 million on his RKO collection alone over a three-year period—roughly twice what the federal government will give in the same time to all the U.S. archives combined. There is no altruism involved, of course. "Failure to proceed," one critic notes, "could leave Turner owning a pile of dust." But then, as I have said, previous owners of film libraries haven't seemed too worried about that. If Turner is willing to spend $2 million to save his RKO films, it is for the reasons Ronald Haver mentioned: color conversion has now made the investment seem profitable.

Moreover, Turner's investment in film preservation has led him into direct contact with the archives. In 1989, having copied his Warner Bros. holdings for use on television, Turner deposited the nitrate fine-grain masters of some 450 features with the MoMA archive, along with the Popeye and Looney Tunes libraries and about 800 short subjects. This was an enormous donation. Combined with Turner's other deposits of Warner materials— prints have gone to the UCLA archive, and the negatives are in the Library of Congress—it means that the entire output of an American studio has been preserved, for the first time.

Beyond that, Turner is cooperating with MoMA and the UCLA archive on the restoration of some older films, such as the Technicolor *Meet Me in St. Louis* and the two-color Vitaphone *Under a Texas Moon*. Turner has also proved cooperative about supplying projection prints to the revival houses, even striking new prints when needed. As Frank Rowley of the Biograph Cinema notes, Turner is "willing to license nearly any title I select, and in many cases this means one-of-a-kind archive prints. No other distributor is willing or able to supply us with such a variety of high-quality films."

Unlike most of the diatribes against colorization, Rowley's sentiments have a firm basis in fact. Sooner or later such level-headed arguments will catch on; and when that happens, people will see that color conversion was nothing worse than an inconvenience or (if I may play prophet) a short-lived fad. As of this writing, both CST and Colorization Inc. have lost millions. Demand (except from Turner) has been lower than expected; costs have proved to be higher. Faced with bankruptcy, the owners of the color-conversion labs now seem to want to abandon film and concentrate again on their original source of raw material, old television series. As that happens, and as emotions die down, the filmgoing public might look again at Turner's contributions to the archives and revival houses and admit that colorization did have some pleasant side effects.

But no one, unfortunately, is likely to mention the more troubling point: that Turner, or the next person to buy these films, will have no obligation to preserve them, to show them, to account for them in any way. If the price of guitar picks should suddenly rise, the fine-grain master of *Captain Blood* could wind up in the fingers of 130,000 aspiring rock musicians; and nobody will have a right to say no.

Misguided crusades must end in misguided conclusions. No doubt a good many of my former neighbors, upset at leaving their old homes and blind to their own collusion in the move, went on to vote for Ronald Reagan. He was certain to keep the colored down; and, indeed, he did it so effectively that black Americans lost much of what they had gained in the civil-rights movement. Today white Americans look at the desperation of the ghetto and congratulate themselves on having been right all along—those lazy, irresponsible, dope-peddling, murdering blacks bring misery wherever they go.

Misguided notions about colorization are less noxious, of course, but they have been part of a similar social dynamic. Members of the Directors Guild felt economic pressure, from the dominance of television over film; but they saw only color. Soon their hallucination about timeless, austerely black-and-white "classics" took on a life of its own, dooming their efforts to confusion. Organized to save film "classics," the anti-colorization struggle drained money and attention from real efforts to preserve films. Organized to assert the integrity of films, it reinforced public confusion over the difference between film and video. Organized as an appeal for moral rights, it dissipated much of the energy behind the drive for copyright reform.

But of all the false impressions that rose like smoke from the colorization war, none is likely to be so damaging as the final one: the inevitable conclusion that the great god Market, working through his servant Turner, has saved America's film heritage. Until we finally learn to recognize rights besides those of owner-ship, our film heritage will continue to be endangered—and not by anything so trivial as an uglified videotape.

*E*nd
of Story

MARK CRISPIN MILLER

"**T**HIS APPROACH TO human beings strikes me as utterly cynical, and directly contrary to the democratic ideal." Such was the sharp response of Dr. Lewis Webster Jones, head of the National Conference of Christians and Jews. Other clergymen agreed: this new technique could mean the twilight of democracy. "Such a weapon," wrote one rabbi, "could result in the molding of our population's social and political attitudes and beliefs to the point where democracy would be a mockery and freedom meaningless." Nor was it only God's ministers who sensed a terminal threat: "Put to political propaganda purposes," warned Republican congressman William A. Dawson of Utah, this infamous device "would be made to order for the establishment and maintenance of a totalitarian government." Many intellectuals were equally perturbed by this new instrument, which could, suggested Aldous Huxley, make "nonsense of the whole democratic procedure, which is based on conscious choice on rational ground." Huxley had not, he said, foreseen this invention when writing *Brave New World*—which, he feared, might now come true.

Such were the apprehensions not only of a few edgy pundits but of the nation generally. The public protest was immense. The National Association of Radio and Television Broadcasters felt obliged to ban the use of the technique by any of its members, and the three major television networks also publicly rejected it. The New York State Senate unanimously passed a bill outlawing the technique. When KTLA, an independent TV station in Los Angeles, announced that it would soon start using the invention to discourage littering and unsafe driving, the station "received such a torrent of adverse mail," *Life* magazine reported, "that it cancelled the campaign."

Meanwhile, there were some who were not emitting "yelps of alarm," according to the *Wall Street Journal.* Indeed, certain forward-looking managers were rather taken with the idea, despite its dangers, or perhaps because of them. These men regarded the new instrument not with foreboding but with a wry and jovial fascination. "Chuckles one TV executive with a conscious eye on the future," reported *Time* magazine in its coverage of the controversy, " 'It smacks of brainwashing, but of course it would be tempting.' "

The invention that had sparked the national panic, and that was also quietly thrilling certain corporate salesmen, was "subliminal advertising"—a phrase coined by the first of its practitioners, James M. Vicary, "a young motivational researcher and amateur psychologist," as the *Journal* dubbed him. On September 12, 1957, Vicary, vice-president of Subliminal Projection Company, held a press conference to tout the results of an experiment he had just concluded at a movie theater in Fort Lee, New Jersey. For six weeks, using special equipment, he had flashed imperceptible allurements onto the screen during the theater's showings of *Picnic,* a Columbia release. Projected every five seconds for one three-thousandth of a second, those unnoticed coaxings, Vicary said, had dramatically boosted sales out at the concession stand of the items subliminally hyped. Vicary had projected two terse bits of copy: "Hungry? Eat popcorn" and "Drink Coca-Cola."

Today what matters most about Vicary's experiment is not its "findings"—which Vicary fabricated. His device turned out to have had no effect at all on how much Coke or popcorn people swallowed but was a mere sales gimmick used to promote the Subliminal Projection Company itself. However, while Vicary's "results" were valueless, the outrage stirred by his announcement was important. Back in 1957 the rumor that one movie had been temporarily polluted with an advertising pitch—"Drink Coca-Cola"—was enough to elicit a great wave of angry protest from the American public. Let us now look at two clips from the movies of the eighties—movies that nobody protested.

In *Murphy's Romance* (1985), a Columbia release, Sally Field is a youngish divorcée, poor but plucky, who has just moved with her sweet preadolescent son to this calm and frien'ly Texas town. At the start of the film she wanders into an old-fashioned sort of general store, owned, we soon discover, by James Garner, a very benevolent curmudgeon ("Murphy"). On her way in, Field passes (slowly, so we'll see them) not one but *three* bright Coca-Cola signs (the merry red, the bold white script)—one on each front window, one on the front door; and then, as Field plunks herself down cutely at the soda counter, and as the seemingly brusque but really very kindly Garner comes to serve her, there is the following exchange:

FIELD: I'll have a banana split. No, I won't. I'll have a Coke.
GARNER: A Coke?
FIELD: A lemon Coke.

Much is later made of Garner's cherished 1927 Studebaker, which sits out front—he refuses to put it elsewhere, despite a daily parking ticket. Although this business does say something obvious about Garner's character ("That Murphy! Stubborn as a mule!"), its implicit visual function is to say "Drink Coca-Cola," since it shares the frame with, and is itself the same deep merry red as, those three prominent signs for Coca-Cola. (The movie, incidentally, has a happy ending.)

Toward the beginning of *Who's Harry Crumb?* (1989), another Columbia release, John Candy sits next to Jim Belushi on a bus. A fantastically inept detective, Candy is on his way to meet his employers in a big kidnapping case. Here, in all its comic brilliance, is the entire scene with Belushi:

CANDY *(eating cherries, offers one)*: Cherry?
BELUSHI *(reading)*: No fruit, thank you.
    Candy pulls a can of Diet Coke (silvery cylinder, red block letters) out of his valise.
CANDY: Coke?
BELUSHI: No, thank you.
CANDY: Mix 'em together, ya got a cherry Coke. Ah ha ha ha ha! A cherry Coke, ha ha ha ha!

Later, dining with his wealthy clients, Candy pours a can of Diet Coke into a brandy snifter full of ice cream, holding the (silvery) can up high so that its (red) name is not just legible but unavoidable. (Despite his imbecility, Candy finally cracks the case, saves many lives, and becomes rich and famous as the head of his own detective agency.)

What is the difference between James Vicary's ploy and these later cinematic tricks to make an audience "Drink Coca-Cola"? In 1957, Vicary tried to boost his business by implanting a commercial message in a Columbia release (and then by making false claims for the failed experiment). In 1982, Coca-Cola purchased 49 percent of Columbia Pictures and began at once to plug (its own) products in (its own) movies—trying, just like Vicary, to profit by turning movies into advertising. (The company kept it up until it sold Columbia Pictures to Sony in 1989.) Certainly, there is a difference in degree. Whereas Vicary's method was a furtive imposition on the movie, used only in one theater, and only temporarily, the come-ons embedded in Coke's movies are there forever, in whatever prints or tapes you choose to see, because they are worked—overtly—right into the movies' scripts and *mise-en-scène.*

These later exhortations to "Drink Coca-Cola," one might argue, differ crucially from Vicary's gimmick, since his appeal was "subliminal," whereas the later cans and signs beckon us openly, like illuminated billboards. Such a distinction, however, rests on too crude an understanding of "subliminal" effects— which result not from invisible "implants" but from words and/ or images that are explicitly presented yet only, at best, half-perceived. These latter-day plugs for Coca-Cola work as "subliminal" inducements because their context is—ostensibly— the movie, not the ad, so that each of them comes sidling toward us dressed as something not an ad and therefore welcome, just as other kinds of ads nowadays rountinely come at us disguised as "magalogues" and "advertorials," rock videos, "educational" broadcasts and newsletters, filmstrips and posters, as well as many concerts, art exhibits, sports events, magazines, newspapers, books, TV shows, and a good deal of your daily mail—in short, as anything and everything but advertising.

The "subliminal" impact of the Coke plugs arises not only from their cinematic camouflage but from the rich and pleasant welter of associations that, within each movie, efficiently glamorizes every Coca-Cola can or logo: James Garner's personal warmth and fine old car, and John Candy's would-be riotous antics (as well as each man's patent stardom) are attractions serving as oblique—that is, "subliminal"—enhancements to the all-important product. Precisely because of this benefit, Coca-Cola has been very careful in its choice of cinematic vehicles. And for the same reason, Coca-Cola also used the movies to stigmatize the competition.

This practice represented a sly refinement on official company policy. Shortly after buying into Columbia in 1982, the managers of Coca-Cola sent the studio executives a memo forbidding the use, at company events as well as (by implication) in Columbia productions, of any goods produced by PepsiCo or Philip Morris: Pepsi, Miller, Löwenbräu, 7-Up, Stolichnaya vodka, and Frito-Lay potato chips. Columbia, however, sometimes went beyond mere omission to the deliberate sabotage of rival images. In *Murphy's Romance,* for instance, Field's nice son goes looking for a job; and while "Coca-Cola" sheds its deep-red warmth throughout Murphy's homey general store, in a big supermarket where the kid is told abruptly that he isn't needed, two (blue) Pepsi signs loom coldly on the wall like a couple of swastikas. In fact, the company used such tactics before its purchase of Columbia. In Costa-Gavras's *Missing* (1982), made just before the acquisition, Jack Lemmon plays a very decent father searching in Chile for his son, who has been kidnapped by Pinochet's soldiers. In one scene this haggard, loyal dad, while talking things out, takes rare (and noticeable) solace in a bottle of Coke—whereas inside the nightmare stadium where the army does its torturing and murdering, there stands a mammoth Pepsi machine, towering within this underworld like a dark idol.

Although PepsiCo owns no movie studio (yet), its officers began fighting back at once. A special manager tackled the job of keeping Pepsi on the silver screen, and from that moment the circular Pepsi logo (white/blue/red) became a film presence almost as ubiquitous as big handguns. In the movies Pepsi is the choice of a new generation—that is, of every generation. The suburban kids are drinking Pepsi in *Ferris Bueller's Day Off,* the poor kids are drinking Pepsi in *Stand and Deliver* and in *Lean on Me,* the old folks are drinking Pepsi in *Cocoon: The Return.* Jennifer Beals is drinking Diet Pepsi in *Flashdance,* Kathy Baker is buying Pepsi in *Clean and Sober,* and in *Legal Eagles* Debra Winger keeps her Pepsi cold and blatant in a refrigerator otherwise full of blank containers. Pepsi glides through the Texas of the fifties in *Everybody's All-American,* Pepsi glows among the Texans of today in *True Stories,* Pepsi pops into the cute Manhattan of *Crossing Delancey,* Pepsi drops in on Norman Bates's milieu in *Psycho II* and *Psycho III. In Cobra* a huge neon

Pepsi logo shines right outside Sylvester Stallone's apartment (he kicks some ass, fatally, in its cool light), and in *batteries not included* a huge neon Pepsi logo high above Times Square forms the immediate backdrop to a pivotal scene (in which cuddly metal critters zoom back down to save the day, and frolic in the Pepsi sign's warm light). And PepsiCo, too, has tried to move against its major rival, refusing to place a Pepsi ad on the cassette of *Dirty Dancing* unless Vestron, the video company, would cut every scene that showed a Coca-Cola sign. Vestron passed. (All these movies have happy endings.)

Such "subliminal" tactics are certainly not peculiar to the mighty cola rivals, for they are also used today—aggressively—by every other major advertiser. Indeed, cinematic "product placement" has become so common in the eighties that it now sustains a veritable industry. Formerly, plugging was a marginal (if common) practice in the movie industry, the result of direct bartering between studio and advertiser: MGM (say) would use a box of (say) Rice Krispies in a movie, and for such exposure Kellogg's would keep the studio commissary stocked with cold cereals for a year. Although a serviceable system, it was not wholly pleasing to the advertiser, who had no guarantee that the all-important footage would not be cut before the film's release, or that the product would be set off vividly enough.

In the eighties the plugging process became "rationalized" as dozens of companies formed to broker deals between advertisers and film producers. Such companies, said one "product placement" manager in 1984, "are getting specific guarantees of exposure now. It's no longer a hit-or-miss situation with the producers or prop masters." Usually the advertisers keep the brokers on retainer with an annual fee and are then charged extra for specific "placements." In return for the plug the manufacturer will help defray the ever-rising costs of filmmaking, not only by providing props or costumes but—more important—by mounting a tie-in promotional campaign that will sell the movie in many ads, in thousands of bright aisles, on millions of clean boxes.

Plugs vary in blatancy, and so the amount paid by the advertiser depends on the length and strength of the product's apparition. In 1989, for example, one broker was charging $2,500 to slip a product into the background of a scene and $18,000 for the Plug DeLuxe: "hands-on use" combined with "verbal mention." (Those were very modest prices.) The greatest prize of all, of course, would be the can's or jar's or pack's protracted "use" and flagrant "mention" by the celebrity who gets top billing. "There is no greater promotional value—short of a direct endorsement—than having a major motion picture star use a product in a big budget film," attests a prominent plugster.

The arrangement seems to work wonders for the budgets of all concerned. Advertisers love it: "More and more companies now recognize that movies are an alternative advertising and promotional medium," exults one plugster. And this offer is one that financially pressed filmmakers can't refuse. "Hollywood has changed its tune," crows *Incentive* magazine ("Managing and Marketing Through Motivation"). "Obsessed with the bottom line, studios no longer snub promotion tie-ins—much to the delight of marketers eager to reach the last captive media audience." Beams an executive at Disney, "Add the magic of movies to a promotion, and you can rise above the clutter to get people's attention."

Always in search of the perfectly closed-off setting, advertisers have for decades been eyeing cinema, whose viewers can't flip the page or turn their chairs away. It is this coercive interest in a "captive audience," and not the apparent "magic" of the spectacle itself, that has the marketers "delighting" in the movies—which, now crammed with plugs, offer about as much "magic" as you would find at K-Mart, or at Lord and Taylor. Watching them, there is no way that *you* can "rise above the clutter," because they *are* "the clutter." Consider one of Sylvester Stallone's big hits, *Rocky III* (1982), which plugs, in passing, not only Coca-Cola but Sanyo, Nike, Wheaties, TWA, Marantz and Wurlitzer, *and*—in actual ads within the film, with Rocky as endorser—Nikon, Harley-Davidson, Budweiser, Maserati,

Gatorade, and American Express. Or consider *Over the Top* (1987), a box-office disaster in which Stallone plays a humble trucker who, estranged from his son, finally wins the lad back by taking first prize in a major arm-wrestling tournament. Even before the opening credits are over, the movie has already plugged Budweiser, Colgate shaving cream, and Michelin tires; and Stallone's giant rig has daubed across its side a huge, full-color ad for Brut cologne, which shows up grandly in all the film's big landscape shots. (Brut and the film's producers had a tie-in deal.) The many arm-wrestlers who roar and shudder at the Big Event, moreover, each bear the imprint of some corporate sponsor, so that the movie also plugs not only Hilton Hotels, TWA, Nintendo, Leaseway Corp., Alpine car stereos—and Pepsi—but both Volvo *and* Toyota, both Nike *and* Adidas, as well as Valvoline, Duracell, Soloflex, and Alka-Seltzer. (Both films, of course, have happy endings.)

These are two examples of Hollywood's renewed commercialism at its most grotesque—and there are many others, such as the dismal *Johnny Be Good* (1988), which purports to satirize the commercial rip-off of college sports yet features, straight, an entire commercial for Adidas; or the latest 007 entry, *License to Kill* (1989), in which James Bond ostentatiously smokes Larks—a plug for which Philip Morris paid $350,000; or, *Back to the Future II* (1989), a very loud and manic "romp" that lovingly showcases the futuristic wares of at least a dozen corporate advertisers, including Nike, Black and Decker, Pizza Hut, AT&T, CBS Records, Mattel, and Pepsi; or *The Wizard* (1989), a children's movie that is essentially a long commercial for Nintendo; or the children's movie *MAC & Me* (1988), a shameless *E.T.* knockoff, in which a handicapped child befriends an alien, MAC, who lives on Coca-Cola. Young Eric (cf. *E.T.*'s "Elliott") takes MAC (a Yoda look-alike) to a birthday party at McDonald's and then, fleeing federal agents, escapes into the local Sears (which, in real life, sells clothes that advertise McDonald's, which, of course, sells Coca-Cola). The two then find MAC's family, languishing from lack of Coca-Cola, and nurse them back to life with Coca-

Cola. At the (happy) end(ing) the aliens, wearing McKids T-shirts, become U.S. citizens. (In just over a month, this movie grossed over $34 million.)

Such cartoonish films show product plugging at its most egregious. However, the practice is just as evident throughout movies that do not resemble comic books. Take *Bull Durham* (1988), which begins with the cute rookie pitcher Nuke LaLoosh (Tim Robbins) on the mound, the Pepsi logo not only plain as day on the outfield wall behind him but with its colors reproduced exactly on his uniform. As the film proceeds, it also plugs—repeatedly—Budweiser, Miller, Jim Beam, Oscar Mayer, and a host of Alberto-Culver products. (*Bull Durham* has a happy ending.) Or take *Mr. Mom* (1983), a feeble "issue" comedy about the travails of a green house-husband, which plugs McDonald's, Domino's pizza, Terminix exterminators, Folger's coffee, Miller's Lite Beer, Jack Daniels, Van Camp's chili, Ban Roll-On, Windex—and Tide, Spray 'n' Wash, Borax, Clorox 2, and Downy Fabric Softener. (*Mr. Mom* has a happy ending.) Or, finally, take *Murphy's Romance,* which plugs (aside from Coke) Purina, Heinz Steak Sauce, Wesson Oil, Nike, Huggies, Vanish Toilet Bowl Cleaner, Fuji Film, and Miller Beer. There are also *two* bottles of Ivory Liquid at Sally Field's kitchen sink, and at one point she asks James Garner, "Could I have two Extra-Strength Tylenol and a glass of water, please?" At another point she shouts enticingly, "Campbell's Tomato Soup!"

Such bald intrusions into dialogue have a near-aphrodisiac effect on advertisers, who will therefore pay heavily for such upbeat "verbal mention." Sometimes a character will do a naked pitch, lauding her Hefty Bags or Tender Vittles. Usually, however, the spoken plug comes in the form of a casual request: "Want a Coke?" Elliott asks E.T. (1982). "D'ja pack extra Pampers?" asks Steve Guttenberg in *Three Men and a Baby* (1987). "Gimme a Pepsi Free," Michael J. Fox tells the soda jerk in *Back to the Future*—and since they didn't have that *choice* back in 1955, the jerk's snide retort is really funny. To the advertisers such a soft gag is ideal, especially if it quotes an established piece of copy. For instance, in *Vice Versa,* one of 1987's several comedies about dads and sons exchanging bodies, the apparent child, on line at the school cafeteria, betrays his inner maturity in this way: "I don't suppose you have any Grey Poupon?" (All these movies have happy endings.)

As in the low-budget *Johnny Be Good,* so in the expensive *Wall Street* (1987) the product plug can easily pervade the dialogue even of a film that sermonizes against "greed." "Bring a Molson Light for the kid, will ya?" rasps Martin Sheen, the good working-class dad, sittin' with his stockbroker son in the homey tavern where he hangs out after work—a great moment for Molson Breweries, since it "subliminally" bolsters the product's sweaty nimbus of blue-collar authenticity. And on the other side of the class struggle, Charlie Sheen, the son (who drinks Pepsi), refers at one point to *Fortune* magazine as "the bible," and there is also a shot of *Fortune* showing the movie's charismatic villain, Gordon Gekko, on its cover—a double plug that *Fortune* bought by giving Twentieth Century Fox two free ad pages, worth $94,000, to plug *Wall Street* (which has, basically, a happy albeit somber ending).

Thus movies in the eighties became a huckstering device far pushier even than network TV, whose programs, routinely interrupted by pure ads, need not themselves display the labels quite so often, nor so dramatically (although they do display them). The American movies, however, do have a televisual counterpart: the Brazilian soap opera, a daily spectacle in which the products play so large a role that some multinationals, like Coca-Cola, sign annual contracts with TV Globo to keep their wares incessantly written into the shows' ongoing "stories." Down there in Rio the practice, which the Brazilians call (by the English word) "merchandising," is defended just as Hollywood defends it here—by attesting to its powerful *naturalism.* "Most soap operas are about daily life in which people go shopping and drive cars and drink beer," says TV Globo's head of product placement. "That's why it is so natural." Likewise, a Hollywood plugster argues that because the movies "are pushing more toward reality," plugging is an imperative: "A can that says 'Beer' isn't going to make it anymore." "Product placement," agrees another specialist, "comes out of a creative need—filmmakers are only trying to reflect life."

In a few recent films, the subtle use of products does make the fictive milieu more believable than generic items would. Usually, however, "product placement" does not seem "natural" at all but is, in fact, deliberately *anti-*realistic: its sole purpose is to enhance the product by meticulously placing it within the sort of idealized display that occurs nowhere in real life but everywhere in advertising—which is itself just such display. In the world as advertised, the label or logo always shines forth like the full moon, whereas in our world, where "people go shopping and drive cars and drink beer," the crucial symbols reach us (if at all) with none of that sudden, startling clarity: for the very ubiquitousness of advertising has also, paradoxically, worked to hide it from us. To live the "daily life in which people go shopping" is to be bombarded into numbness; and it is this stupefaction that movie plugs (like advertising proper) have been devised to penetrate.

Sailing through the movies, the multitudinous labels and logos of our daily lives appear (or so the advertisers hope) renewed, their stale solicitations freshened up by the movie's magical, revivifying light—and by the careful steps taken to glamorize them. As such plugs are anti-realistic, so are they also anti-narrative, for the same movie-glow that exalts each product high above the "clutter" of the everyday also lifts it out of, and thereby makes it work against, the movie's story (if any). Even when half-turned toward us, coquettishly, and/or placed in some marginal position, the crucial can or box or bottle tends (as it were) to make a scene. An expert rhetorical missile in the first place, and with its force enhanced a thousandfold by advertising, the product cannot even sneak by without distracting us at least a little, its vivid, pleasant features calling, *"Hey! It's me!"* Thus it is with the bottles of Evian and Budweiser permeating 1989's hit comedy *Parenthood* (which has a long and desperate happy ending).

And when shoved right into the spotlight, the product not only upstages the star but can even stop the narrative. In *Uncle Buck* (1989) John Candy appears sitting on a sofa, holding a big box of Kellogg's Frosted Flakes at his side, as prominent and boldly hued as an armorial shield—and on that sight the camera lingers. At such a moment the loud package wipes out its costars and surroundings, becoming the only thing we notice; and so, in such extreme cases, it is not the movie that plugs the commodity but the commodity that plugs the movie: that is, abruptly stops its flow, breaking in on the story just to make a sale—exactly as TV commercials do. (*Uncle Buck* has a happy ending.)

The rise of "product placement" has, however, damaged movie narrative not only through the shattering effect of individual plugs but, more profoundly, through the fundamental shift of power that the practice has wrought within the movie industry: the transfer of creative authority out of the hands of filmmaking professionals and into the purely quantitative universe of the CEOs. All the scenes, shots, and lines mentioned above overemphasizing Coca-Cola, Pepsi, *Fortune,* Pampers, Tylenol, Grey Poupon, Nike, Molson Light, etc., represent the usurpation, by advertising, of those authorial prerogatives once held by directors and screenwriters, art directors and set designers—and by studio heads, who at least cared (with widely varying results) about how their films were put together, whereas the managers now in charge are thinking only of their annual reports. "Hollywood has changed," says Edward Meyer of ad agency Saatchi & Saatchi DFS Compton. "Unlike the old days, the bankers and MBAs are calling the shots, and producers have discovered that product placements and tie-in promotions can help cut the movies' production and advertising costs."

Thus the basic decisions of filmmaking are now often made, indirectly, by the advertisers, who are focused not on a movie's narrative integrity but *only* on its viability as a means of pushing products. Take the case of costume designers, who have often, in the eighties, been displaced by "promo-costuming"—an arrangement that, reports *Premiere* magazine, either boosts the wares of name designers (Oscar de la Renta did *Bright Lights, Big*

City, Giorgio Armani did *The Untouchables*) or, more often, "involves manufacturers of such branded staples as jeans and sneakers, which have visible logos that make them much easier to promote." In 1987, for example, it was Adidas that shod and clad many of the characters in "some sixty movies, including *Beverly Hills Cop II, The Running Man, Superman IV,* and *Throw Momma from the Train.*" (All six movies named above have happy endings.)

The plugging process is as thorough and exacting as the work of those professionals whose work it has long since superseded. The preproduction effort is exhaustive: "Friendly producers send scripts to [Associated Film Promotions] weeks and even months before filming starts, and the company analyzes them scene by scene to see if it can place a product—or advertising material, a billboard perhaps—on, under or behind the stars." Such agencies "review some 400 film scripts a year looking for promotional opportunities for current or potential clients," and while those clients may not be as idealistic about movies as, say, David O. Selznick, they are just as dictatorial: "We choose projects where we have maximum control," says one plugster. "We break a film down and tell the producers exactly where we want to see our clients' brands."

What the advertisers want, finally, is unqualified display. To them, a drama's most exhilarating moments are the least dramatic, the most stunningly promotional, which is why one product placement firm decided to pass on *Big Business* (1988), whose producer, reports the *Wall Street Journal,* "refused to alter the characters' dialogue to plug Eastern Airlines' flights through Atlanta." As the would-be broker of the tie-in put it, "The creative forces conflicted with our marketing goals, and we backed out." (*Big Business,* it should be added, plugs plenty of other companies, and also has a happy ending.) That the proposed change in dialogue would have set up an abysmal moment (for anyone other than Eastern Airlines) mattered not at all either to the plugster or his client, because to such entities the plug itself is all that counts—more than a movie's quality, of course, but sometimes even more than its success: "I'd rather be associated with a hit," remarks the head of tie-ins for Miller Brewing Company, "but ultimately it doesn't make a big difference. A movie is just a theme."

Such subordination of the movie is essential to the plugging process, which assumes that the movie will in no way contradict—will, indeed, do nothing but enhance—the product's costly, all-important aura. The plug, in other words, must not just foreground but flatter the crucial name or image: that is, brightly reaffirm the product's advertising. When its brokers argue that plugging is an aid to greater "realism," they are implying that "reality" is only where the products mean just what their advertising says they mean: "power" or "safety" or "old-fashioned goodness"—and nothing else. Thus PepsiCo, for example, would have made no tie-in deals for Mike Figgis's *Stormy Monday* (Great Britain, 1988), in which a giant Pepsi bottle symbolizes, rather than "the choice of a new generation," the invasion of Newcastle by a shady American tycoon allied with a horde of unctuous Thatcherites.

Now and then in the eighties an American movie has invoked products critically, or at least in a way that is poetically telling and not just promotional. The eerie satire *Heathers* (1988) credibly (and—aptly—without obtrusive plugging) evokes an affluent Midwestern suburb, a cold, consumeristic Eden where the most popular girls in the local high school are, as the heroine puts it acidly, "a bunch of Swatch dogs and Diet Coke–heads." And in Garry Marshall's *Nothing in Common* (1986), a surprisingly grim and moving (if uneven) comedy about a successful young adman (Tom Hanks) and his dying scoundrel of a father (Jackie Gleason), the same product appears in two shots—not to sell it but as both a chilling metaphysical implication and a visual hint that father and son, despite their mutual loathing and antithetical "life-styles," are fundamentally alike. Placed casually in each man's kitchen—the one bare and slovenly, the other tidy and state-of-the-art—is a box of the same cereal, Life, the mock-gaiety of the name's Crayola colors suggesting in this context something more troubling than an easy breakfast. (These films do not have happy endings.)

Such dark suggestiveness, however, is precisely what the advertisers do not want; and so they, or their brokers, will back away from any movie that might somehow cast a shadow on their advertising. Of course, they will avoid anything that might, they fear, gross people out. For instance, it could have been Milk Duds, and not Reese's Pieces, that Elliott uses to lure E.T. out of hiding, but the broker had his qualms: "In the script we saw, we thought [E.T.] would be unappetizing." Similarly, in 1985 a manager at General Foods thus predicted Kool-Aid's impending screen career: "We may place it in as many as six movies, but [each] movie must be just right. We can't turn up in something like *The Texas Chainsaw Massacre.*" As with gore, so is it often (not always) with villainy: "[We] have a rule of thumb," remarked a Mercedes-Benz official in 1982, "that the bad guy never drives a Mercedes." And of course, there are certain behaviors that must never seem to be condoned by, much less aligned with, the upstanding label: Anheuser-Busch refused to place Budweiser anywhere in *Making Love* (1982), a restrained tale of homosexual seduction.

Such fretting is understandable. Advertisers do not want their sweets made nauseating by association, their elegant cars to symbolize the criminal mind, their manly beers to glint suspiciously. Since such preservation is their main concern, however, advertisers are far too timid, and too trivially absorbed, to be allowed to wield "creative" influence on the movies. And yet, precisely because of their conservatism, their sway extends far beyond an excessive interest in this running shoe or that hood ornament. For advertisers are obsessed not just with selling their own specific images but with universalizing the whole hermetic ambience for selling itself: the pseudo-festive, mildly jolting, ultimately tranquilizing atmosphere of TV and its bright epiphenomena, the theme park and the shopping mall.

END OF STORY: THE MOVIE

Even if, armed with some marvelous zapping gizmo, you could sit and blast away every obvious product as it passed through the frame or glowed in close-up, today's Hollywood movie would still seem like an ad. This is in part because the movies tend now to look and sound a lot like TV commercials, as if the major film schools were teaching not (say) the best movies out of Warner Brothers but the latest campaign by the Saatchi brothers. Like ads, movies each tend now to have a perfectly coordinated *total look,* as if they'd been designed rather than directed—a tendency so marked in some cases that a movie and some well-known ad can hardly be distinguished. Thus *The Color Purple* (1985), with its lush score, hazy golden images, and long climactic round of teary hugs, leaves you thinking not that you should read the novel but that you really ought to call your mother ("Reach out . . ."), while the parodic *Raising Arizona* (1987) uses precisely the same wide-angle distortion and hyped-up, deadpan acting that Joel Sedelmaier used in his famous ads for Federal Express ("When it abso*lute*ly, posi*tive*ly . . ."), while *Top Gun* (1986), the blockbuster salute to Navy fliers, has action sequences identical to those spectacular commercials that allured the young with "It's Not Just a Job—It's an Adventure!" or (yes!) "Be All You Can Be!"—expert flashes of recruitment propaganda that were probably well known to the film's director, Tony Scott, who came to the movie business as a famed director of TV ads, most notably for Diet Pepsi. (These three movies leave you feeling good.)

Such crossovers are the usual thing in today's media industry, many of whose filmmakers learned their craft (and continue) in the world of advertising. Around the turn of the decade a stellar group of such professionals migrated from the ad shops of London to the studios of Hollywood, where they helped alter modern cinema. Like brother Tony (who also directed, in 1987, the repetitious *Beverly Hills Cop II*), Ridley Scott is a prolific admaker, most notably for Chanel, W. R. Grace, and Apple Computer, and also *auteur* of the inspired and nauseating *Alien* (1979), the brilliant *Blade Runner* (1982), then a thriller designed, as if by computer, to stroke lonely women, *Someone to Watch over Me* (1987), and finally the unforgivable *Black Rain* (1989). Ad-maker Hugh Hudson has turned out such gorgeous, empty films as *Chariots of Fire* (1981) and *Greystoke: The Legend of Tarzan, Lord of the Apes* (1984). Having made hundreds of short ads, Adrian Lyne came and made such longer ones as *Flashdance* (1983) and *9½ Weeks* (1986), as well as the gynophobic crowd-pleaser *Fatal Attraction* (1987). Alan Parker, whose films include *Midnight Express* (1978), *Fame* (1980), and *Mississippi Burning* (1988), is easily the most successful of the British émigrés because the most adept at stirring our worst impulses. And many American ad-makers have also become filmmakers, including Stan Dragoti, director of the "I Love New York" ads as well as the plug-ridden *Mr. Mom*; Howard Zieff, director of Alka-Seltzer's "Spicy Meatball" ad and the incoherent *Private Benjamin* (1980); Joe Pytka, director of numerous Pepsi ads and the deadly racetrack comedy *Let It Ride* (1989). (The ending of *Alien* is slightly ambiguous, the ending of *9½ Weeks* a little melancholy.)

Meanwhile, as more and more admen direct the films, more and more filmmakers are directing ads—in order to keep working, now that the huge costs of moviemaking have made it near-impossible to get a project going. Pressed for opportunities, directors no longer can afford to scorn the sixty-second pitch: "There *was* a stigma in the past," observed, in 1988, the head of the Association of Independent Commercial Producers. "There was a time when even actors wouldn't do commercials. The feeling was it was not a great art form." That "feeling" is passé, if not extinct, now that Robert Altman, Martin Scorsese (Armani), Federico Fellini, Jean-Luc Godard, Francis Coppola (Fuji), John Frankenheimer, John Badham, Tony Bill (Bud Light), John Schlesinger, David Lynch, Penny Marshall (Revlon), David Steinberg, Stephen Frears, and Errol Morris (Ford), among others, are making ads. (Leftist director Haskell Wexler has been doing commercials since the sixties.) Cinematographers, too, have turned to advertising: Sven Nykvist, Nestor Almendros, Gordon Willis, Eric Saarinen, Vilmos Zsigmond, among others. And filmmakers have even been doing celebrity turns in ads: Richard Donner in several ads for Amaretto di Saronno; Spike Lee in an ad for the Gap, and in a commercial (which he also directed) for Nike (which he also plugs through-out his movies); Bernardo Bertolucci and George Lucas in print ads for Pioneer.

If movies now look like ads, then, the transformation may owe something to this exchange of personnel—which delights the powers of advertising, who want their ads to look like movies (so that the restless TV-viewer won't zap them). "Advertisers and agencies want their commercials designed with the look of the hottest features," says one ad producer. The crossover has helped erase the old distinctions between movies and commercials: "The two disciplines—feature films and commercial films—have blended together to the point now where it's just filmmaking," says a senior vice-president at DDB Needham, Chicago. Through this convergence it might seem that, theoretically, each "discipline" would somehow benefit the other; but in the era of the VCR it is advertising that has affected cinema, not the other way around. Now that most movies are produced with an eye toward their eventual re-release on videocassette, and now that TV, moreover, has induced a universal taste for its own pace and tone, the new "filmmaking" takes its lead primarily from those who create the small screen's most hypnotic images. "There's not a good filmmaker alive who doesn't look to us for inspiration," claimed Bob Giraldi, director of ad spots for GE, Sperry Rand, McDonald's, and many other corporations, in 1984.

Just as the product plug halts or weakens the movie narrative, so has this general drift toward ad technique reduced, drastically, the movies' narrative potential: for cinematic narrative works, first of all, through a range of visual conventions or devices, and the recent rise of ad technique has all but wiped out that earlier diversity, coarsening a various and nuanced prior form into a poundingly hypnotic instrument—a mere *stimulus* (and an ugly one, at that).

There is, first of all, the sheer—and all-important—difference in scale. "This is just like doing a small feature," Ridley Scott assured his crew, in 1984, on the set of a Pepsi ad. "My goal" as an ad director, Howard Zieff proclaimed in 1989, "was to make little movies." "I see commercials as short films," Adrian Lyne told *Advertising Age* in 1985. But to suggest that commercials are just like movies, only smaller (both in space and time), is to negate the crucial ground of cinematic art: an expansive visual field, broad enough to imply a world beyond, behind, more varied than the glamorous item in midframe. TV is, to say the least, different. Watching *The Last Emperor* on your Sony is like trying to survey the Sistine Chapel ceiling by peeping at it through a toilet paper roll. TV, however, has reduced the movies not just by putting blinders on the viewers of wide-screen epics but by establishing a compositional norm of close-ups, two-shots, and other setups whereby the action is (just as in advertising) repetitiously *foregrounded.*

Such is now the norm of cinema. Today there are few scenes shot in deep focus, as in Renoir and Welles, *Vertigo* and *The Godfather Part II*, or, for that matter, in *Night of the Living Dead.* Likewise, we rarely see the kind of panoramic composition that allows a generous impression of quasi-global simultaneity, as (most elaborately) in the movies of Robert Altman and Jacques Tati, but that also, more subtly, enriches the frame in most great movies, whose makers have offered *pictures* comprising pleasurable "touches," legible detail, moving tableaux that often (as Bazin argued) give their viewers some choice, and require some (often minimal) interpretive attention. Only now and then, and in films that don't come out of Hollywood—Terry Gilliam's *Brazil* (1985), Stanley Kubrick's *Full Metal Jacket* (1987)—do we perceive such exhilarating fullness. By contrast, today's Hollywood movie works without, or against, the potential depth and latitude of cinema, in favor of that systematic overemphasis deployed in advertising (and all other propaganda). Each shot presents a content closed and unified, like a fist, and makes the point right in your face: big gun, big car, nice ass, full moon, a chase (great shoes!), big crash (blood, glass), a lobby (doorman), sarcasm, drinks, a tonguey, pugilistic kiss (nice sheets!), and so on.

Thus today's movie not only foregrounds but serializes: for, just as TV's narrowness has superannuated deep focus and the

movies' (sometime) lateral complexity, so has the speedy pace of
TV's ads superannuated most of cinema's earlier transitional devices. As John Frankenheimer (*The Manchurian Candidate,* Fiat,
AT&T) told *Advertising Age* in 1989, "No longer do films use the
fade to black and the slow dissolve the way they used to." This
laconic, and correct, observation hints at a grievous cinematic
loss, because the fade and the dissolve are no quaint old-movie
mannerisms like the wipes that George Lucas used "nostalgically" in *Star Wars.* Rather, the dissolve is a succinct, and often
beautiful, means of conveying the passage of time, or the onset
of a memory; to drop it from the movies would be (although it
has no exact linguistic counterpart) somewhat like dropping the
past tense from verbal language. The fade to black works like a
curtain dropped to cover some event too painful and/or intimate
for exhibition, or as a means of conveying loss of consciousness;
or as a somber sort of visual cadence, a way of saying, "It's over:
now consider what you've seen." In today's ad-saturated "filmmaking" these devices seem too slow and (in different ways) too
suggestive of mortality for the movies' bright mall-atmosphere,
and so they have been dumped in favor of that most basic of
connectives, the simple cut, whose overuse has helped transform
the movies into adlike serial displays.

Such displays show us nothing, not only because each image
in the series is as unambiguous as a brand-new belt but because
that serial rush itself is mesmerizing, and so it blinds us to the
flashing items it comprises. Large, stark, and fast, the mere contrast stuns us pleasantly—a response that is (as it were) subvisual,
as the ad-makers know very well. Thus, both marketing and
advertising always aim directly at the lowest levels of the mass
(i.e., your) brain, seeking a reaction that is at once "positive,"
unconscious, and immediate. Although the pillars of the ad world
still use the word "persuasion" to (mis)represent their business,
the whole selling project now depends on moves that are less
rhetorical than neurological: "Color goes immediately to the
psyche and can be a direct sales stimulus," says one typical package designer. Such blithe (and simplistic) Pavlovianism is wholly

characteristic of the ad-makers and marketers, who like it when we "respond" without even knowing it, much less knowing why. Thus BBDO's Philip Dusenberry claims to have learned (from making Pepsi ads) "that it wasn't important that the viewer read every scene—just that they get the impact of the message."

That last remark could just as easily apply to the movies, which now, like advertising, rely heavily, if not exclusively, on techniques that work directly on the nervous system. Of course, the movies have always used gratuitous tricks to keep viewers riveted: pointless close-ups of a baby's smile to get the women cooing, martial music to tense up the men, sad violins to get the whole house sniffling. Indeed, some of cinema's basic rhetorical devices, it could be argued, are inherently non-narrative, subvisual: cross-cutting for suspense, say, or the weepy reaction shot (which moves the viewers to weep). The point, however, is not that such tricks are new but that they now are all-important—for their power has been fantastically augmented by computer science, Dolby sound, great strides forward in the art of mock mayhem, and other technological advances. Whereas they once served, by and large, as adjuncts or enhancements to the visual narrative, such grabbers have now replaced the narrative, with irresistible nonvisual effects.

Music, for example, has long been overused by Hollywood, as James Agee noted in 1945. Watching John Huston's war documentary *San Pietro,* which he admired immensely, Agee found it "as infuriating to have to fight off the emotional sales pressure of the Mormon Choir as it would be if all the honored watches and nasal aphrodisiacs insisted on marketing themselves against a Toscanini broadcast." At its pushiest, movie music "weakens the emotional imagination both of maker and onlooker, and makes it virtually impossible to communicate or receive ideas. It sells too cheaply and far too sensually all the things it is the business of the screen itself to present."

Watching the movies that Agee found overscored, most now would probably agree with him, since the aesthetic errors of the past are easy to laugh at decades later. What may be less obvious today is the persistent relevance of Agee's argument, for the movies have, as visual events, been largely devastated by their "music"—a vast and irresistible barrage of synthesized sound, a hyperrhythmic full-body stimulus far more effective, and a whole lot louder, than the old choral yawpings or symphonic sweeps that now seem so corny. Starting somewhere out and back there to the left, the "music" thrums and zooms and zips and jumps and jangles right on through you, clearing out your head with such efficiency that not only is it "impossible to receive ideas," but the whole movie, once over, seems to have gone in one ear and out the other—except that it's not just your head that's functioned as a throughway. Before it leaves, the "music" ripples lightly over every vital organ, an inhuman massage whereby that sound works not just subvisually but even subaurally, doing a gigantic hum job on you, like a vibrating bed.

It is the Dolby system, sometimes enhanced by George Lucas's system THX, that gives the music such prostrating force. Even on cassette, however, the music works an anti-visual effect (just as it does throughout TV's shows and ads), imposing a certain mood (upbeat) on images that are, per se, so mundane that they would bore or even depress you if the music weren't there telling you to dance. In *St. Elmo's Fire* (1985) Emilio Estevez drives off in a car, and the music makes it sound as if he'd just won gold at the Olympics. At the end of *Private Benjamin* Goldie Hawn walks down a lonely road, and the score exults as if she were attending her own coronation. In movie after movie there's some guy ambling up a driveway or waiting for the bus, and the music has our bodies jerking pointlessly in sympathetic ecstasy. And there are many, many times when the music orders you not just to boogie but to boogie on down Memory Lane, as in *True Believer* (1988), wherein at one point James Woods goes and sits down in the other room as Jimi Hendrix breaks into "All Along the Watchtower"—a typically blinding moment, hiding the void before us with a song that has us dancing through the past. (Those three movies have happy endings.)

More and more, the movies' very images are also—paradoxically—nonvisual, since, like the music, they try to force our interest, or reaction, through a visceral jolt that stuns the mind and shuts the eyes. Some of the movies' latest grabbers are very old, like the gooey close-up of some smiling baby ("Awwww!"), a device no less sickening in *Ghostbusters II* (1989) than it was in *Bachelor Daddy* (1941). Generally, however, the grabbers are both more technologically sophisticated and (a lot) more violent than those sentimental moments—and far more commonplace, now that movie narrative has been supplanted by such blinding jabs. (Of course, *Ghostbusters II* ends happily.)

As the special effects have, since *Star Wars,* become more mind-blowing and yet more believable, they have also advanced in their importance to the spectacle, and have changed in tone. First of all, the effects, in many instances, now *are* the movie, whether it's *Indiana Jones and the Last Crusade* or *Nightmare on Elm Street 3*, films you can sleep through for twenty minutes without then having to ask, "What did I miss?" And as the effects have become the whole show, they have ceased to represent some ambiguous looming force, uncanny or apocalyptic—as in the first *King Kong, The Day the Earth Stood Still,* or *2001: A Space Odyssey*—and have instead become the tools for a light-show that both stimulates and reassures, like fireworks on the Fourth.

Whereas the effects, in other words, were once used, by and large, to fake some scary Threat to All Humanity, they now routinely fake, in one way or another, someone's annihilation—and it is *good.* The wipeout might be violent, as at the end of *Raiders of the Lost Ark* (1981), the Nazis melted down or shriveled up by the wrathful ark light, or as in the horror movies where (say) Jason burns, zaps, and mangles several teens, until some teen then zaps or burns or mangles Jason. Whether the killing force is righteous or demonic, the spectacle of its/his/her destructiveness/destruction invites your rapt gaze of wondering assent—just like those movies that present the wipeout as a sweet translation into outer space (i.e., Heaven): *E.T., Close Encounters of the Third Kind, Cocoon, Cocoon: The Return*—films whose (grateful) characters finally disappear into the all-important light show, just like the films themselves.

For all their visual sophistication, these effects are meant to move us beyond, or back from, visual experience, either by having us nearly *feel* those razors rake that throat, or having us *feel* as if we were dissolving in a celestial bath of light. The same kind of "experience"—anti-visual, non-narrative—is commonplace even in films that have no supernatural/"alien" component. In the eighties, the car chase, for instance, became the movie's definitive story substitute, offering both the illusion of dreamlike forward speed and the gratifying sight/sound/feeling of machinery bucking, squealing, even blowing up—elements that have become so frequent that to list them here would fill a page, since they constitute whole sections not only of the cop films *(The Presidio, Cobra, Lethal Weapon 1/2, Beverly Hills Cop I/II, Red Heat)* but also of many comedies, even those that didn't need such filler *(Midnight Run, The Blues Brothers, Throw Momma from the Train).* The pleasure here is far less visual than physically empathic—the centrifugal tug, that pleasing *crash!*: mock thrills that have only gotten punchier and more elaborate as the car stuff has become all too familiar. Likewise, screen violence in general, a relentless story substitute, has become both commonplace and often horribly sadistic. (The movies named in the above two paragraphs all have happy endings.)

The empathic function of today's screen violence has changed the character of movie heroics. In *Bullitt* (1968) and *The French Connection* (1971), in *The Searchers* (1956) and in the movies of Sam Peckinpah, the violence was, however graphic, muted by a deep ambivalence that shadowed even the most righteous-seeming acts of vengeance, and that therefore suppressed the (male) viewer's urge to join in kicking. Now, by contrast, screen violence primarily invites the viewer—man or woman—to enjoy the *feel* of killing, beating, mutilating. This is most obvious in the slasher films, in which the camera takes the stalking murderer's point of view, but the same empathic project goes on throughout the genres. There is no point to Rambo's long climactic rage, or Cobra's, or Chuck Norris's, other than its open invitation to *become him* at that moment—to ape that sneer of hate, to feel the way it feels to stand there tensed up with the Uzi. The hero's

inner kinship with the villain used to seem uncanny, as in Hitchcock's and Fritz Lang's movies, and in Clint Eastwood's excellent
Tightrope (1984)—whereas Stallone's Cobra gets a charge out of
being *exactly* like the psychopaths he chases, just as we are meant
to feel *exactly* like him.

Nor is it just the overt paeans to machismo that thus incite us
but also films that seem politically unlike, say, *Rambo III*. Midway
through *The Accused* (1988) gang-rape victim Jodie Foster meets,
in a record store, one of the men who had watched and cheered
the crime, and who now recalls it. Jeering hatefully, he trails her
out to the parking lot, where she gets into her car and—protrac-
tedly—keeps backing up and plowing full-speed into the side of
his truck (crunch! . . . *crunch!*), with him sitting in it. The moment
puts us sweetly in the driver's seat and therefore seems improper
in a movie that otherwise so forcefully decries the spectatorial act
of sitting by and urging pain on others—a vicarious attack that
is, of course, commonly directed against women, but that is not
redeemed when the attacker is a woman and the victim is a man
(or another woman, as in those pseudo-feminist assaults of 1988,
Working Girl and *Dangerous Liaisons*).

And then there's *Mississippi Burning* (1988). Hailed, by some,
for having based its plot on a key event in the history of the
civil-rights movement, it actually has no plot, nor is it even
slightly faithful to that history. The movie is, in fact, nothing
more than one long grabber. After an hour of watching white
trash inflict atrocities on helpless blacks (and a nice white
woman), we watch the kick-ass Gene Hackman argue hotly with
his FBI superior, the tight-assed Willem Dafoe, who from the
outset has rebutted Hackman's vigilantist urgings with the boring
creed of rules-and-regulations. They fight at length (shouts,
punches)—and then, suddenly, Dafoe just up and *changes:* "New
rules. We nail 'em any way we can. Even your way." This absolute reversal, although absurd in terms of character, makes sense
rhetorically, since it's now time to have the three of us (audience,
Dafoe, Hackman) all fold into Hackman, who is thereby freed
to punish all those ugly rednecks in the ugliest of ways: crushing

their testicles, threatening them with castration, maiming them with razor blades, and otherwise permitting "us" to act, through him, just like the Klansmen we presumably detest, while the blacks remain helpless throughout. (*Mississippi Burning* has a happy ending.)

Over and over, conventional narrative requirements are broken down by the imperative of violence—which need not only be inflicted by "us," through the movie's hero, but which is just as often used against us, by the movie's anti-hero: for what matters above all, it seems, is that we feel the stimulus. Thus we are victimized by the "sight" of the vampires in *The Lost Boys* (1987) biting off bright-red gobbets of their victims' heads ("Ow!"), or by the sound of Freddy Krueger's razor-nails scraping metal just like fingernails raked across a blackboard, or by the sight/sound of the good guy having his fingers broken (*Blade Runner, Blue Thunder*) or receiving a ballistic kick between the legs (*Shoot the Moon, Black Moon Rising*). Likewise, the movies now, more than ever, shock us with the old (nonvisual) trick of going "Boo!", a crude startler once used mainly in horror films (and sparingly at that) but now recurring in thriller after thriller (often heightened by the deep "*lub*-dub-*lub*-dub" that simulates your fearful heartbeart).

The primacy of stimulation has, in short, made the movies more and more cartoonlike. In the cartoon world, nothing stands between the wish to see/feel violence and the enactment of that violence: no demands of plot or character, no physical limitations (space, gravity), no mortality. Ingeniously, and with cruel wit, the cartoon presents a universe wherein the predatory are, over and over, punished for their appetite by the very trees and doors and crockery. Full of rage and purpose, those victim/predators get nowhere and yet never die, pushing on forever, despite the anvils landing on their heads, the steamrollers flattening their bodies out like massive pancakes, the cannonballs zooming down their throats—torments at once severe and harmless, and that occur exclusively because we want to see them happen.

It is not just *Batman* and *Who Framed Roger Rabbit* that invoke the cartoon but all those movies that present a universe wherein the stimulus is gross, never-ending, and immediate, the human "characters" appearing just as easily tormentable, as cruel themselves, and yet (usually) as indestructible as Wile E. Coyote or Yosemite Sam. Thus *Lethal Weapon 2*, which begins with the old Looney Tunes theme playing over the familiar Warners logo, includes several scenes in which Mel Gibson casually brutalizes Joe Pesci—squeezing his badly injured nose, for instance. And thus in *Dragnet*, as a car runs over Dan Ackroyd's feet, there is a sound as of the crushing of a bag of walnuts, and Ackroyd pales and winces. And thus in *The Witches of Eastwick* (1987), Veronica Cartwright keeps painfully vomiting gallons of cherry pits (until her husband finally kills her). And thus Jason, although dead, keeps coming back to life, like Freddy Krueger, like Michael Myers—and (for that matter) like the dead ballplayers in *Field of Dreams*, like the vanished old folks in *Cocoon: The Return*, like the dead E.T., and so on, all of them coming back forever and ever—because the cartoon always has a happy ending.

WHEN YOU WISH UPON A STAR

The convergence of the movies with both cartoons and ads makes sense, because the ad and the cartoon each present a fantasy of perfect wish fulfillment: that is, a wish fulfillment that seems both immediate and absolute, arising, on the one hand, from a purchase (which will make life perfect *now*) or, on the other hand, from the animated spectacle itself (in which the universe appears responsive to your wishes). This has been compounded in the movies, which now purvey a wish fulfillment fantasy as extreme as, and far more compelling than, any Coke spot or Tom and Jerry free-for-all.

Although as old as Hollywood itself, the fantasy has, since the late seventies, changed in several crucial ways. First of all, the element of wish fulfillment no longer recurs primarily in a last-minute payoff, obviously tacked on, as it did in so many movies of the past—most notably Hitchcock's *Suspicion* and Frank

Capra's *Meet John Doe* (both 1941)—where troubling implications would then have to be negated through some sudden, terminal change of heart or unexpected gift of money. This kind of
hasty ending is still used today, although the "problems" dramatized, and then dismissed, are generally much slighter than they
used to be, and the "solutions" are even more perfunctory. In
St. Elmo's Fire, for instance, the well-dressed Ally Sheedy is loved
equally by the hoglike Judd Nelson and the poetic Andrew
McCarthy—a triangle that permits much petty "suffering" by all
three, and that dissolves at the end, when Sheedy tells the guys,
"I think I have to be by myself for a while," adding, "I hope we
can still be friends," and—hey, no problem! The guys just grin
and shrug and mumble, "Sure!"

Often, however, today's cinematic wish fulfillment comes not
in an abrupt and gratuitous final moment, as if the writer(s) didn't
know what else to do, but as an obviously calculated piling up of
surplus triumphs—triumph upon triumph upon triumph—not as
a quick way to end the film, in other words, but as its very
purpose. Many movies now purvey such surplus wish fulfillment,
film after film repeatedly screaming: "You *can* have it all!" Thus
in *Hoosiers* (1986), the small-town basketball team, coached by
newcomer Gene Hackman (whom the townsfolk don't much like
at first), starts winning games, and then keeps winning, and wins
and wins and wins and wins until the movie finally ends—on a
photo-portrait of the winning team, as Hackman's voice-over
quavers tenderly, "I love you guys!" And thus in *3 O'Clock High*
(1987), high-school student Casey Siemaszko manages to beat up
the towering near-homicidal nut who had vowed to pulverize
him, while the whole student body cheers, and cheers again as
his girlfriend kisses him adoringly, and then the next day all the
kids (the nut, too!) show up with lots of money (to bail Casey out,
since he'd robbed the school store to buy the bully off), and then
the winner's tall and dishy English teacher—in front of everyone—rewards the winner further with a long, hot, womanly kiss:
"Un-buh-*leev*-a-bull!" breathes an admiring teen.

The same surplus wish fulfillment occurs in movies that seem

more respectable. In *sex, lies, and videotape* (1989) Andie Mac-
Dowell is, although well-off and gorgeous, an unhappy person:
a bored housewife, racked by anxieties, sexually repressed, and
married to an evil yuppie lawyer who (she doesn't know this yet)
is screwing her own sister, a hostile tart who does it sheerly out
of sibling rivalry. Into this situation floats James Spader, an old
college pal of the husband's and now a wandering semi-bohemian
who, impotent, spends all his time either videotaping the sexual
confessions of female acquaintances or, we gather, masturbating
before one tape or another. Spader befriends MacDowell, who
feels drawn to the pale, vague onanist, although she disapproves
of his hobby.

Much talk ensues, and eventually MacDowell finds, under her
own bed, her sister's earring. Irate, she rushes off to Spader's
house and demands that he now videotape *her* confessions—in
the midst of which she starts interrogating *him*. Suddenly bold,
certain, and desirous, she initiates lovemaking and cures his impotence. Spader, redeemed, wrecks his tapes and camera. Mac-
Dowell swiftly leaves her husband and gets herself a job (and a
new car). With cool forgiveness she then brings a rhododendron
to her sister, who, having hated MacDowell's guts throughout
the movie, now sheepishly adores her. The husband, meanwhile,
gets fired, as if by God Himself. At the end MacDowell and
Spader make a calm and handsome couple—like Ben and Elaine
at the end of *The Graduate,* but without the irony.

Each of these movies has the feel of narrative only for as long
as it takes to set up the basic situation, and then it starts to seem
less like a story than a daydream. The fantasy contains only the
(many) victories of the attractive viewer surrogate within the
film—and that fantastic element is not just paramount within
the movie but, finally, its whole content. In this way film narrative
has been displaced by the pseudo-narrative of advertising, whose
idealizing and disjointed images cannot constitute a story, no
matter how much the ad world has, in the eighties, tried to exalt
such images to narrative status. Boosting a number of new ad
spreads (for Calvin Klein, Ralph Lauren, and others) in the fash-

ion magazines, *Advertising Age* thus concluded: "In essence, they tell a story, and the story is, buy these clothes and create your own highly personal scenario."

There was, of course, no narrative of any kind discernible in those series, whose disparate images sustained no plot, presented no ongoing characters. Within each spread the shots shared nothing but the line of goods they were promoting and that implicit come-on: "Create your own highly personal scenario." From any conventional standpoint that phrase is a very dubious one: a "creation" derived solely from Ralph Lauren's clothes and ad suggestions can be neither "your own" nor "highly personal." "Scenario" itself seems strikingly misused, since any screenplay based on such a concept ("Buy these clothes and look like this") should leave us cold—as other people's daydreams tend to do.

The ad's reference to "your scenario," however, and those solipsistic cinematic "stories" point us toward a crucial change in the nature of the movies' wish fulfillment fantasy. Formerly the movie was (like many ads before the seventies) a sort of exit visa from the working world, proffering an "escape" through empathy with some intrepid hero/heroine, who has a lofty job to do in some exotic or aristocratic setting. By contrast, today's movies tend to extol not the lucky, plucky character who marries up or wins a war but the star who plays that character—and who shines as the true object of your empathy, sheerly because s/he is the center of attention. The change is evident in all those closing-credit sequences that feature outtakes of the stars euphorically kidding on the set, and in those numerous sequences of teen heroes lip-synching famous hits and posturing like rock stars before imaginary crowds of loving fans, and in the frequent "comic" bit that has a character do the rapturous sportscast commentary on his own athletic horseplay, also performed before imaginary cheering crowds. In short, *feeling warmly watched by everyone* now seems a sweeter fantasy than the fictitious heroisms of past cinema, in which the star's fame helped to glamorize the story—whereas celebrity now is the story, just as in the ads.

Reinforcing the surplus wish fulfillment, this foregrounding of celebrity has also helped erode film narrative, for all that's needed now (aside from the grabbers) is a series of setups that convey the feel of being watched by an admiring audience. Thus *Hoosiers* is filled in with all those slo-mo sequences of deft, victorious athletics, as in an ad for *Sports Illustrated,* just like the *Rocky* films, like each *Karate Kid*—or like *Fame* (1980), *Flashdance* (1983), *Footloose* (1984), *White Nights* (1985), *Tap* (1989), and other storyless montages of stars boogying. Likewise, the movie is often a comedian's plotless metaperformance, like *Good Morning, Vietnam* (1987), which mainly shows us Robin Williams doing shtick for audience after audience, or like *Beverly Hills Cop II* (1987) and *The Golden Child* (1986), in both of which Eddie Murphy is . . . just Eddie Murphy, cracking wise in between, and during, the bloody and/or dazzling parts—just like Bill Murray as a Ghostbuster and in *Scrooged* (1988). (All end happily.)

Even if not an athlete or a comic, the star tends, through his/her new centrality, to obviate any self-sufficient narrative context. Sitting through one of his/her vehicles, you can almost hear the way some agent pitched it years before—because the pitch is all you see: "Fonda's this floozy. She wakes up next to a dead guy"—and that's it for *The Morning After* (1986), which begins with Fonda, playing a floozy, waking up next to a dead guy, and which then . . . goes on for a while, with Fonda looking *real* in every shot, until it all concludes with some thin business too inane to remember. Likewise: "Jimmy Woods is this lawyer from the sixties—with a ponytail? *Now* he's defending *pushers!* Uh . . ." And that's about the whole of *True Believer* (1988), in which nothing memorable occurs (although the ponytail is great!) until the overcomplicated climax, which is as credible as it is entertaining.

The glamorization of stardom has required that celebrity be not only relentlessly foregrounded but invidiously set off, through systematic hostile contrast with the numerous jerks, creeps, dweebs, dorks, dips, freaks, shmucks, bitches, bastards, phoneys, fags, and sleazeballs that now surround the star. The belittlement of everyone except the central character is a strategy that goes way, way back in the narrative tradition, occurring in, say, *Pride and Prejudice* as well as in innumerable texts that are a lot less readable today (and that do it far less artfully than Jane Austen did). It is not that this cheap trick is peculiar to today's movies, but that, in the movies, the trick is incessant, automatic, and extreme—each putz or jackass serving only, through his/her perfect worthlessness, to make the star look, and us feel, cooler.

Thus the townsfolk who at first oppose Gene Hackman are, of course, a bunch of funny-looking hicks, just as Casey Siemaszko is, of course, surrounded by a mob of nerds and brats and fatsoes (even his friends), just as Andie MacDowell's randy, lying husband and mean sister are, of course, depicted as pure scum (although the sister is redeemed at the happy ending). In most movies, only the star—and, sometimes, his/her special friend—is not an utter joke. In *Baby Boom* (1987) rising corporate manager Diane Keaton, unexpectedly left with a baby (not her own), is thereby enabled to seem terribly superior to the young ass-kissing crud who finally gets her job, then to the two dull, dumpy yokels (from Deleuth!) who almost adopt the precious baby girl (but Keaton saves her!), then to various thick-witted rubes up in Vermont (where Keaton goes when she loses her job, moving to a fifty-two-acre estate), then to four laughably affected yuppie fools who blow into the general store where Keaton's homemade applesauce is on display, and who buy several dozen jars, thereby initiating Keaton's rise to entrepreneurial greatness, which allows her, first, to be courted fawningly by those phoney pigs who'd let her go, and then, majestically, to turn them down.

The same (as it were) promiscuous ridicule occurs in movie after movie: John Landis's *Coming to America* (1988), Rob Reiner's *The Sure Thing* (1985) and *When Harry Met Sally . . .* (1989), John Hughes's *Pretty in Pink* (1986) and *Ferris Bueller's Day Off* (1986), and countless others. Often the star's prerogative permits him/her to do more than smirk at those flakes and nitwits. In Mike Nichols's *Working Girl* (1988) chilly, two-faced bitch Sigourney Weaver, having thwarted warm, hard-working (two-faced) sweet thing Melanie Griffith, is humiliated out of all proportion to her "crime," in a scene that is unbearable to watch unless you see things as the movie means you to—that is, as the heroine sees things, herself included.

Then there's John Hughes's *Uncle Buck* (1989), in which big, lovable slob John Candy, having found his teen-aged niece's sneaky, creepy-looking, overprivileged little snot-nose of a boyfriend lying atop some other girl, moves in on him with a devilish smile, and with a live power drill in his hand: cut. Candy, now cruising the suburban night, finds his niece (who's out walking, heartbroken) and tells her that he has something to show her. He opens the car trunk to reveal the two-timing little puke, his hands bound tightly with electrical tape and another piece across his mouth. Candy rips off that piece of tape (*"Oww!!"* yells the little prick), then hoists the kid up by the arm and drops him on the street *(thud!—"Ow!")*. The kid runs away, then turns around and (what a doofus!) starts taunting Candy, who calmly hefts a golf club, tees up on the street, and sends that ball right at the little wienie's skull *(thunk!—"Ouch!")*. Then he does it again.

Such gratuitous sadism, played for laughs, has only recently become a standard feature of the movies, along with that compulsive, adolescent jeering at everyone who's not the star. Even with all their painful stereotypes, the movies, on the whole, used to purvey a kinder view of people than they do today, now that the sitcom has universalized the sneering putdown: and—more important—now that the movies have converged with advertising, which divides all humanity into the cool few and everybody else, all others utterly contemptible.

THE EPOCH OF REVISION

The general surplus character of today's fantasies was not, in fact, a common feature of the movies until the late seventies, when *Rocky* (1976), *Star Wars, Close Encounters of the Third Kind* (both 1977), and *Superman* (1978) kicked off the current age of systematic big-screen infantilism. Indeed, for several years before that time (and in ever-fewer exceptions after it) American film was remarkable for the tentative mood or outright darkness that often marked the final scenes of its most memorable works: the masterpieces of Francis Ford Coppola, Robert Altman, Roman Polanski, Stanley Kubrick, and Sam Peckinpah, the best films of Hal Ashby, Jerry Schatzberg, Bob Fosse, William Friedkin, and Alan Pakula, and dozens of other powerful (if often flawed) movies that collectively rebut the claim that Hollywood has "always" sold cotton candy: Michael Ritchie's *The Candidate* (1972), Arthur Penn's *Night Moves* (1975), Sydney Pollack's *Three Days of the Condor* (1975), Nicholas Roeg's *Don't Look Now* (1973) and *The Man Who Fell to Earth* (1976), George Roy Hill's *Slap Shot* (1977), Karel Reisz's *The Gambler* (1974) and *Who'll Stop the Rain?* (1978), Peter Yates's *The Friends of Eddie Coyle* (1973), Alfred Hitchcock's *Frenzy* (1972), Bryan Forbes's *The Stepford Wives* (1975), Paul Schrader's *Blue Collar* (1978), Mike Nichols's *Carnal Knowledge* (1971), Ted Kotcheff's *North Dallas Forty* (1979), Elia Kazan's *The Last Tycoon* (1976), Martin Scorsese's *Alice Doesn't Live Here Anymore* (1975) and *Taxi Driver* (1976), Michael Douglas's and James Bridges's *The China Syndrome* (1979), Woody Allen's *Interiors* (1978) and *Stardust Memories* (1980), Brian De Palma's *Carrie* (1976), Ulu Grosbard's *Straight Time* (1978), Warren Beatty's *Reds* (1982), Philip Kaufman's *Invasion of the Body Snatchers* (1978), and Sidney Lumet's *The Anderson Tapes* (1971), *Serpico* (1973), *Dog Day Afternoon* (1975), and *Network* (1976)—among others, including George Lucas's *American Graffiti* (1973) and Stephen Spielberg's *The Sugarland Express* (1974).

It would be wrong, however, to imply that before the late sixties all Hollywood pictures ended in the same warm glow of factitious "bliss." There were many big-budget movies that did not end as the movies do today: a fact that we would recognize at once if any of those earlier films were remade now. Today Rhett and Scarlett would patch things up and have a baby, Shane would come back, Charles Foster Kane would find his sled, Tom Joad would get to be a CEO, and Mildred Pierce would send her daughter out for counseling (and the two of them would end up in a freeze-frame, hugging).

This is, unfortunately, no idle satire—for Hollywood has, since the late seventies, systematically bowdlerized the best of its own heritage, over and over whiting out the darkness of some earlier film in order to create yet one more total wish fulfillment fantasy. Thus has Hollywood's old banalizing instinct not only gotten worse but now turned in on Hollywood's own canon. Once it was only plays and novels that the studios would buy up and (often) standardize—a process that in 1950 Gilbert Seldes called "the art of licking." For elaboration he quoted Evelyn Waugh: "Each book purchased for motion pictures has some individual quality, good or bad, that has made it remarkable. It is the work of a great array of highly paid and incompatible writers to distinguish the quality, separate it, and obliterate it."

Since the seventies Hollywood has resumed "the art of licking," post-sweetening plays and novels just as Mayer or Zanuck would have done—only now the audience is deemed (and deems itself) "sophisticated," since the speed and gloss of new technique make even the hokiest tricks seem somehow not hokey. Here, for example, is an ending that never made it to the screen:

> "Say it ain't true, Roy."
> When Roy looked into the boy's eyes he wanted to say it wasn't but couldn't, and he lifted his hands to his face and wept many bitter tears.

Such are the last lines of Bernard Malamud's *The Natural* (1952), whereas the Robert Redford vehicle of 1984 climaxes with Roy Hobbs—although morally compromised, and with an open wound—belting one last meteoric homer (slow motion, fireworks, music, cheering crowds), thereby winning—that is, *not* throwing—the big game: a finale of bogus jubilation that we might expect in a TV commercial, which figures, since the movie's script was written by BBDO's Phil Dusenberry, maker of many ads for, among other products, Diet Pepsi and Ronald Reagan.

Other melancholy texts have been likewise renovated: Edmond Rostand's *Cyrano de Bergerac,* adapted with due pathos by the Hollywood of 1950, was played for laughs, or chuckles, by

Steve Martin in *Roxanne* (1987), which ends with the modern cavalier not dying but "having it all," as in an ad for Visa. Now, however, Hollywood not only turns good literature into bad movies but also turns good movies into advertising. This advance reflects Hollywood's general shift away from its old dependency on literary sources and into automatic self-cannibalization, as the deals and movies have come to be made by personnel who know nothing much but some earlier movies and the TV programs of their childhood—works that are endlessly recycled in the great downpour of sequels and remakes (both implicit and overt) that is American film today. Obviously, this endless self-revival betrays a general uninventiveness; less apparent is the continual bright erasure, in this process, of all uncanny moments, all discordant notes—those elements that had made the originals compelling in the first place. Thus the (rare) excitements of cinematic art—the reawakened sense of physical reality, and the apprehension of some truths that lie too deep to be articulated, or that are too disquieting to mention—have been replaced by another, lesser sort of pleasure, now that the movies all appeal, deliberately, to one regressive longing: the wish to see a thing brought back, this time without the sad parts.

For instance, Hollywood has revised the somber urban parable of the great athlete used up, or driven out, by the gangsters who control the game. Here the epoch of revision starts with the (first) rise of Rocky Balboa (1976). Despite the artful squalor of its setting, *Rocky* is a simple stimulant, conveying none of the fatalism that had been the whole point of boxing films from *Golden Boy* (1939) and *Body and Soul* (1947) to *The Harder They Fall* (1956) and *Requiem for a Heavyweight* (1962). That tragic genre pointed up the champ's brief hour of glory, his manipulation by corrupt old men, the slow wreckage of his mind and frame. (Thus the boxer recalls the entertainer—a simile that Martin Scorsese worked into his superb and antithetical *Raging Bull* [1980].) For Rocky, on the other hand, boxing is, although colorfully seedy, a sport as clean as tiddlywinks, involving no bets, no dives, no crooked action. Nor does Rocky seem at all

affected by the numerous head punches that have crippled so
many other boxers real and fictional, but keeps his sleepy *cin-
quecento* mug pristine through sequel after sequel.

By mere force of personal stardom, the movie hero now easily
negates what's bothersome about the past, and so transcends the
vicious world: Rocky simply outshines the gloomy legacy of the
boxing movies, Roy Hobbs simply bats his way beyond the tragic
novel that had told his story, and "Fast Eddie" Felson/Paul New-
man, the virtuoso pool player, simply cues his way beyond the
monstrous power of dirty money—the force that, in *The Hustler*
(1961), finally drove Fast Eddie from the game, but that is simply
not a problem in *The Color of Money* (1986), Martin Scorsese's
Rocky-like sequel to, and revision of, Robert Rossen's movie.
What troubles Eddie now is not the callousness of capital but his
own advancing age—which he defeats in a jarring coda, clearly
tacked on, that shows him Getting Back in Shape: consulting his
optometrist, jumping off a high-dive, and otherwise narrowly
cavorting à la Sly Stallone.

Throughout the epoch of revision, earlier filmed indictments,
or examinations, of the state or status quo recur—but now as
adlike affirmations of Our Way of Life. Thus Eisenstein's nightmare vision, in *Potemkin* (1925), of the Czarist massacre on the
Odessa steps becomes a crude adrenalizing bit in Brian De
Palma's *The Untouchables* (1987), its gruesome climax negated by
a happy ending that perversely (albeit "playfully") demonstrates
the God-like goodness of the FBI (one of whose agents *saves* the
baby in the runaway carriage). And thus Jean Renoir's wry and
complex vision of the bourgeoisie in *Boudu Saved from Drowning*
(1932) is inverted in Paul Mazursky's remake, *Down and Out in
Beverly Hills* (1986), which ends not with the tramp impulsively
deserting his adoptive family but with Nick Nolte trying and
failing to escape the affluent and cuddly Whitemans. And thus
Nicholas Ray's *Rebel Without a Cause* (1955), a rich, bleak story
of how the young are inexorably broken by their fearful parents,
comes back as *Footloose* (1984), in which young Kevin Bacon
finally gets the whole town *dancing!*—a pseudo-celebration of

such bad faith that it inspired a number of TV commercials for McDonald's. And thus Roman Polanski's *Chinatown* (1974), a devastating allegory of corporate power and American dominion, recurs as the jolly tale of Toontown in *Who Framed Roger Rabbit* (1988)—a simple, goofy fantasy, despite its frequent wit, and therefore just the thing for pushing Diet Coke.

What with all their high-speed montage, their state-of-the-art rock scores slamming through us, the movies seem hipper than hip, and yet for sheer parochialism they outdo Pangloss himself: not only is this the best of all possible worlds, they teach us—this is the only world possible! No more bitter Eddie Felson no more cynical Roy Hobbs, no wayward Boudu, no disillusioned J. J. Gittes! In the eighties the critical outsider has been thoroughly revised out of the movies; and so has that overpowering sense of the uncanny which marks certain prior movies—the feeling that makes those films seem so unusual, and even dangerous (especially today).

Like the Balboan emendation of the boxing genre, this other grand revision also starts in the late seventies: *Star Wars* (1977) is a deliberate renovation of Stanley Kubrick's *2001: A Space Odyssey* (1968)—which George Lucas deemed "the ultimate sci-fi film," although, notes his biographer, "too obscure and downbeat for his tastes." What most impressed Lucas in *2001* was its "technical craftsmanship," and yet only a few of Kubrick's effects recur in the *Star Wars* movies: believable gadgetry and the video game sensation of delicious forward speed. Absent, however, is the abyssal feeling of deep space—its utter quiet, its dark infinitude, and the absurdity, out there, of terms like "up" and "down." By contrast, the universe of *Star Wars* is like a big, warm room, or like a grand, smooth web of freeways weaving through the western night.

What Lucas and his Hollywood had to revise out of Kubrick's film was its uncanniness, which arises not only from that eerie evocation of the void but from the film's oblique reflection on ourselves. Within a clean, cold module facing toward the stars, we—like the astronauts—assume ourselves to be heroically headed in a new direction: *away* from the familiar earth, *away* from our own bestial origins, by our own spotless technologies now prepared for some great "discovery"—and yet, as the film's subtitle suggests, we cannot finally leave ourselves behind. Nor can we viewers trust in that Promethean conviction of our own distinctness, because *2001* raises too many unsettling questions: Who is the more "human" character? The affectless Dave Bowman or the polite, demented HAL? The cagey Dr. Heywood Floyd or his hairy, murderous ancestor (the first to kill and walk erect)? And was that act of killing "good" or "bad"? In fact, the film implies, the trace of "animal" aggression is inextricable, compelling even the best-trained engineer, the coolest scientist— and it always will drive us, and drive our descendants. Thus we are not unlike our simian predecessors—nor, weirdly, are we unlike those disembodied beings that put Dave Bowman on display. Finally, the higher intelligence is an inchoate watching entity, itself unseen, full of curiosity and malice: a projection (like the ghosts in *The Shining*) of the viewing audience itself. Although its close is enigmatic, *2001* does complete the "odyssey" when, in the final shot, the star-child gazes directly, and with transcendent calm, back into our own bewildered eyes.

All these difficulties are repressed in the *Star Wars* trilogy. For Lucas, "human" and "good" are terms as obvious as stoplights, and technology is just a big trove of empowering toys. In order to revise the menace out of Kubrick's film, Lucas had to sentimentalize those nonhuman creatures whose "human" traits make *2001* so uncanny an experience: thus the hairy, murderous early man recurs as the hairy and benevolent Chewbacca, now no simian rival but Han Solo's doglike sidekick; and the homicidal HAL, with his superior manner and his secret dream of taking charge, recurs both diminished and divided, as the two cute little "droids" C-3PO and R2D2, technological assistants now un-threateningly dated, the one looking like a fire hydrant in an old cartoon, the other like the Tin Man in *The Wizard of Oz* (and forever jabbering in a voice like Franklin Pangborn's). Thus put (back) in their respective places, the ape and the machine no longer crowd the human heroes, who are therefore free not just to save the day but to feel good about themselves again.

Throughout the epoch of revision, *2001* has been repeatedly negated in movies made above all to flatter and console. In Stephen Spielberg's *Close Encounters of the Third Kind* (1977) the universe's higher beings are not Nietzschean phantoms but emanations of pure friendliness—just like the human characters who seek (and resemble) them. Whereas Kubrick's scientists can never approach the big mystery, Spielberg's army of schoolboyish technocrats trades many a beep and wink and teary grin with the mellow, penile aliens, who at the end lift off with Richard Dreyfuss weeping joyfully aboard their glowing "mother ship" (to the strains, on the VCR version, of "When You Wish upon a Star").

And so the void unforgettably conveyed by Kubrick's film becomes a little easier to forget, since the revisions assure us that the universe is just a supermall—and that we are, or should be, happy, totlike shoppers beaming at the stars. These revisions converge wholly with the widespread advertising fantasy of perfect wish fulfillment. Whereas Kubrick's characters (in all his films) are thwarted by the very fact of their humanity, in the *Stars Wars* movies there is no necessity at all. At the end of *Return of the Jedi* (1983), the dead (Kenobi, Yoda, Vader) are partying along with everybody else; and when, in *The Empire Strikes Back* (1980), Luke has his arm cut off—hey! No problem! He gets a new one!

Like *2001,* Hitchcock's *Psycho* (1960) has been multiply revised because it, too, is an uncanny masterpiece, reflecting eerily on those who watch it (as each of Hitchcock's best films does). Years later, and even after all the big-screen deaths so much more graphic, the sudden slaughtering of Marion Crane is still a moment of unequaled horror, pathos, and surprise—a horror deepened all the more by the radical empathic shift that occurs right afterward. That thing had come into the *shower* and—for no reason—slashed at her so viciously, and just when she'd decided to (in every sense) come clean. The event terrifies because we side with her, empathizing with her terror, her nakedness. But then the young man comes in, sees the carnage, shows revulsion—and as he starts to tidy up, we side with *him,* now feeling oddly gratified to see the blood rinsed down the drain, the tiles mopped clean, her body wrapped and stowed so neatly, and then her white car slowly, slowly sinking until it's finally gone, deliciously obliterated, perfectly submerged in that nocturnal pool behind the Bates Motel.

What Norman offers us, in short, is the pleasure of complete repression. Armed either with clean linens and a mop and bucket or with that knife (which of course he cannot remember using), he wipes out every hint of corporeality that might disturb the antiseptic "calm" of life with mother: mildew, bloodstains, sexual desire. Efficiently he dumps all troublesome matter down the drain, or sinks it deep into the swamp; and as a hobby, he stuffs birds. Thus, over and over, he fulfills the wish to see a thing brought back, this time without the sad parts—that is, without any messy indications of mortality.

Driven by a puritanical hatred that he denies in himself, Norman, the apparent "psycho," is not unlike the movie's other, "normal" characters, who are also kept from pleasure by the dead hand of the past. What is eeriest about Norman's madness, however, is its similarity to our spectatorship as Hitchcock reflects upon it: for we, like Norman, are also driven by aggressions that we let fictitious others act out on our behalf. Thus Norman does for us what "Mother" does for him—an analogy that he himself reveals to us (and that the psychiatrist obscures with his anticlimactic lecture). When Marion suggests that Norman have his mother put away, he reacts with cold fury: "Have you ever seen the inside of one of those places? The laughter and the tears! The cruel eyes studying you!"—a chilling linkage of the madhouse with the movie theater. In the end, his/our whole project of absolute repression breaks down in a terminal montage of unsurpassed uncanniness, as that boyish face smiles up at us through Mother's bony rictus, and then the white car reemerges startlingly, yanked up and lunging toward us from the depths.

In the epoch of revision the uncanniness of *Psycho* has itself been repressed—in the very films devised to exploit it. By serializing the original, both *Psycho II* (1983) and *Psycho III* (1986) actually do the work of Norman Bates. Serialized, that peculiar horror of 1960 becomes another Golden Oldie, and Norman's psychic arrest, once an oblique and terrifying challenge to the audience, recurs as an outright desideratum: "He's back!" both films exult, "and everything's the same!"—the regressive fantasy embellished with a lot of campy humor, which plays the early horror for a knowing laugh. Thus through nostalgic repetition and compulsive winking, the sequels turn Hitchcock's assault into a chuck under the chin; and in so doing they do not now depict as horrible but (fittingly) celebrate serial butchery—the butchery of women.

Psycho II begins with the original shower sequence, torn out of its narrative context and trimmed down to make it punchier, so that it now comes as a mere tidbit of familiar porn. From there, both sequels treat us to a series of outlandish murders, as a number of delicious curvy bimbos (among others) are variously sliced and punctured, dying with many a hoarse scream and rich arterial spurt. Frankly pandering to the misogynistic animus, the sequels mark a full retreat from Hitchcock's challenge to the audience. At the end of *Psycho III,* as he is driven back to the asylum, Norman smiles up at us again as at the end of *Psycho*— only not, this time, as our uncanny double but as our faithful servant, our old pal. No skeletal grin converges on that (aging) face, no figure lunges at us from the depths, for in these bright, bloody films there are no depths.

Hitchcock has been thus invoked and contradicted throughout this era, in dozens of thrillers, both costly and low-budget, that adapt some of Hitchcock's tricks, perversely, to work up, then mollify, the hateful parent-imago within each one of us. In the slasher films it is the horny, active boys and girls who tend to get it in the neck/chest/stomach/eyes/nape/etc., whereas it is the chaste teen heroine who (temporarily) burns or blows up or drowns the vengeful Jason, Freddy, Michael (a defeat that indicates no crypto-feminist reversal, since it is a serial necessity, stoking the sense of sexist grievance that will impel the murderer's next comeback). For the putative grown-ups there has been *Fatal Attraction,* in which Michael Douglas is nightmarishly pursued by Glenn Close after—as punishment for—their illicit weekend of hot sex (an interlude of passion that is itself depicted as a farce). After lots of provocation, Glenn Close/Mrs. Bates— rising out of Douglas's bathtub, knife in hand—is enjoyably bumped off (and her unborn baby handily aborted) by Anne Archer, Douglas's sweet, asexual wife, who nails the harpy midtorso with a big handgun. Other directors have also invoked Hitchcock in films that punish women for their sexual allure or appetite: Brian De Palma in *Body Double* (1984), a *Vertigo/Rear Window* rehash whose dramatic high point is the impalement of Deborah Shelton with a massive power drill, and David Lynch in *Blue Velvet* (1986), wherein Dennis Hopper brutalizes Isabella Rossellini with a zest that is not quite justified by the film's apparent aim to represent the "dark side" of reality.

There is plenty of such outlandish sexual cruelty in the movies. Meanwhile, the true pain of Eros has been revised out of many earlier films. Thus Hitchcock's *Strangers on a Train* (1951) recurs as Danny DeVito's *Throw Momma from the Train* (1987), which, although a smart and often very funny movie, whites out the homoerotic tensions in the original (and in Patricia Highsmith's novel), setting up instead a sort of father/son relationship between Billy Crystal and the childlike DeVito. Moreover, the anxious mood of Hitchcock's ending (Bruno's death on the carousel, Guy's nervous exit with his bride) here gives way to a sentimental change of heart ("My momma!") and then an overtidy wrap-up that has the two men (now both successful writers) frolicking in the surf along with Crystal's girlfriend.

If there is no heartache in Hollywood's recycled love stories, neither, of course, is there any tragic passion; Cyrano's fate is not the only one that's been "improved." Adrian Lyne's *9½ Weeks* (1986), a glossy, static update of Bernardo Bertolucci's *Last Tango in Paris* (1972), is about as sexy as a locked warehouse full of designer shoes, whereas the original did generate some heat, despite its tedious artiness and many passages of utter bull. While there is plenty of abuse, there is no sense of inner torment in Lyne's fashion show, which ends, or stops, with Kim Basinger simply walking out on lover Mickey Rourke and then traipsing homeward in the rain, weeping "soulfully" and looking like ten million dollars. Compare this adlike close to Bertolucci's harsh and psychologically incisive ending, in which Jeanne (Maria Schneider) shoots and kills her lover (Marlon Brando) at the very moment that she first tells him her name.

And then there's Rob Reiner's *When Harry Met Sally . . .* (1989), a lite version of Woody Allen's *Manhattan* (1979) so close in plot to the original that it could be deemed a plagiarism if it were not so bald an act of homage—and so grossly antithetical in tone and message. Contradicting Allen's movie (and the drift of its own story, such as it is), the film ends up denying the melancholy of erotic life. In the last sequence of *Manhattan,* Allen, musing fondly on the much younger girl he'd earlier loved and dropped, races out of his apartment and through the city streets, needing to see and reclaim her—but finds her on her way to Europe and knows that, once there, she'll forget about him, despite her heartbreaking reassurance (and the film's last line): "You've got to have faith in people sometimes." On the contrary, Billy Crystal, having dumped old friend Meg Ryan after a night of lovemaking, and despite his heavily established inability to "commit" to any woman he's had sex with, suddenly races through the city streets, needing to see and reclaim her, and—hey! No sweat! She takes him back, and they get married!

MERGERS

The epoch of revision, with its perfect comebacks, dancin' populations, kindly aliens, lovers marrying, athletes scoring, winners winning, has in fact reflected an intense and widespread fear of loss. In Hollywood (as throughout the corporate world) this fear of loss has found its outlet in an all-consuming drive for profits that makes even the vast avarice of the old studio heads seem restrained. It is this drive, necessitated by the global competition of the media monopolists, that has compelled the industry VPs again and again to resell whatever sold before, just as the advertisers do. "Movies are becoming a product-line business, like Detroit or the cereal business," lamented Harlan Jacobsen, editor of *Film Comment,* in 1989. This was no exaggeration, reflecting as it did on an industry whose executives refer to movie stars as "assets" and to each run of sequels as a "franchise." The packaged-goods analogy would not offend the studio heads, who want their movies to be as well liked and predictable as any other winning item. "Eddie Murphy is our Kellogg's Corn Flakes," remarked Frank Mancuso, chairman of Paramount, in 1989. "The biggest reason to make an old television series into a movie is title identification," explained Scott Rudin, Fox's president of production, in 1987. "You have immediate presence in the marketplace." Such movies "are a pre-sold commodity," claimed Rob Cohen of Taft-Barish Productions, developers of *Johnny Quest, The Fugitive,* and *The Flintstones.*

Such purely economic "reasons," however, do not fully explain the movies' grand regression in the eighties; for that compulsive movement backward is not just a money-making exploit but a nostalgic reflex—or rather, the move makes money *because* of its nostalgic import, which is what draws those executives (personally as well as capitalistically) to such projects in the first place. That backward gaze reveals, in part, the escapist longing of the so-called baby-boomers, or at least those in Hollywood, to reenter the imaginary Eden of their own adolescence (c. 1958–67): "I loved 'Dragnet,' " says the producer of the movie. "I'm 37 years old," admits the vice-chairman of Taft-Barish, "and I started watching 'The Flintstones' when I was 10, the year it went on the air." This nostalgic urge also explains the weird prevalence of fifties/sixties rock & roll in today's movies—even in films about kids too young to remember, much less care about, the Shirelles, Tommy James, or the Golden Age of Doo-Wop.

It is, however, our whole axial generation of consumers, and not just those within the movie industry, who want somehow to go back—a yearning now exploited by the total media spectacle. TV is no less regressive than cinema, having revived *The Munsters, Adam-12, Star Trek, Kojak,* and *Columbo,* among others (including *Dragnet*), in an effort to reclaim the same (aging) audience that watched them fifteen, twenty, thirty years ago. "This is an uncanny time, when people are looking backward to go forward," comments the executive producer of the new *Lassie.* The ads, of course, make the same appeal: "Now that it's accepted that nostalgia is the way to reach baby-boomers, that has become the norm" in advertising, observed Young & Rubicam's creative director in 1986. Repeatedly the ads now sell their sugary treats by linking them with the TV/movie imagery of yesteryear: "The enduring [TV] characters of the '50s are still vivid," a Sara Lee ad soothes us, "because they are the legends we grew up with—the heroes, villains, and clowns of our youth."

Like TV and the movies, those inexpensive, yummy items—from Hershey, Nestlé, Sara Lee—have become overly precious to a cohort of consumers who cannot afford the more substantial comforts, or, therefore, the sense of relative stability, that their parents could attain on only one income: the house and yard, the car(s) and swings and barbecue. The affluent yuppie, ironic and serene, is an advertising figment, meant both to flatter and exploit the actual baby-boomers—who are mostly moving *downward.* Between 1973 and 1986 housing prices doubled as more and more young workers were forced to take lower-paying jobs. "In the same years," Katy Butler reports, "the real median income of all families headed by someone under 30 fell by 26 percent." Thus pressed, and yet remembering the softer life provided by their parents, many boomers have, notes Butler, given up "necessities and comforted themselves with cheap luxuries: flowers, Dove bars, Haagen-Dazs, Cuisinarts, dinners out"—and TV shows and movies, which, when they aren't showing wealthy yuppies eating Haagen-Dazs and having dinner out, are invoking that Golden Age when mom was always in the house and you could play outside without a bank card.

As the boomers go, so goes the consuming nation, whose people generally are also "looking backward to go forward"—if the success not only of those nostalgic shows and movies but of Reagan/Bush is any indication. Those images console us with well-crafted invocations of the Good Old Days when we were all allegedly well off—and when the U.S.A. was still, to quote Dan Quayle, "the envy of the world," its postwar empire undiminished. In the jingoistic sequences of *Top Gun* and the Rambo movies, in the quaint performances of Indiana Jones and Ronald Reagan, as well as in the many boomer-oriented remakes and revivals of the hit songs and TV shows of the Ike/Kennedy interlude, we hear the incessant reassurance that we Americans have *not* lost *anything*—that *Americans can never lose!*

There is more to Hollywood's regression, however, than simple postimperial nostalgia. Although backward-looking, Hollywood does not return us to the spectacle of yesteryear; rather, as we have seen, it systematically *negates* the narrative force of the originals. We are watching not what people watched when Ike was president but a spectacle that has been meticulously engineered to "gratify" at every single moment: the movies now (like the ads and our political theatrics) are deliberately concocted as relentless uppers, their images devised to keep us happy, thereby composing a heavy atmosphere of continual stand-up, easy shocks along with constant solace, flattery, and affirmation, a new global belt of laughing gas, which seems to have induced, among the viewers (and reviewers) who've been breathing it, a desperate taste for more of the same.

Where the movies once could dramatize a painful choice, the new fear of loss prohibits such a story; and whereas the prior movies could, at times, reflect, albeit obliquely, on dark forces outside (and inside) the theater, the new taste refuses any such bad news. Indeed, the fear of loss seems so intense that it now rejects not just a downbeat story but any story whatsoever, as if the crucial difference between fiction and reality were too much to bear. Whereas narrative requires that you maintain some sense of distance from it, what the movies offer, and what their viewers seem to crave, is the infantilizing promise of *no distance*: no separation, never any feeling of exclusion—not even from the spectacle itself.

The advertising industry has noticed this new flight from story into spectacle. Discussing the largest, most free-spending bloc of viewer/consumers in America today, the researchers at Grey Advertising explain that, having been "raised on daily doses of television imagery," these "UltraConsumers" have minds that "are primed to blur the boundaries that separate fiction from fact." Dependent on the images they watch nonstop, and always trying to emulate them, however much it costs, the "Ultras" are the most desirable of markets, to be avidly pursued for their confusion. "Today, as they infuse their lives with an action-packed schedule of drama, adventure, variety and, of course, costume changes, Ultras are merging their glamorous fantasies with everyday reality. All things considered, it's not so surprising that after years of exposure to electronic heroes, the average UltraConsumer wants to be one."

Hollywood now offers, explicitly, to fulfill that longing: at its theme parks—those efficient recreational environments whose expansion, in the eighties, has coincided with Hollywood's grand revision of the movies. (The biggest parks, appropriately, are owned by the biggest media companies—Disney and Universal.)

Modeled after Disneyland and Disney World, these theme parks are designed to infantilize the paying crowds. "Walt's thing was reassurance," recounted Disney's chief designer, John Hench, in 1989. "The message is, 'You're going to be okay.'" This "reassurance" glows from the very colors of the place, the very architecture. Because black, Hench noted, "is associated with mystery and holes and things," there is no black in Disneyland. Striving to suppress all negativity, Disney favored circular designs: "Round shapes are generally softer," Hench pointed out. "They evoke clouds, hills, babies and so forth." The "Victorian" buildings on Main Street, moreover, fulfill the wish to see a thing brought back, this time without the sad parts. "We take what the original architects were trying to say about optimism and give it a push." The theme park induces a quasi-oceanic feeling in its visitors, who are meant to find themselves as if comfortably suspended beyond time. "They say, 'Gee, we had a good time.' They don't know why. It's because they dropped those two things they'd been carrying. They forget tomorrow and they forget yesterday."

In the late eighties, the major theme parks became extensively movie-based—not only those owned by Disney and Universal but Hershey Park, Knott's Berry Farm, Six Flags, and all the rest, whose "rides" were now, increasingly, both adaptations of and ads for the biggest blockbusters of the epoch of revision. The aim, one ride designer said, is "to do live things that are like a Spielberg movie." Through this convergence the parks' attractions have become a lot more knuckle-whitening—and yet the whole experience is (still) fundamentally consoling, because the very wildest of these cinematic rides provides a quick nostalgia bath while appearing to close that painful gap between the viewer and the screen. "The Walt Disney Imagineers," shouts an ad for the Great Movie Ride at the Disney/MGM Studios Theme Park, "have brought your favorite films to life as you journey *into* the movies you love!"—a ride that pulls you into *Alien* as well as *Mary Poppins*.

The theme park stands as an apt paradigm for today's movies. Like the park, the movies offer, *instead* of narrative, a series of visceral jolts far stronger than any ever sold before; and yet, paradoxically, the abuse is finally nullified in an all-healing, all-inclusive merger—a rousing/tranquilizing moment of manifold collapse. Just as the theme park promises to take us right "*into* the movies," the movies themselves now fake our integration with the spectacle; they even go the parks one better, by simultaneously dissolving the apparent differences between their own main characters. In short, the film eliminates both its own intrinsic differences and (seemingly) the extrinsic distance between itself and us. Such is Hollywood's new happy ending: a moment of euphoric melding, as the audience within the frame looks on and cheers.

In other words, a type of ending once reserved (fittingly) for musicals now terminates movies of all kinds, which routinely climax in a shot or scene of spectatorial ecstasy that is clearly meant to work us into the same rapture. In this way the movies—and not just such neo-musicals as *Coal Miner's Daughter* (1980), *Purple Rain* (1984), and *Dirty Dancing* (1987)—actually applaud themselves. Thus both *Ghostbusters* movies climax with the same salute to *Ghostbusters,* whose hip stars arrive to save the day as grateful citizens chant, "Ghostbusters! Ghostbusters! Ghostbusters!" And thus in *Rocky IV* Stallone stands victorious (again), Old Glory draped heroically around his giant shoulders, as the usual trumpets bop and blare and all of Moscow chants the movie's name. And thus the crowds *erupt!* at the climax of each *Karate Kid* (I, II, and III), just as the crowd *erupts!* at the climax of *The Natural, Hoosiers,* and *Three O'Clock High,* of *Scrooged* and *Major League* (1989) and *Lean on Me* (1989), of *Bill and Ted's Excellent Adventure* (1989) and *Born on the Fourth of July* (1989), and so many more.

And yet the new happy ending reveals more than Hollywood's rising need for big hits: for there is more to this repetitious climax than its bald solicitation to go clap clap clap. More often than not, what the crowd-within-the-frame applauds is, specifically, another merger: the melding of two "opposites" into a unity.

At the end of *An Officer and a Gentlemen* (1982), Richard Gere, now very much the officer and gentleman in his crisp dress whites, sweeps masterfully into the factory where the lower-class Debra Winger, dressed real funky, operates a big machine. As such a hero would have done in 1947, Gere sweeps the wide-eyed Winger off her feet and carries her away—only now, instead of its being left to the actual women in the audience to clap and sigh, Gere/Winger is applauded by the other women in the factory, who (an integrated group) are also dressed funky. (The movie's theme—an Oscar-winner—screams over this last shot.)

At the end of *Crocodile Dundee* (1986), the urbane and fleshy Linda Kozlowski, a glamorous American reporter, runs after the lean and leathery Paul Hogan, the blunt Aussie adventurer whom she'd brought back to the States, made famous, and now loves (and who has decided to go home). She hurries down into a subway station and, halting on the stairs, sees Hogan standing at the far end of the platform, which is so jammed with everyday people that she can't get near him. She calls to him, but he can't hear her, nor she him, so each of their love shouts is repeated twice, semaphore-style, by two obliging *Untermenschen*: a bearded Jamaican and a beefily stereotypic "construction worker." Finally, the leads having reconciled, Hogan hoists himself up and makes his way over to Kozlowski by tramping on the shoulders of the intervening crowd, who look up in delight as Hogan steps on them and break into loud cheers when the stars finally form Kozlowski/Hogan. (The music too is loud and happy.)

At the end of *Married to the Mob* (1988), Italo-American spitfire Michelle Pfeiffer, a Mafia ex-wife, sits pertly on the lap of even-tempered WASP Matthew Modine, a by-the-book FBI agent, who has come to see her (and apologize for having posed as not a cop) in the beauty parlor where she works (and where, with a really hip makeover, they got her looking less Italian). She has him sitting in one of the chairs, with a sheet over him, as if he's going to get a perm, and, having bawled him out good-naturedly, she bends down and kisses him. The camera dollies back to show the other women in the place (an integrated group) applauding Pfeiffer/Modine warmly, and then there's the beauty parlor's owner, a hip Jamaican mammy, facing the camera. Knowingly she winks at us. (Hip salsa music rocks loudly over this last shot.)

Thus used commonly to climax love stories, the new happy ending recurs no less frequently in action pictures. At the end of *Indiana Jones and the Temple of Doom* (1984), intrepid Harrison Ford finally grabs and kisses girly-girl Kate Capshaw (they've been squabbling for two hours), as the observing crowd of Indian villagers goes clap clap clap. At the end of "The Running Man" (1987), the robotic Teuton Arnold Schwarzenegger, having won the gruesome TV game show called "The Running Man" (a gladiatorial contest, broadcast by the state), appears on a giant outdoor TV screen, beside his co-contestant, Maria Conchita Alonso, a voluptuous Hispanic. Throughout the film the applause of the bloodthirsty TV audience has been portrayed as stupid and barbaric, but now there is no problem whatsoever as, gazing up exultantly at the victorious Alonso/Schwarzenegger, that same crowd goes clap clap clap.

Over and over, "opposites" converge as everyone applauds— as (also) in *The Color Purple, Heartbreak Ridge* (1986), *Everybody's All-American* (1988), *Young Einstein* (1989), *The Secret of My Success* (1987), *Over the Top,* the first three Rocky movies, *True Believer,* each *Karate Kid, Stripes* (1981), *My Favorite Year* (1982), *Overboard* (1988), *Cocktail* (1988), *Without a Clue* (1988), *Desperately Seeking Susan* (1985), and *Outrageous Fortune* (1987), among others, in all of which two "different" types end up hugging and/or dancing close and/or strolling off together, as a knot or mob of watchers claps and/or yells "Yeah!" and/or "Hurray!"

Differences within the frame, it seems, are just as threatening as our distance from it; and so, just as the new happy ending seems to let us jump that gap through an empathic merger with those filmed applauders, so does it merge all the figures on the screen into one big happy family, or rather, into a seeming group portrait in which every figure is identical—an image that strikes eerily at the end of *All About Eve* (1950) but that has come to represent a gross desideratum since the seventies: the baseball players merging in ecstatic slo-mo at the climax of *The Natural;* at the end of *Chariots of Fire,* the privileged runners seeming, as they glide along the distant shore, to form a hovering pastel cloud; at the climax of *Top Gun,* Tom Cruise (with Old Glory stitched across the shoulder of his flight suit) trading manly hugs and high-fives with his joyous peers as the score rocks screamingly and many sailors also stand there cheering.

The terminal erasure of all "difference" can, and often does, require a killing, as when the cracked, desirous Glenn Close is blown away by chaste Anne Archer—the kind of fate that almost always (still) befalls the few libidinous characters in movies. More often, however, there is no need for such extreme preju-

dice, because it is the purpose of the new happy ending to obviate
the threat of difference through the very figures that seem to pose
it so schematically. Those melding "opposites," of course, turn
out never to have been very different from each other in the first
place. When Rocky hugs his Adrian, for instance, the seeming
disjunction (bulging boxer/timid anti-boxing wife) is at once
subverted by the marked likeness of Stallone to Talia Shire, both
of them dark-haired and mournful-looking, similarly coiffed and
wearing the same nose (in different sizes). And the apparent
mismatch in *Married to the Mob* is undercut by the clear ethnic
sameness of Modine and Pfeiffer, who, despite the widow's peak
and tinted contact lenses, does not exactly look Italian.

Of course, the fundamental likeness of the "opposites" involves more than looks. Film after film is based on, its "plot"
enabled by, a tendentious pairing, as two antithetical stereotypes
are pushed together (white man/black man, Harry/Sally, earth-
ling/alien, old Asian/U.S. kid) so that, through their "conflicts,"
they can banter, until they merge and end the story. Certainly,
some such play of opposites recurs throughout the history of
modern comedy, from Shakespeare and Congreve to *His Girl
Friday* and *The Odd Couple;* and there are a few post-seventies
movies that have also found some truth, and therefore real
humor, in the clash of disjunct temperaments: John Cassavetes's
Gloria (1980), John Sayles's acute and subtle *Baby, It's You*
(1982), the exquisitely acted *Midnight Run* (1988). Generally,
however, the clash of "opposites" is based not on any human
traits but on sheer commercial necessity. Prior Hollywood also
had a penchant for the stereotypic pairing—as in *The Cowboy and
the Lady* (1938), *Her Highness and the Bellboy* (1945), *The Prince
and the Showgirl* (1957), and other dogs—but it was only in the
eighties that the device came to be used incessantly, and almost
always as a way to represent, and celebrate, the same difference.

In short, the usual pairings have the same bogus character
(and, ultimately, the same purpose) as the "opposites" portrayed
in ads. ("He likes hardware. She likes software. BUT THERE'S
ONE THING THEY AGREE ON.") Thus we have that staple

of the cop movie, the loose/tight combination: in *Lethal Weapon 1* (1987) and *2* (1989) black and proper Danny Glover, who goes by the book, is paired up with wild, white Mel Gibson, who breaks the rules, as in *Dragnet* (1987), wherein proper Dan Ackroyd goes by the book, while wild Tom Hanks breaks the rules, as in *The Big Easy* (1986), which has wild cop Dennis Quaid routinely break the rules, while Ellen Barkin, the starchy DA, goes by the book, much as in *Shoot to Kill* (1988), which has black urbanite Sidney Poitier, who goes by the book, teamed up with white backwoodsman Tom Berenger, who follows his own rules, whereas in *Red Heat* (1988) we have the proper Arnold Schwarzenegger, a "Soviet" policeman, break the rules, while it's his sloppy U.S. partner, Jim Belushi of Chicago, who would prefer to use that book.

The cop combo now pervades the genres, or what passes for them. In *Married to the Mob* she breaks the rules, he goes by the book—as in *Something Wild* (1986), also directed by Jonathan Demme, and also about a mild male clone liberated by a hot-shoppin' female, which happens also to be the premise of *Desperately Seeking Susan,* although it's not a male who's freed by the sultry, go-for-it Madonna but the naïve suburbanite Rosanna Arquette, who does here what prim Shelley Long does in *Outrageous Fortune,* while it's Long's "opposite," Bette Midler, who breaks the rules, rather like James Woods, the lawyer in *True Believer* (1988), a cynical pot-head paired up with sober, earnest Robert Downey, Jr., who goes by the book, whereas in *Twins* (1988) it's the short and sleazy Danny DeVito who breaks the rules, whereas large, innocent Arnold Schwarzenegger, DeVito's twin brother (get it?), goes by the book—like the short, pathologically tidy Dustin Hoffman in *Rain Man* (1989), paired up with his tall, normal, impulsive brother Tom Cruise, or like the tidy gentile Sally, whose hyperneatness is the object of much joshing by the (tidy) Jewish Harry (and at the end Hoffman/Cruise push heads together, Downey/Woods stroll off together, twins converge and double, Sally/Harry marry).

Through this repetitious contrast the pairings each sell, first of all, the same liberatory promise sold by advertising, which routinely shows you one who's hot and one who's not—and if the wild one doesn't win the dull one over (to the product), that very failure ought to win *you* over—since *you* don't want to be a dullard (do you?). In the spectacle of Tight and Loose (whether ad or movie), Loose—Madonna/Gibson/Pfeiffer/Griffith—is usually the funny one, and the smarter shopper, hipper dresser, hotter lover, cooler dancer: that is, the one you'd rather be, although the choice is finally easy in the movies, since Tight/Loose merge in any case.

And while the pairing sells us shopping as a means toward liberation, it also sells us on the work world that you must inhabit if you want to keep your Visa(s). The pairing sells, in other words, not just the corporate product (movie, Larks, Pepsi, Bud) but the very structure of the corporation: bureaucracy, which always prevails in these movies, finally absorbing both its "wild" child and the anal one, who, with his/her bureaucratic affect, will also be rewarded—and who will never be dismissed, even if, postmerger, s/he becomes a little "crazier." Despite the movie heroes' frequent grumblings about "red tape" and "the bureaucrats," the movies actually extol the system that produces them, for the usual pairing demonstrates the breadth and tolerance of bureaucracy, which always turns out to have everything in common with its "wildest" employee: for the most explosive cops and soldiers—Rambo, Cobra, "Maverick" (in *Top Gun*)—are always "crazy" not in opposition to bureaucracy but in its service. Toward the end, some crusty, decent papa comes down from high atop the company or service or department, grins knowingly upon the pseudo-dissident, and often gives him/her a break—the kind of move that used to be portrayed as cynical *(Meet John Doe, A Face in the Crowd, A Clockwork Orange, The China Syndrome)* but that now serves as winking propaganda for the bureaucratic state, in which, high up, some nice dad is allegedly looking after you and all others who "perform."

The new happy ending offers the same reassurance, at once authoritarian and easygoing, that we discern in advertising. The cool mayor who blesses Eddie Murphy at the end of *Beverly Hills Cop II,* the sharp mayor who values those Ghostbusters, the CEO who, in *Working Girl,* promotes Melanie Griffith, the top boss who, in *Big,* promotes Tom Hanks, the warm general who, in *Good Morning, Vietnam,* chuckles craggily at the shtick of Robin Williams, the calm officer who keeps turning up to soothe the veiny, pop-eyed Rambo, and the movies' numerous other managerial *dei ex machina* betray the paternalistic bias of the media monopoly—as do those cheering crowds, whose subjugation shows not only in their loud unanimous assent but in their manifest subject status. In nearly every case the crowds are either quaintly working-class or adorably Third World—or else showily *grateful* citizens, overjoyed to be there in the movie.

Abrupt, illogical, unmotivated, the new happy ending is, as narrative, a total washout. And that is precisely what it's meant to be: each cheery climax functions not to end the story but to liquefy it. As everybody seems to melt into the spectacle, the "problems" that had kept the story going, however minimally, need no longer be resolved, because this sweetest of all pleasures has *dissolved* them: the bliss of being in the spectacle, of being (like the stars) lovingly looked up to and (also like the stars) watched over. This narcissistic meltdown is, in itself, not new, having also been used long ago, and by some good directors: King Vidor's *The Crowd* (1928), having told a painful modern story, ends absurdly with a mawkish tribute to the act of watching a swell show, much as Preston Sturges's dark tale of a film director's wanderings, *Sullivan's Travels* (1942), ends by submerging its bitter vision in a sugary montage of chuckling moviegoers.

Nowadays, however, this cop-out seems to wash out every movie, finally obliterating, in a flash flood of affirmative theatricality, all memory of whatever gross event or cartoonish plight the movie has presented. Whether it's Michael Keaton's heavy woes (job loss, chick totaled) in *Clean and Sober* (1988), or Barbara Hershey's slow, untimely death in *Beaches* (1988), or the numerous domestic worries limned so heavy-handedly in *Parenthood* (tense kids, failed marriage, job loss), or Robin Williams's

sad dismissal in *Dead Poets Society* (1989), or the lurid tangle of
Bad Things (philandery, embezzlement, coprophilia, suicide, as-
sassination) that constitutes the plot of Woody Allen's *Crimes and
Misdemeanors* (1989), all the pain is suddenly negated by some
putatively deft performance: a kid makes a great catch at Little
League, Bette Midler "mourns" Hershey's death by belting out
"The Glory of Love"—or some watching crowd just breaks out
into meaningless applause, each movie thereby leaving us with
this self-referential bit of reassurance: "If you can wow an audience, it doesn't matter *what* your problems are!"

Thus the movies promise us no distance, no difference—and
no ending. Made for, and helping to create, an audience terrified
of time itself, an audience eager to "forget tomorrow and forget
yesterday," the movies now conclude their "narratives" without
seeming to terminate them, as if to assure us that the spectacle
will never end at all. Such is the implicit promise of the gimmick
that now ends, or rather stops, most movies, a gimmick that, in
film after film, follows even the new happy ending, as a bit of (as
it were) surplus reassurance: the freeze-frame, whereby the
movie actually negates the crucial power of its own cameras to
make a keen, enduring record of the passage of time.

An old device, the terminal freeze-frame has enabled countless
charged and suggestive final images, especially since François
Truffaut used it to confront us with the wounded gaze of Jean-
Pierre Léaud at the end of *The 400 Blows* (1959). Powerful
freeze-frames end (to name just a few) Sam Peckinpah's *The Wild
Bunch* (1969), Nicholas Roeg's *The Man Who Fell to Earth*
(1976), Sydney Pollack's *Three Days of the Condor* (1975), Paul
Schrader's *Blue Collar* (1978)—and yet no such memorable
freeze-frame ends any movie in the epoch of revision, although
the device has never been so overused. Over and over, the convergence *freezes* at the end—Rocky and Adrian, Mr. Miyagi and
the Karate Kid, Long/Midler in *Outrageous Fortune*, Caine/
Kingsley in *Without a Clue*, Hines/Baryshnikov in *White Nights*
(1985), Gibson/Pfeiffer in *Tequila Sunrise* (1988), Amy Irving/
Peter Riegert in *Crossing Delancey* (1988), Elizabeth Shue and her

dream date in *Adventures in Babysitting* (1987), Kozlowski/
Hogan in *"Crocodile" Dundee II* (1988). Often the convergence
comes in a mock-photographic format (as at the end of *Hoosiers*),
freezing DeVito/Schwarzenegger *en famille* to stop *Twins,* Her-
shey/Midler to stop *Beaches,* Lange/Spacek/D. Keaton to stop
Crimes of the Heart (1986), Arquette/Madonna to stop *Desperately
Seeking Susan.*

And if it's not the convergence, then it's just the star himself,
famed face transfixed in a wide, phoney smile (or real cool
smirk), as if posing for a series of publicity shots: John Candy at
the end of *Uncle Buck,* Bill Murray at the end of *Stripes,* Prince
at the end of *Purple Rain,* Matthew Broderick at the end of *Ferris
Bueller's Day Off*, Chevy Chase at the end of *Fletch Lives* (1989),
Morgan Freeman at the end of *Lean on Me*, Eddie Murphy at the
end of *Beverly Hills Cop* and *Beverly Hills Cop II.*

In every case, the movie finally dead-ends into a promotional
photo, an image that—all at once—extols (some) celebrity, denies (your) mortality, and (so) invites you to identify with that
bright entity—like any ad that features someone famous.

"IF HISTORY HAS TAUGHT US ANYTHING . . ."

Formerly the movies sold a vision of utopia, allowing—indeed,
exploiting—the impulse to escape into another place: a balmy
land of plenty, where the people would be kind (and, in most
movies, all the same). This vision often made the movies memorable. In 1939, for instance, the best big productions ended—
albeit naïvely, or dishonestly—with their gazes outward, looking
past the whole dispiriting mechanism of production: toward that
place "across the border" where Dallas and the Ringo Kid are
headed, or toward that Paradise beyond the snows where Heath-
cliff will love Cathy for all time, or toward Jefferson Smith's
rejuvenated nation, or toward that new Union wherein Rhett and
Scarlett now will go their separate ways, or toward that homey
farm where Dorothy *will* now find her "heart's desire."

Today's movies offer no utopia, since everything you'd ever

want, they say, is here on sale. They make this pitch first of all by concentrating on, and glamorizing, the closed sites of shopping and consumption: nice restaurants and luminous department stores, and the clean and roomy cell wherein the star keeps his/her posters, sweaters, jackets, copper pots, appliances. And the movie makes the pitch by packaging *itself* as a commodity—as an item, like any smoke or Coke or burger, whose appeal does not outlast the moment that it takes to suck it in.

And so going to the movies now is about as memorable as going to the airport. Conceived and sold as "product," just like the many products that it sells, so does the movie pass right through you, leaving nothing in you but the vague, angry craving for another one. Today, that craving is what keeps the movies going—and so the movies sell that kind of appetite, that infantile ravenousness, even as they offer you a daydream of your own tremendous strength. Reconsider the famous bat sign that, in 1989, sold *Batman* on several million bits of merchandise. Seen the obvious way, that logo is a stylized emblem of the bat in flight, a sign inviting you to think of Batman and to feel yourself as zooming likewise high above the lethal city. Seen another way, it shows the open mouth of an insatiable half-wit: Pac-Man seen from the front, about to take another bite.

But this is much too grim an ending; because the movies, at their best, have reminded us, forcefully, that things should be otherwise—which is why advertising urges us to laugh them off, to "see right through them." Those movies have to be suppressed, revised, their power forgotten, because they don't just bedazzle us with a blurred promissory vision of utopia but actually enable us to *see,* through them, the real workings of the very system that produced them, and that is now degrading them and us.

"The cinema is a more or less modern thing, and it ought to be used, now and again, as a means of getting something clear about the life that takes hold of us, and our attempts to pretend that the hold is a handshake." Thus, in 1936, one critic expressed the promise of the movies, which have, at times, made good: by treating us not as wired "consumers" but respectfully, as persons (somehow) still outside that system, and so still able to be moved and challenged by its devastations—by the shame and terror of James Allen, chain-gang fugitive, shocked face disappearing into blackness; by the efficient murder of Joanna Eberhardt, killed by, and replaced with, that "perfect wife" now gliding toward us down the supermarket aisle in sunny Stepford; by the final helplessness of J. J. Gittes, unable to abort the terminal rise of Noah Cross, author of the dark flood gathering over Chinatown; and by the deep, uncomprehending pain of Michael Corleone, who, having finally gained so much and yet lost everything, sits in the dusk behind his big, sepulchral house, brooding in the unexpected cold of this clean country, and realizing, all alone, that it was not supposed to end like this.

*N*otes

INTRODUCTION: THE BIG PICTURE
by MARK CRISPIN MILLER

page 4 **"for the future"/"constant ideas"**: Harry Warner's testament was reprinted in the *Christian Science Monitor* under the headline "The Filmmaker's Obligations As One Producer Saw It," April 26, 1989. Eisner's vision was recorded in "Adman of the Year: Michael Eisner," *Advertising Age,* January 2, 1989, p. 23.

"the Bible does": *Fortune,* December 1937, p. 220, quoted in Neal Gabler's *An Empire of Their Own: How the Jews Invented Hollywood* (New York: Crown Publishers, 1988), p. 196. This book offers an indispensable analysis of the moguls' respective backgrounds and personalities, as well as their peculiar plight.

5 **"separate earnings"**: "Now Lawyers Are Hollywood Superstars," *New York Times,* January 11, 1987. On the recent rise of the blockbuster obsession, see Thomas Schatz, "The Hit," *Gannett Center Journal,* vol. 3, no. 3 (summer 1989), pp. 29–44.

7 **collective sway**: There are, at this writing, two other studios: the small Orion and the virtually defunct MGM/UA. For a good overview of each studio's current situation and their respective plans for the nineties, see Aljean Harmetz, "Now Showing: Survival of the Fittest," *New York Times,* October 22, 1989.

number two export: Alex Brummer, "A Curious El Papa Meets the Fast Buck Head-on," *Manchester Guardian Weekly,* October 4, 1987.

8 **"and getting the script written"**: L. J. Davis, "Hollywood's Most Secret Agent," *New York Times Magazine,* July 9, 1989, p. 27.

"maximize commercial effect": Sean Mitchell, "Why the News from Hollywood Always Wears a Tan," *Washington Journalism Review,* July/August 1989, p. 30.

8 **"positive, Pollyannaish pap"**: Quoted by Jonathan Alter in "Tales from the Dark Side," *Premiere,* October 1989, p. 143.

9 **"advertising and publicity offices"**: "Industry Watches the Movies for Public Trends," *Nation's Business,* July 1940, p. 20.

THE MEDIUM: DOWN THE TUBES, by TODD GITLIN

Thanks to Tom Engelhardt, Aljean Harmetz, Jeremy Larner, Mark Crispin Miller, and Ruth Rosen for sitting and seeing through movies with me.

page 14 **"The 'content' of TV":** McLuhan, *Understanding Media* (New York: Mentor, 1964), p. ix.

"the 'content' of any medium": McLuhan, p. 23.

Ed Sullivan: Actually, McLuhan did notice Sullivan (p. 288), but only the characteristics of his face, not of his form.

16 **Tim Brooks and Earle Marsh:** *The Complete Directory to Prime Time Network TV Shows, 1946–Present,* revised and enlarged ed. (New York: Ballantine, 1981), p. 510.

19 **insatiable hunger for hits:** See the excellent analysis in Thomas Schatz, "The Hit," *Gannett Center Journal,* vol. 3, no. 3 (Summer 1989), pp. 29–44.

60 percent: David Bollier, "The Future in Home Video for Niche Programming," Aspen Institute Communications and Society Forum Report, 1989, pp. 9–10.

Between 1946 and 1957: Christopher H. Sterling and Timothy R. Haight, *The Mass Media: Aspen Institute Guide to Communication Industry Trends* (New York: Praeger, 1978), p. 352. As late as 1985, the latest year for which statistics are available, movie attendance had barely scrambled back to a mere half of the 1957 figure—23 million per week. (Computed from *International Motion Picture Almanac* [New York: Quigley Publishing Co.] for 1975 through 1978 and from 1979 through 1987, when it is known as *The Motion Picture Almanac.*)

20 **studios got huffy:** Todd Gitlin, *Inside Prime Time* (New York: Pantheon, 1983), p. 145.

21 **Two movies:** And a third bashed another side of the entertainment business. The bad guy in *Sweet Smell of Success* (directed by Alexander Mackendrick with a script by Clifford Odets and Ernest Lehman) is J. J. Hunsaker (Burt Lancaster, in perhaps his most vivid role), a powerful and unscrupulous gossip columnist for a New York City tabloid. Hunsaker has something on everybody; he makes and breaks entertainers, hangers-on, everyone. The drama revolves around Hunsaker's diabolical scheme to corrupt a small-time publicist played by Tony Curtis. The movies had often depicted reporters as glib and cynical characters, but the entertainment figure as moral monster was something else—a sign of how eager a moviemaker could be to distinguish himself from the gutter side of show biz.

23 **clunker of a speech:** In his memoir Kazan writes that he wishes he had excised this speech. *Elia Kazan: A Life* (New York: Knopf, 1988), p. 206.

25 **Sidney Lumet once told me:** Interview with the author, November 2, 1987.

28 **overnight Nielsen ratings:** Gitlin, *Inside Prime Time,* pp. 47–48.

29 **Starting in 1954:** Erik Barnouw, *The Image Empire* (New York: Oxford University Press, 1970), pp. 25–40.

30 **society of the spectacle:** Guy Debord, *Society of the Spectacle* (Detroit: Black and Red, 1966).
   American television's regular tone: Daniel C. Hallin, "We Keep America on Top of the World," in Todd Gitlin, ed., *Watching Television* (New York: Pantheon, 1987), pp. 34–35.

32 **Broadcast News emerged:** Some of my discussion of *Broadcast News* appeared in different form in *Threepenny Review,* Summer 1988, pp. 22–23.

35 **Dan Rather:** On the convulsions at CBS News in the eighties, see Peter J. Boyer, *Who Killed CBS?* (New York: Random House, 1988), and Edward Joyce, *Prime Times, Bad Times* (New York: Doubleday, 1988).

39 **Television was almost entirely:** Mark Hertsgaard, *On Bended Knee: The Press and the Reagan Presidency* (New York: Farrar, Straus and Giroux, 1988), pp. 302–16.

42 **Videocassette royalties and pay-cable fees:** Schatz, "The Hit," p. 42.

43 **plots recombine pretested elements:** On recombinant culture in television and elsewhere, see Gitlin, *Inside Prime Time,* pp. 77–81.

44 **Pauline Kael:** *Kiss Kiss Bang Bang* (New York: Bantam, 1969), p. 79 (first published in the *New Yorker,* October 21, 1967).
   had "great jeopardy": Interview with the author, March 23, 1981.

45 **children's TV cartoons:** See Tom Engelhardt, "The Shortcake Strategy," in Gitlin, ed., *Watching Television,* pp. 68–110.

47 **Steven Spielberg:** Speech of March 30, 1987. Transcript made available by the library of the Academy of Motion Picture Arts and Sciences.
   efficiently directed episodes: David Thomson, *A Biographical Dictionary of Film,* 2nd ed., revised (New York: Morrow, 1981), p. 575.

48 **choose between pictures and words:** Theory has a certain responsibility for this perverse development. Much of today's film theory, drawing credentials from the glib psychoanalytic sketches of Jacques Lacan, presumes that the look of a movie is everything; since the self is incoherent, "character" is nothing other than a sequence of gestures. In an act of intellectual terrorism—the act in which French intellectual life specializes and on which a good deal of American university life hangs at second remove—an interesting notion hardens into a doctrine, at least until the next counterdoctrine forms. In the meantime, practical consequences have been drawn, fulfilling themselves. If the image is everything, the word has been made into nothing. To return to our starting point: this is the reductive, deceptive logic that, even before Lacan, Marshall McLuhan made respectable in America and still circulates in movie circles, gets taught in film schools and passed on as advice to aspiring directors who long to find a place in the history of "pure cinema."

THE THEATER: IF YOU'VE SEEN ONE, YOU'VE SEEN THE MALL, by DOUGLAS GOMERY

I wish to thank Marilyn Moon, Cassie Moon, Mark Crispin Miller, and Tom Engelhardt for their comments and encouragement.

page 50 "of dreams": Ben M. Hall, *The Best Remaining Seats* (New York: Bramhall House, 1961), p. 93.

51 "unrespectable people": The quotation is taken from James Agee's *Agee on Film* (Boston: Beacon, 1968), pp. 6–7.

"a headache": The reflections of one of America's early filmgoers can be found in letters reprinted in his "1907" in *Esquire,* September 1989, pp. 132–134.

54 "live here?": Published in the *New Yorker* in 1929 and reproduced in Hall, *Best Remaining Seats,* p. 123.

edge of town: We are only now beginning to appreciate the impact of Sears, Roebuck on American life. For a much-needed reevaluation see James Worthy's *Shaping an American Institution* (Urbana: University of Illinois Press, 1984).

55 Maxwell Street ghetto: For more on the social life in this extraordinary community see Louis Wirth's *The Ghetto* (Chicago: University of Chicago Press, 1928).

57 "spelled CHICAGO!": Meyer Levin, *The Old Bunch* (New York: Citadel Press, 1937), p. 58.

"is waiting": E. C. A. Bullock, "Theatre Entrances and Lobbies," *The Architectural Form,* vol. 17, no. 6 (June 1925), p. 372.

at Versailles: George L. Rapp, "History of Cinema Theatre Architecture," in Arthur Woltersdorf, ed., *Living Architecture* (Chicago: Kroch, 1930), pp. 55–64.

59 Chicago's tabloids: For a history of the organist as superstar see John W. Landon's *Jesse Crawford: Poet of the Organ* (Vestal, N.Y.: Vestal Press, 1974).

60 "at the movies": To fully appreciate the impact Balaban & Katz's innovation had, see "Air Conditioning" in the technical journal *Ice and Refrigeration* for November 1925.

61 "of a maid": Frank H. Ricketson, Jr., *The Management of Theatres* (New York: McGraw-Hill, 1938), p. 126.

increased attendance: For more on this fascinating era see Robert W. Chambers, "The Double Feature as a Sales Problem," *Harvard Business Review,* vol. 16, no. 2 (Winter 1938), pp. 226–236.

63 "around it": Arthur Bartlett, "Popcorn Crazy," *Saturday Evening Post,* vol. 221 (May 21, 1949), pp. 36, 141.

66 movie viewers: A well-documented history of the drive-in can be found in Bruce A. Austin's "The Development and Decline of the Drive-in Movie Theatre" in his *Current Research in Film,* vol. 1 (Norwood, N.J.: Ablex, 1985).

68 Hollywood's attentions: Indeed, some argue that the mall has

become the locus of Western civilization. See, for example, "Why Everyone Goes to the Mall," by N. R. Kleinfeld in the *New York Times* for December 21, 1986, section III, pp. 1, 33.

in the basement: Downtown, those picture palaces that remained were invariably "twinned" by dividing up the main auditorium into two or three screening spaces and even adding new auditoria in former backstage, restroom, or stage spaces.

69 distracting attention: George Lucas's organization, indeed, was one of the most progressive in developing a superior theatrical sound system, which they named THX, after his first film, *THX-1138.*

70 in the mall: The loathsome character of the modern multiplex has been commented on by any number of critics, but none with more pointed examples than Vincent Canby in his "When Movie Theatres and Patrons Are Obnoxious" in the *New York Times* for Sunday, February 7, 1982, section II, pp. 19, 24.

75 authorized biographers: See *Variety,* April 26–May 2, 1989, pp. 47–120, for Drabinsky's own take on the rise of Cineplex Odeon.

76 of protest: *Advertising Age* blames the rise of advertising in movie theaters on the declining viewership of network television. There is a limit, however: "Research shows that we could run five commercials. But the audience begins to get noticeably restless at that point." See Marcy Magiera, "Advertisers Crowd onto Big Screen," *Advertising Age,* September 18, 1989, pp. 14–15.

78 to offer: I present a detailed history of movie screenings on television in my article *"Brian's Song:* Television, Hollywood, and the Evolution of the Movie Made for Television," found in John E. O'Connor's anthology *American History, American Television* (New York: Ungar, 1983).

VIETNAM: GOOD SOLDIERS, by PAT AUFDERHEIDE

page 82 sympathy for Vietnam vets: Welcome-home marches in New York in 1985 and in Los Angeles in 1987 showcased this sentiment. Public opinion was shifting by the beginning of the eighties toward a growing rejection of Vietnam as, for whatever reasons, a bad war—a rejection that was already quite substantial. For instance, one poll showed that in 1971, 62 percent agreed with the statement "Veterans who served in Vietnam are part of a war that went bad," while in 1979 that percentage rose to 81 percent. U.S. Congress. Senate. Committee on Veterans' Affairs. *Hearings.* 96th Cong., 2d sess. February 21, March 4, May 21, 1980 (Washington, D.C.: GPO, 1980), p. 87.

academic research: In "The Vietnam War: Perceptions Through Literature, Film and Television," *American Quarterly* 36:3 (1984), pp. 419–32, Peter C. Rollins chronicles recent work and describes archival resources such as the Vietnam War Veteran Archives at Olin Library, the Institute of East Asian Studies, Indochina Studies Project, and the Association for Asian Studies, Southeast Asia Council Vietnam Studies Group. A survey of recent work is found in Catherine Calloway, "Vietnam War Literature and Film: A Bibliography of Secondary Sources," *Bulletin of Bibliography* 43:3 (September 1986), pp. 149–58. Conferences on the image of Vietnam in the arts include "War and Memory: In the Aftermath of Vietnam," Washington Project for the Arts, Washington, D.C., 1987; and "The War Film: Contexts and Images," Center for the Study of War and Its Social Consequences, University of Massachusetts, Boston, March 24–25, 1988. Harper's Index for December 1988 announces that an estimated 400 courses on "the sixties" were offered at U.S. colleges and universities in 1988. Books such as Bill McCloud, ed., *What Should We Tell Our Children about Vietnam?* (Norman: University of Oklahoma Press, 1989), serve that market. Albert Auster and Leonard Quart's *How the War Was Remembered: Hollywood and Vietnam* (New York: Praeger, 1988), despite a plethora of typos and some errors of film dates, provides an impressive survey of films on the war, as well as background information on the history of war films and a bibliography. Rob Silberman, "The Art of War: Vietnam Terminable and Interminable," *Afterimage,* September 1988, p. 10f., discusses the recovery of the war as a personal experience to be mediated therapeutically.

dreamlike unreality: Jonathan Schell, *Observing the Nixon Years* (New York: Pantheon, 1989), p. 8.

"America seemed omnipotent": Quoted in Auster and Quart, *How the War Was Remembered,* p. 83.

"not a winning combination": Loren Baritz, *Backfire: A History of How American Culture Led Us into Vietnam and Made Us Fight the Way We Did* (New York: Morrow), p. 54.

83 **rupture in expectations:** As Todd Gitlin put it, "History was ruptured, passions have been expended, belief has become difficult; heroes have died and been replaced by celebrities. The 1960s exploded our belief in progress, which underlay the classical faith in linear order and moral clarity. Old verities crumbled, but new ones have not settled in." *New York Times Book Review,* November 6, 1988, p. 1f., adapted from his essay in Ian Angus and Sut Jhally, eds. *Cultural Politics in Contemporary America* (London: Routledge, 1989).

the sixties reevaluation: See, for instance, Todd Gitlin's definitive history, *The Sixties* (New York: Bantam, 1988). As sixties radical Mickey Kaus said in *Newsweek's* September 5, 1988, cover story, "It all does come down to the war . . . Ultimately, opposing the war—not sex or drugs or rock and roll or Marx—was what gave a clarity and purpose to our lives that, for many, has been missing ever since" (p. 28).

84 **"the Generic Vietnam War Narrative":** C.D.B. Bryan, "Barely Suppressed Screams: Getting a Bead on Vietnam Literature," *Harpers,*

June 1984, pp. 67–72, discussed in Auster and Quart, *How the War Was Remembered,* p. 84.

86 **"purely heroic":** Mark Morrison, " 'China Beach' Salutes the Women of Vietnam," *Rolling Stone,* May 19, 1988, pp. 75–79.

88 **two views of the war:** Oliver Stone, introduction to *Platoon and Salvador: The Original Screenplays* (New York: Vintage Books, 1987), p. 9.

  emotional legacy: Bruce Weber, "Cool Head, Hot Images," *New York Times Magazine,* May 21, 1989, p. 24f.

92 **stepping-stone:** Karen Jaehne, "Company Man," *Film Comment,* March–April 1989, p. 12.

93 **"U.S. leaves Vietnam" theme:** Edward J. Epstein, *News from Nowhere: Television and the News* (New York: Random House, 1974).

94 **veteran broadcaster:** See my "Paul Harvey, Good Day!" *Progressive,* July 1986, pp. 20–25.

96 **"both good and evil":** Stone, introduction to *Platoon and Salvador,* p. 9.

  "vision of personal responsibility": Jaehne, *op. cit.*

  "a twisted, upside-down world": Press kit, *Casualties of War,* 8.

98 **"fought for each other":** Press kit, *Hamburger Hill.*

  "tormented libidinal economy": J. Hoberman, "Hi, Nam," *Village Voice,* December 29, 1987, p. 63. See also his "Vietnam: The Remake," in Barbara Kruger and Phil Mariani, eds., *Remaking History* (Seattle: Bay Press, 1989), pp. 175-96. Gender issues in Vietnam films have also been a subject of academic discussion. Michael Comber and Margaret O'Brien (in "Evading the War: The Politics of the Hollywood Vietnam Film," *History* 73:238 [June 1988], pp. 248–60) maintain, "The anxiety about what it is to be a hero slides into an anxiety about what it is to be a man." Susan Jeffords in *The Remasculinization of America: Gender and the Vietnam War* (Bloomington: Indiana University Press, 1989) sees the new Vietnam films as an environment within which to restore a dominant masculinity under challenge by changing mores; the role of soldier—emblematic, for her, of American males— as victim places the American female in the position of other and enemy.

99 **World War II combat film:** Jeanine Basinger, *The World War II Combat Film: Anatomy of a Genre* (New York: Columbia University Press, 1986).

101 **jumble of disturbing images:** See D. C. Hallin, *The 'Uncensored War': The Media and Vietnam* (New York: Oxford University Press, 1986).

  inverted the reigning clichés: Michael Renov's "Imaging the Other: Representations of Vietnam in '60s Political Documentary," *Afterimage,* December 1988, discusses ways in which images of Vietnam were used in left documentaries of the time.

103 **underdog-warrior theme:** See Vivian Sobchack, *Screening Space* (New York: Ungar, 1987), p. 228.

110 **"a warrior without a war"**: *Washington Post,* October 17, 1988, p. B2.
111 **"brave the opening expanse"**: Peter Marin, "What the Vietnam Vets Can Teach Us," *Nation,* November 27, 1982, p. 562; John Hellman, *American Myth and the Legacy of Vietnam* (New York: Columbia University Press, 1986), p. 224.

BLOCKBUSTER: THE LAST CRUSADE, by PETER BISKIND

I am indebted to Mark Crispin Miller, Tom Engelhardt, and J. Hoberman for their suggestions.

page 113 **permeated by countercultural values**: Spielberg has said he was making home movies while everybody else was out demonstrating against the Vietnam War, but he unquestionably was shaped by the sixties, and there is more than enough evidence to establish the biographical component in his films. "Everything that I do in my movies is a product of my homelife in suburban U.S.A.," says Spielberg. "I can always trace a movie idea back to my childhood." ("The Autobiography of Peter Pan," *Time,* July 15, 1985, p. 62.) His various childhood fears and phobias have all been enshrined in his movies: sharks *(Jaws),* snakes *(Raiders),* insects *(Temple of Doom),* flying *(Temple of Doom).* Writer Lynn Hirschberg has observed that all his movies are "exercises in counterphobic behavior." ("Will Hollywood's Mr. Perfect Ever Grow Up?" *Rolling Stone,* July 19–August 2, 1984.)
appropriate studio executives: Dale Pollock, *Skywalking* (New York: Harmony Books, 1983).
"countless Indians have stuttered": Ariel Dorfman, "Norteamericanos, Call Home," *Village Voice,* August 24, 1982, pp. 39–40. Spielberg apparently agreed with Dorfman. "*E.T.* was a broad-based story about an ugly duckling who didn't belong," he said. "Someone who wasn't like everyone else . . . I always felt *E.T.* was a minority story." (David Breskin, "Steven Spielberg," *Rolling Stone,* July 22, 1982, p. 70.)
114 **"chemical exhaust fumes"**: James Kahn, *Return of the Jedi* (New York: Ballantine Books, 1983), p. 122.
"I liked that": Pollock, *Skywalking,* p. 138.
115 **fought social control**: Peter Biskind, *Seeing Is Believing: How Hollywood Taught Us to Stop Worrying and Love the Fifties* (New York: Pantheon, 1983).
118 **"nobody would laugh"**: Pollock, *Skywalking,* p. 176.
"this is wrong": *Ibid.,* p. 144.
120 **"previously fulfilled by narrative"**: Richard Maltby, *Harmless Entertainment: Hollywood and the Ideology of Consensus* (Metuchen, N.J.: The Scarecrow Press, 1983), p. 311.
121 **"really roll with it"**: Pollock, *Skywalking,* p. 186.

124 **deconstructed and demystified itself:** Spielberg himself has called attention to the connection between the movie and the extraterrestrials. "I've never had a close encounter of any kind—except with a $19,000,000 movie. (Mitch Tuchman, "Close Encounter With Steven Spielberg," *Film Comment,* January/February 1978, pp. 49–55.) **"even if his script seemed to call for it":** Pollock, *Skywalking,* p. 164. **"I wanted it to be real":** Paul Scanlon, "The Force Behind George Lucas," *Rolling Stone,* August 25, 1977, p. 48.

125 **not Peckinpah's:** Cf. Richard Corliss, "I Dream for a Living," *Time,* July 15, 1985, p. 54.

126 **of the Force:** Pollock, *Skywalking,* p. 140.

127 **"glows in the dark":** Dan Rubey, "Star Wars: Not So Far Away," *Jump Cut,* no. 18, pp. 9–14. This is the best article on *Star Wars* and is basic to any discussion of the film.

128 **"no jiggling in the Empire":** Pollock, *Skywalking,* p. 165.

129 **often called Lucas "Kid":** *Ibid.,* pp. 128ff.

132 **labor were a by-product:** Neil Postman, *The Disappearance of Childhood* (New York: Delacorte Press, 1982).

133 **uncomplicated moviegoing:** Speaking in another context, Spielberg said, "I think the outcry [against *Heaven's Gate*] was a primal scream from movie lovers, saying 'Please . . . give us better ideas and more entertainment . . .'" (Michael Sragow, "A Conversation with Steven Spielberg," *Rolling Stone,* July 22, 1982, p. 28.)

137 **a lot had changed:** Today we so take the domination of Hollywood by kids for granted that it's hard to recall it was ever any different. Here's Spielberg, remembering how things were when he broke in: "I did sneak on the Universal lot—it was 1967 . . . but actually it was a cul-de-sac experience for me, because, once in, I discovered nobody really wanted anything I had to offer, that it was still a middle-aged man's profession. The only young people on the lot were actors. It was just the beginning of the youth rennaissance." (Tuchman, *op. cit.*) **overthrowing the Republic:** The films conceal their nostalgic glow by managing to portray conservatism as "revolutionary." Cf. Michael Ryan and Douglas Kellner, *Camera Politica: The Politics and Ideology of Contemporary Hollywood Film* (Bloomington: University of Indiana Press, 1988), p. 234.

141 **"his family from evil":** Dave Kehr, "The Star," *Gannett Center Journal,* Summer 1989, p. 57. **"television replaced the father":** Breskin, "Steven Spielberg," p. 69. **"in James Bond":** Richard B. Woodward, "Meanwhile, Back at the Ranch," *New York Times,* Arts and Leisure, May 21, 1989.

142 **"I think it's dangerous":** Breskin, "Steven Spielberg," p. 72. **"how we feel":** Michael Rogin, *Ronald Reagan, the Movie and Other Episodes in Political Demonology* (Berkeley: University of California Press, 1988), p. 262.

143 **"go to Washington":** *Ibid.,* p. 263.

"claimed to represent": *Ibid.,* p. xvi.

"in back of anything": *Ibid.,* p. 7.

144 "results of those choices": Maltby, *Harmless Entertainment,* p. 331.

145 (or illogic) of the films: Another way of looking at it is that since the ideological struggle between corporate liberals who wanted to use persuasion and conservatives who wanted to use force had been won by the right, this was no longer a live ideological issue and there was nothing much at stake.

"outspectacle each other": Sragow, "A Conversation with Steven Spielberg," p. 26.

146 "they want good stories": Chris Hodenfield, "The Sky Is Full of Questions!!" *Rolling Stone,* January 26, 1978, p. 37.

"a buffet": Tuchman, "Close Encounter with Steven Spielberg," pp. 49–55.

"of television": *Ibid.*

147 "to overwhelm me": Breskin, "Steven Spielberg," p. 80.

COLORIZATION: ROSE-TINTED SPECTACLES, by STUART KLAWANS

Much of the source material for this essay came from the files of the Film Study Center of the Museum of Modern Art, New York, to whose staff I am very grateful. I have also relied on a compilation titled "Computer Colorizing Clippings," circulated by the National Center for Film and Video Preservation, American Film Institute. Among the writers not cited by name in the notes below, I owe the most to Barbara Aarsteinsen of the *Globe and Mail* (Toronto), Bob Thomas of Associated Press, Tom Nolan of the *Philadelphia Inquirer,* and all the reporters for the two papers of record, *Variety* and *Daily Variety.*

page 153 "You couldn't make *Wyatt Earp*": Sharon Singer, "Finding the Gold in Black and White," *Toronto Star Magazine,* November 4, 1984.

154 "ensure color quality": Michael Silverman, " 'Dandy' 1st From MGM/UA Due For Color Conversion," *Daily Variety,* January 30, 1985.

155 people in their teens and twenties walk out: Interview with Frank Rowley, March 24, 1989.

157 realized they didn't need Capra: Stephen M. Silverman, "Over the Rainbow: Debate Erupts on Coloring Old Black-&-White Movies," *New York Post,* April 18, 1985.

"I chose to shoot it in black-and-white": Leslie Bennetts, " 'Colorizing' Film Classics: A Boon or a Bane?," *New York Times,* August 5, 1986.

159 "The last time I checked": Robert M. Andrews (Associated Press), "A Growing Challenge to Film Coloring," *Philadelphia Inquirer,* November 5, 1986.

"you cannot talk morals with money people": "Fred Zinnemann

Sees Red Over Colorizing Classics," *Daily Variety,* September 10, 1986.

160 **"an ugly practice":** Bennetts, " 'Colorizing' Film Classics."
"People can't go to the archive": *Ibid.*
"History lives on tape": Todd McCarthy, "AFI Squares Off Against Coloring," *Variety,* October 8, 1986.

162 **"We made the first mistake":** *Ibid.*
"If directors had their way": Maureen Dowd, "Film Stars Protest Colorizing," *New York Times,* May 13, 1987.
"We were looking for a platform": Telephone interview with Elliot Silverstein, July 6, 1989.
"the straw that broke the camel's back": *Ibid.*

164 **"cultural butchery":** Jack Mathews, "Film Directors See Red Over Ted Turner's Movie Tinting," *Los Angeles Times,* September 12, 1986.
"to use its full resources": "Directors Guild Takes Official Stand Against Film Colorization," *Variety,* October 22, 1986.
"spirited, emotional press conference": McCarthy, "AFI Squares Off Against Coloring."
NEA chairman Frank Hodsoll: Irvin Molotsky, "Council Opposes Coloring Old Films," *New York Times,* November 4, 1986.

165 **"Seated in a wheelchair":** Aljean Harmetz, "Huston Protests Coloring of 'Falcon,' " *New York Times,* November 14, 1986.
"tone of righteousness": Vincent Canby, "Through a Tinted Glass, Darkly," *New York Times,* November 30, 1986.
"seems doomed to stalk the earth": Vincent Canby, " 'Colorization' Is Defacing Black and White Film Classics," *New York Times,* November 2, 1986.

166 **"They're get-rich-quick schemes":** Canby, November 30, 1986.

167 **"No professional film archivist":** Harmetz, "Huston Protests Coloring of 'Falcon.' "

168 **"is a boon to preservation":** *Ibid.*
"Colorization is a mindless obscenity": Ellen Cohn, "Tint Men," *Village Voice,* February 7, 1989; Letters, *Village Voice,* February 21, 1989.

169 **"a film enthusiast took what he could get":** Andrew Sarris, "The Color of Money," *Village Voice,* February 24, 1987.

170 **"Old movies *are* the past":** *Ibid.*
"as great an impertinence": "Directors Guild Takes Official Stand Against Film Colorization," *Variety,* October 22, 1986.

171 **The word *classic* first appeared:** See Ernst Robert Curtius, *European Literature and the Latin Middle Ages,* trans. Willard R. Trask (Princeton: Princeton University Press, 1973), *passim.*
the "classics" were a small group of antique sculptures: See Francis Haskell and Nicholas Penny, *Taste and the Antique: The Lure of Classical Sculpture 1500–1900* (New Haven: Yale University Press, 1981), *passim.*

173 **"Hair, eyes, lips, and dress":** John Boardman, *Greek Sculpture: The*

Classical Period (London: Thames and Hudson, 1985), pp. 11–12. Thanks to David H. Rosenthal for suggesting this line of inquiry and to Amelia Arenas and John McLaren for helping me pursue it.

175 **"It's only feasible to convert to color":** Singer, "Finding the Gold in Black and White."

176 **The issue of moral rights:** Eric J. Schwartz, "The National Film Preservation Act of 1988: A Copyright Case Study in the Legislative Process," *Journal of the Copyright Society of the USA*, vol. 36, no. 2 (January 1989), pp. 138–159. I have followed Schwartz's account throughout. My thanks to Lawrence Joseph for helping me pursue this subject.

In the words of Leon Friedman: Herbert Mitgang, "Old Copyright Treaty: New Shield for U.S. Artists," *New York Times*, March 10, 1989.

178 **"settled for the foreseeable future":** Schwartz, *op. cit.*, p. 152.

"show Jimmy Stewart": *Ibid.*, p. 145.

180 **"the companies gave the films to the archives":** Interview with Mary Lea Bandy, March 28, 1989.

181 **a cost to the public of approximately $225 billion:** See Anthony Lewis, "But We Are Going to Pay," *New York Times*, February 9, 1989; and Nathaniel C. Nash, "House and Senate Pass Plan to Rescue Savings and Loans," *New York Times*, August 5, 1989.

"the laws of appropriation": Karl Marx, *Capital: A Critique of Political Economy*, trans. Samuel Moore and Edward Aveling (New York: Modern Library, 1936), pp. 639–40.

182 **nearly half of the American people saw their incomes decline:** These figures, which are adjusted for inflation, come from a House of Representatives study, "Background Material and Data on Programs Within the Jurisdiction of the Committee on Ways and Means." See Martin Tolchin, "Richest Got Richer and Poorest Poorer in 1979–87," *New York Times*, March 23, 1989.

183 **"Failure to proceed":** Cohn, "Tint Men."

"willing to license nearly any title": Letters, *Village Voice*, February 21, 1989.

CST and Colorization Inc. have lost millions: Michael Lev, "Little Gold in Coloring Old Films," *New York Times*, November 11, 1989.

ADVERTISING: END OF STORY, by MARK CRISPIN MILLER

I want especially to thank Jean McGarry and Tom Engelhardt for their strong support and critical assistance. I am also indebted to Jeff Chester, Marc Lapadula, Emily Leventhal, Ross Posnock, Kim Rusin, and the people at Video Americain, in Baltimore.

page 186 "the democratic ideal": "Brainwash Peril Seen over Nation," *New York Times*, November 11, 1958.

"and freedom meaningless": *New York Times Magazine,* Letters section, January 26, 1958.

187 "a totalitarian government": "Psychic Hucksterism Stirs Calls for Inquiry," *New York Times,* October 6, 1957.

"on rational ground": Huxley made his remarks on *The Mike Wallace Interview,* May 18, 1958: "Huxley Fears New Persuasion Methods Could Subvert Democratic Procedures," *New York Times,* May 19, 1958.

"cancelled the campaign": "Hidden Sell," *Life,* March 31, 1958.

"yelps of alarm": " 'Subliminal' Salesmen Stalk Consumers via TV, Radio and Movies," *Wall Street Journal,* March 7, 1958.

" 'would be tempting' ": *Time,* September 9, 1957.

188 Vicary's hoax: For an account, see Walter Weir, "Another Look at Subliminal Facts," *Advertising Age,* October 15, 1984.

190 Coca-Cola memo: "Fox to Sell Product Plugs in Its Movies," *New York Times,* December 21, 1983.

192 "or prop masters": "TV Commercials in the Next Century? '2010' Offers Peek," *Advertising Age,* December 2, 1984.

193 "hands-on use": "Questions Raised on 'Product Placements,' " *New York Times,* April 13, 1989.

"big budget film": "Tobacco's Cloudy Image on the Silver Screen," *Christian Science Monitor,* July 28, 1989.

"and promotional medium"; "Hollywood has changed its tune"; "get people's attention": "Movie Tie-Ins," *Incentive,* June 1989, pp. 36–41.

194 *License to Kill:* The plug is so blatant that the film's producer felt obliged to shove the Surgeon General's warning into the closing credits—knowing, of course, that that belated flash of print could not mitigate the visual impact of the star's repeatedly lighting up a Lark. The decision to insert the warning, the producer claimed, did not result from any fears of governmental pressure but merely expressed his own civic-mindedness: "There's a sense of social responsibility," his spokesman told the press. See "Advertising," *New York Times,* July 13, 1989. For more on cigarette-plugging in the movies, see "Tobacco's Cloudy Image on the Silver Screen," *Christian Science Monitor.*

The fact that *License to Kill* was used to sell cigarettes elicited much complaint from consumer groups and at least one congressman—pressures that Philip Morris, predictably, assailed as a threat to civil rights. "You're getting into telling filmmakers how to make their films," a company spokesman said. "It really is a government intrusion into artistic decisions." "Outcry Over Product Placement Worries Movie, Ad Executives," *Wall Street Journal,* July 3, 1989.

MAC & Me: The film was produced by an ex-adman, R. J. Louis, who has also produced *The Karate Kid* and its sequels. See "Brand Names Star in 'MAC & Me,' " *Advertising Age,* September 5, 1988.

196 *Wall Street:* The plug was arranged after some competitive bidding

that also involved *Forbes* magazine. See "How Fortune 'Out-Slicked' Forbes to Win Movie Role," *Wall Street Journal,* February 27, 1988. **"is so natural"**: "On Brazilian TV, the Subtle Sell Pays Off Big, Too," *New York Times,* June 3, 1988.

197 **"make it anymore"**: "Outcry Over Product Placement," *Wall Street Journal.*
  "to reflect life": "Movie Tie-Ins," *Incentive.*

198 **"and advertising costs"**: Quoted in "Consumer Products Become Movie Stars," *Wall Street Journal,* February 27, 1988.

199 **"some sixty movies"**: John Birmingham, "See the Movie, Buy the Suit," *Premiere,* April, 1988, pp. 17–19.
  "behind the stars": "Why Marlon Brando Passed the Milk Duds to George C. Scott," *Wall Street Journal,* May 24, 1982.
  "or potential clients": "Movie Tie-Ins," *Incentive.*
  " 'our clients' brands' ": "Consumer Products Become Movie Stars," *Wall Street Journal,* February 27, 1988.
  "we backed out": "Consumer Products Become Movie Stars," *Wall Street Journal.*

200 **"just a theme"**: "Movie Tie-Ins," *Incentive.*

201 **"would be unappetizing"**: "TV Commercials in the Next Century?" *Advertising Age.*
  "Chainsaw Massacre": "Kool-Aid Man Is Really Cool in New Ads Targeted to Kids," *Wall Street Journal,* May 9, 1985.
  "drives a Mercedes," *Making Love:* "Why Marlon Brando Passed the Milk Duds to George C. Scott," *Wall Street Journal,* May 24, 1982.

203 **"not a great art form"**: Quoted in "Hollywood Buys the Concept," *Advertising Age,* November 9, 1988, p. 158.
  Cinematographers: The rock video, a more expansive form of advertising, has attracted, among others, John Sayles, William Friedkin, Bob Rafelson, John Landis, George Miller, and Brian De Palma.

204 **George Lucas:** These ads were circulated only in Japan.
  "the hottest features": "Ads You Like It," *Premiere,* December 1989.
  "it's just filmmaking": "Major Directors No Longer Shun TV Ads," *Wall Street Journal,* June 14, 1989.
  "look to us for inspiration": "For the Master of TV Brevity, A Minute Can Be Too Long," *New York Times,* February 5, 1984.
  "just like doing a small feature": "Ridley Scott Makes the Details Count," *Advertising Age,* June 21, 1984.

205 **"make little movies"**: "Hollywood Buys the Concept," *Advertising Age,* November 9, 1988.
  "commercials as short films": "Adrian Lyne," *Advertising Age,* August 1, 1985.
  compositional norm: While this particular précis would apply to a cop film directed by Stallone or Walter Hill or Peter Hyams, the fantasies of Lucas/Spielberg, and most big-screen comedies, are, shot by shot, no more nuanced or ambiguous. In nearly every instance the frame is wholly, and therefore propagandistically, filled in with one "idea."

206 **"the way they used to"**: "Hollywood Buys the Concept," *Advertising Age.*
"direct sales stimulus": "Marketing," *Wall Street Journal,* November 29, 1984.

207 **"of the message"**: "Ads with the Dusenberry Touch," *New York Times,* November 16, 1986.
nonvisual effects: Hollywood's increasing reliance on foreign markets has also increased the amount, and intensified the punch, of on-screen violence, which "tends to export better," says one executive, than comedy and other, quieter kinds of spectacle. See "Movies Look Abroad for Profits," *New York Times,* December 17, 1988.
Agee quotes: These observations come from Agee's film essay in the *Nation,* May 26, 1945. *Agee on Film* (New York: McDowell, Obolensky, 1958), p. 164.

210 **empathic violence:** The importance of this project may explain why certain marketers have sometimes let the bad guys use their merchandise. In *Teachers* (1984) a reprehensible coach, wearing a Nike T-shirt, admits to having had sex with a high school student: "A Nike spokesman," *Advertising Age* reported, "declined to discuss the Beaverton, Ore.-based company's product-placement activities." And in *The Terminator* (1984) the killer robot played by Arnold Schwarzenegger "wears Gargoyles-brand sunglasses placed by Associated Film Promotions. 'We're opening lots of new accounts as a result of that movie,' said Russell Remington, marketing director of the small Bellevue, Wash.-based company." ("TV Commercials in the Next Century?" *Advertising Age.*)

212 **cartoonization:** The movies have become both adlike and cartoonlike at the same moment that the old cartoons (both still and animated) have been sold into advertising. In other words, it is not just Mr. and Mrs. Roger Rabbit (Diet Coke) who make the pitch but hardy troupers like Betty Boop (Hershey), Porky Pig (Ruffles), the Road Runner (Purolator), Wile E. Coyote (the Donnelly Directory), Tom and Jerry (Addis in the U.K.), Dick Tracy (A.B. Dick), Olive Oyl (Solo laundry detergent)—and, for Coca-Cola, Ultra Pampers, Chevrolet, McDonald's, Jell-O, M&M's, and lots of other products, the (perhaps) inexhaustible Mickey Mouse, who may well be the Bill Cosby of the animated universe.

216 **"highly personal scenario"**: "Ads Tell a Stylish Story," *Advertising Age,* September 20, 1984, p. 14. Likewise, Benetton's fashion director thus explained her company's multipaged ads: "It's a way to narrate the Benetton image." ("Global Gallery," *Advertising Age,* May 29, 1989, p. 27.)

221 **Evelyn Waugh quote:** Gilbert Seldes, *The Great Audience* (New York: Viking, 1950), p. 50. Waugh made the observation—based on his unhappy experience trying to get the Johnston-Hays Office to approve *Brideshead Revisited* for adaptation—in "Why Hollywood Is a Term of Disparagement," *Daily Telegraph and Morning Post,* April 30/

May 1, 1947. Donat Gallagher, ed., *The Essays, Articles and Reviews of Evelyn Waugh* (London: Methuen, 1983), p. 328.

224 **"technical craftsmanship"**: Dale Pollock, *Skywalking: The Life and Films of George Lucas* (New York: Harmony Books, 1983), p. 142.

226 **emanations of pure friendliness**: The same sameness, as it were, occurs in Spielberg's *E.T. The Extra-Terrestrial* (1982), which represents Elliott and "E.T.," the human child and his alien counterpart, as identical in their sweet innocence.

227 **dead hand of the past**: On this point and others my reading is indebted to Robin Wood's seminal essay on *Psycho* in *Hitchcock's Films* (New York: Barnes and Noble, 1969).

228 **dozens of thrillers**: Concerning latter-day Hollywood *hommages* to Hitchcock, there has been one outstanding departure from the punitive norm: Roman Polanski's *Frantic* (1988), a subtle, unnerving meditation on postmodern culture (including cinema), based on *The Man Who Knew Too Much* (1956) and featuring an extraordinary performance by Harrison Ford. Brian De Palma's *Dressed to Kill* (1980), closely based on *Psycho,* is also thoughtful and inventive, although marred by the obvious relish with which De Palma stages Angie Dickinson's protracted slaughter.

229 **sexist grievance**: See Carol Clover's indispensable overview, "Her Body, Himself: Gender in the Slasher Film," *Representations* 20 (fall 1987), 187–228.

"improved" fates: Concerning eighties repetitions of earlier and darker tales of sexual entanglement, there has been one notable exception to the rule in Lawrence Kasdan's *Body Heat* (1981), a solid remake of Billy Wilder's *Double Indemnity* (1944) enhanced by borrowings from *Vertigo.*

231 **"the cereal business," "Kellogg's Corn Flakes"**: "Sequels and Stars Help Top Movie Studios Avoid Major Risks," *Wall Street Journal,* June 6, 1989.

"in the marketplace," "pre-sold commodity": "Hollywood Recycling Old TV Hits as Films," *New York Times,* February 21, 1987.

"I loved 'Dragnet,' " "on the air": *Ibid.*

232 **"to go forward"**: "TV Is Tuning In to the Past With Revivals of Hit Series," *Baltimore Sun,* July 23, 1989.

"become the norm": "Seems Like Old Times," *New York,* October 20, 1986.

"fell by 26 percent": Katy Butler, "The Great Boomer Bust," *Mother Jones,* June 1989, pp. 32–38.

234 **"the average UltraConsumer"**: "Puttin' on the Glitz," *Grey Matter,* vol. 57, no. 1 (1986), p. 14.

235 **"they forget yesterday"**: "From Disney Fairy Dust, New Realism," *New York Times,* July 20, 1989.

"like a Spielberg movie": "Movie Effects Inspire New Theme-Park Rides," *New York Times,* June 14, 1986.

rousing/tranquilizing collapse: American fiction of the late eighties, notes Michiko Kakutani, repeatedly exploits the same combination: gross, violent effects and then a nice happy ending. (She sees this tendency, however, not as symptomatic of any current cultural developments but as a reversion—purely literary—to Victorian conventions.) "Kill! Burn! Eviscerate! Bludgeon! It's Literary Again to Be Horrible," *New York Times,* November 21, 1989.

238 as everyone applauds: The movie's convergence of opposites need not win explicit applause; and the figures can also converge by doubling one another. At the end of *Field of Dreams* (1989) Kevin Costner finally gets to play catch with his (dead) father—who, owing to the supernatural properties of Costner's ballfield, has reappeared exactly as he was at Costner's age. As the two toss the ball back and forth, looking like a man and his reflection, the camera cranes up and back to show us, in the distance, a long line of cars approaching, their headlights glaring in the dusk. This signals the arrival of the many people who, through supernatural agency, have been moved to come and *pay to watch* the ghostly team play ball on Costner's field. The image suggests nothing so much as the many people who have driven out to catch this movie at the nearest mall.

239 melding "opposites": The animus against clear sexual difference may help explain the preponderance, throughout the postseventies movies, of heroines bearing men's names: both Jennifer Beals and Glenn Close are "Alex" in, respectively, Adrian Lyne's *Flashdance* and *Fatal Attraction*—in which Michael Douglas's sexless little girl, moreover, is named "Frankie," like the heroine of Susan Seidelman's *Making Mr. Right* (1987). In *The Morning After* (1986) Jane Fonda plays "Willie," in *Jagged Edge* (1985) Glenn Close plays "Teddy," in *Clean and Sober* (1988) Kathy Baker plays "Charlie" (Michael Keaton calls her "Chuck"), and in *Vice Versa* (1987) Corinne Bohrer plays "Sam."

It is not only the libidinous female who is ultimately purged, however. In *Outrageous Fortune* (1987) the evil, horny Peter Coyote plummets to his death so that his ex-lovers, "opposites" Shelley Long and Bette Midler, can come together; and in *sex, lies, and videotape* it is the bad husband, not the wicked sister, who gets it in the end. The gender of the scapegoat depends, of course, on the overall gender of the movie's target audience.

241 "crazy" in the service of bureaucracy: Since the seventies, the figure of the authoritarian-as-outlaw has also turned up outside the movies: Ronald Reagan, forever railing against "Washington" as if he were a populist upstart and not the country's president, worked that posture with unsurpassed adroitness. Indeed, the success of Reagan's posture must relate, in various oblique ways, to the recent products of the industry that helped create him.

242 flash flood of affirmative theatricality: One apparent bold exception, Spike Lee's *Do the Right Thing* (1989), offers little encouragement,

since its schematically *un*happy ending is not believable but a broad contrivance flagrantly tacked on to a movie that has, until the climax, offered a view of inner-city life as sunny and stylized as the brighter musicals of Busby Berkeley, whose soul seems to be animating Spike Lee's body.

Several markedly unhappy endings are, in fact, exceptions that turn out to prove the rule since they "subvert" spectatorship in a way that implicitly strokes the viewing audience. Both *Pennies from Heaven* (1981) and Woody Allen's *The Purple Rose of Cairo* (1985) vividly convey both the hopelessness and the delusional nature of the viewer's wide-eyed trust in Hollywood's happy endings—but each critique is softened by those films' concentration on depression-era films and viewers, a marked period emphasis which implies that only *those* spectators had that problem. (In any case, Allen revised the bleakness out of his movie with the 1986 comedy-drama *Hannah and Her Sisters,* in which escapist moviegoing comes across as an existential break-through—evidently because in that film it is Allen himself who does the watching, whereas the character who watches at the end of *Purple Rose* is just a dim little *shiksa* from the outer boroughs.)

Similarly, although Oliver Stone's *Talk Radio* (1988) attacks the passive rage of the American mass audience, that "attack" flatters the movie's audience. At the end, just after the outspoken radio star Barry Champlain has been gunned down by a neo-Nazi (a clear reference to the killing of Alan Berg), there is a long helicopter shot of the nocturnal city, and, over it, a radio broadcast of phone-in reminiscences from many of Champlain's thick-witted listeners. This conclusion assures that the problem lies not with the urban moviegoing public but only with the provincial devotees of late-night radio.

245 **"the hold is a handshake"**: Robert Hering, film reviewer for the *Manchester Guardian,* in his review of *Lonesome* (1936). Reprinted in Alistair Cooke, ed., *Garbo and the Night Watchmen* (rev. ed. London: Martin Secker and Warburg, 1971), p. 27.

The Contributors

Pat Aufderheide is an assistant professor in the School of Communication at The American University and a senior editor at *In These Times.* She also serves on the editorial boards of *Cineaste* and *Black Film Review* and is a member of the film advisory board of the National Gallery of Art. Her essay "The Look of the Sound" appeared in *Watching Television,* edited by Todd Gitlin.

Peter Biskind is the author of *Seeing Is Believing: How Hollywood Taught Us to Stop Worrying and Love the Fifties.* He was formerly editor of *American Film* and is now executive editor of *Premiere.* He has written widely on culture and politics for publications including the *New York Times*, the *Washington Post*, *Vanity Fair*, *Rolling Stone*, *Penthouse*, *The Nation*, the *Village Voice*, and *Grand Street.*

Todd Gitlin is a professor of sociology and director of the mass communications program at the University of California, Berkeley. He is the author of *The Sixties: Years of Hope, Days of Rage, Inside Prime Time,* and *The Whole World Is Watching,* and the editor of *Watching Television.* He has written on culture and politics for the *New York Times Book Review, Tikkun, Dissent, The Nation, Harper's,* the *Columbia Journalism Review,* the *Los Angeles Times,* the *San Francisco Chronicle,* and many other magazines and newspapers.

Douglas Gomery lives in Washington, D.C., and is the author of *The Hollywood Studio System* and co-author of *American Media, Film History: Theory and Practice,* and *The Art of Moving Shadows.* His nearly two hundred articles have appeared in such publications as the *Village Voice, Screen,* the *Gannett Center Journal, Yale French Studies,* the *Wilson Quarterly,* the *SMPTE Journal,* and the *Journal of Contemporary History.*

Stuart Klawans is the film critic for *The Nation.* His essays, reviews, and fiction have appeared in the *Village Voice,* the *Times Literary Supplement,* and *Grand Street;* he has also discussed films and books on the program *Fresh Air* on National Public Radio. His favorite color is blue.

Mark Crispin Miller, who heads the Film Study Program at the Johns Hopkins University, is the author of *Boxed In: The Culture of TV.* He has also written on various aspects of mass culture for *Harper's,* the *Atlantic, The Nation,* the *Village Voice, Film Quarterly,* and other publications. He is now completing a book on American advertising.